The Yorkshire Dales

The Yorkshire Dales

Landscape with Figures

PETER GUNN

CENTURY PUBLISHING
LONDON

First published in Great Britain in 1984
by Century Publishing Co. Ltd,
Portland House,
12–13 Greek Street, London W1V 5LE

British Library Cataloguing in Publication Data

Gunn, Peter
    The Yorkshire Dales.
    1. Yorkshire Dales National Park (England)–
    Description and travel
    I. Title
    914.28'404858   DA670.N68

ISBN 0 7126 0370 0

Jacket photograph courtesy of Fotobank Colour
Library International

Photoset by Rowland Phototypesetting Ltd,
Bury St Edmunds, Suffolk
Printed in Great Britain by
Purnell & Sons (Book Production) Ltd
Paulton, Bristol

Contents

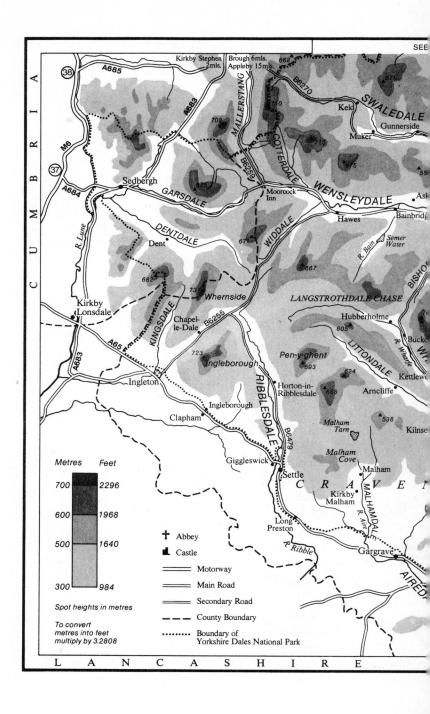

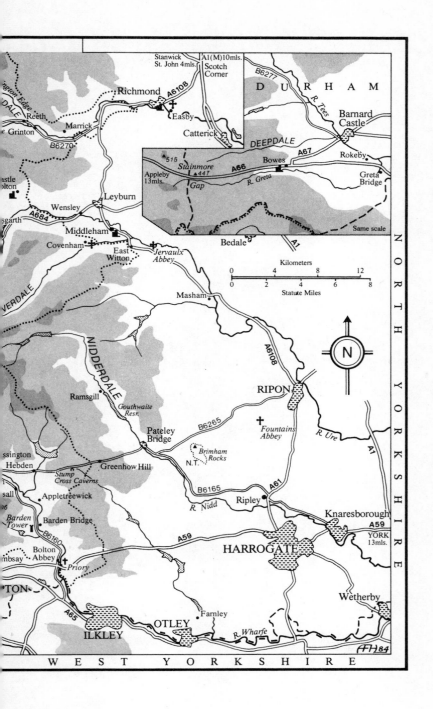

Preface

THAT I HAVE relied heavily on earlier writers on the Yorkshire Dales is evident from the most cursory perusal of these pages. The infinite fascination of this limited region of the British Isles has called forth reams of description and panegyric from the time that Edmund Spencer invited the presence of

> Still Ure, swift Wharfe, and Ouse the most of might,
> High Swale, unquiet Nidd, and troublous Skell

among 'the Sea-gods and their fruitful seed' at the bridal banquet of Thames and Medway to the recent much-read works of H. J. Scott, Dr Arthur Raistrick and the Misses Hartley and Ingilby. How presumptuous I am in adding another book to those of these excellent authors must be left to the readers' judgement. If I owe much to them, I am also deeply indebted to many other dalesmen, who have been willing to put their love and knowledge of the Dales at my disposal. In particular I should like to acknowledge with gratitude the help that I have had from Alan Brown of Haverdale, Mr Robert Brown of Feetham, Dr Thomas Bell and Mrs Batty of Reeth, Mr Gordon Anyan of Low Row, Miss Marie Hartley and Miss Joan Ingilby of Askrigg, Mr S. O. F. Bateman of Mortham Tower, Teesdale; Miss M. Murray of Richmond and Mr Nicholas Horton-Fawkes of Farnley Hall, Wharfedale. Further, I should like to express my appreciation of the unfailing courtesy and attention of the staffs of the London Library and the Durham County Library, Darlington.

Peter Gunn
Swaledale, Yorkshire
December 1983

CHAPTER 1

The Lie of the Uplands

THE YORKSHIRE DALES are a world apart, a world to themselves. The visitor quickly becomes aware of this from whatever direction he has entered them. The dalesman, too, is conscious of the fact; his pride in his native countryside, village or town leads him easily to a sense of his own superiority over all others, however distinguished they may be. If Sir Winston Churchill had come to live in the Dales, he would have been an 'incomer' to the dalesman; not because he was a rich man with a handsome income, but, poor man, for the unrectifiable reason that he was not born and bred in the Dales, that, an outsider, he had come in to dwell there.

Yet what the visitor sees at once, the dalesman seems silently to ignore. The natural beauty all around him—a source of unfailing pleasure to the incomer—seems to be lost on the dalesman: the silhouette of mountains and hills cut out of a blue only a little deeper than that of the sky, the swift, shifting shadows of clouds over the moors, the omnipresence of stone (the browns of Millstone Grit and the weathered whiteness of Limestone), the tarns on the high fells and the rushing becks, the unexpected waterfalls; the river-valleys, so green with their woods and water-meadows, and through them the streams that in winter sweep and swirl in angry spate or in summer idly meander; the fields and roadside verges prinked with wild-flowers, the flight of birds and the sight of wild creatures. If you come across the dalesman by a dry-stone wall, looking intently at the further side of the dale, he will not be sizing up the landscape with a painter's eye for the picturesque; more likely than not he will be assessing the number of animals on the sheepgait opposite or gauging the success of a neighbouring farmer in his perennial feud with the moles. Climate and isolation; it is these that have bred in him that independence and seeming stoical indifference, attitudes born of the conditions of life among these Pennine dales and fells. 'The climate shapes the dales and it shapes the life of the people'; the observation is from Marie Hartley and Joan Ingilby, those gifted researchers and writers to whom all lovers of the Yorkshire Dales owe so much. A contour map of the region shows a surface tormented into mountains and valleys like the great waves and troughs of a tumultuous sea. It is like a continuation of the Atlantic itself, from where the moisture-laden winds prevailing from the west drive in, to be forced upwards by the resistant barricade of these highlands and turn into heavy rain in all seasons and in winter to protracted snow. In summer a sudden downpour far up on the fells can surge in a wall of water down the dales, causing the rivers to overflow their banks and carry away livestock and even the unsuspecting angler in the tormented flurry. But winter in the Dales is the testing time for men and animals alike. What in summer are gales powerful enough to uproot trees and wind against which a man can scarcely keep his feet, leaving sheep to huddle under the shelter of the walls, in winter become searing blizzards, the snow driven to form deep drifts, burying the sheep alive and cutting off outlying farms for weeks on end. Caught in an iron world of snow and ice the dalesman ventures outside to tend his stock to be pierced by a wind that cuts like lancets of frozen steel. Yet generations of men and women have survived such severe climatic conditions. Living isolated on his farm the dalesman has entered into the closest communion with his land, his animals—and his weather. Anything extraneous would be an intrusion—hence his wariness of the incomer. Topography, climate and the character of the inhabitants have made the Yorkshire Dales a world apart, a region, to use John Donne's words, 'intire of its selfe'.

Yet this truth discloses something of a paradox, since it is equally true that the Dales of Yorkshire, despite their insularity, present a surprising and revealing epitome of English history. No important historical event in the nation at large has left the Dales untouched, so that far from being an isolated enclave, every major movement that has changed the face of England has made an imprint on the Dales or left there its transitory trace. In other regions of England the evidences of the past have been obscured or obliterated by material change, especially those brought about by the Industrial Revolution of the eighteenth and nineteenth centuries. In the Yorkshire Dales no such transformation has taken place; all is there, open for those with eyes to see. However, although prehistoric objects and those from historical times, like the tenth-century Viking sword discovered in 1981 near Richmond, are still found there, most of them are preserved today in Dales' or national museums for safety and study. In 1979 a schoolboy, thirteen-year-old Alan Brown, walking by the River Swale near Haverdale, noticed a strange object in the shallow waters of the riverbed, differing in its shape and brown colour from the other water-rounded stones. His curiosity aroused, he lifted it out and carried it home. The local doctor, suspecting the importance of the boy's discovery, took the object to the Zoology Department of Leeds University, where it was identified as a piece of the jaw-bone of a primaeval mammoth, *mammuthus* or *elephans primigenius*. This giant creature must have lived in the region thousands of years ago, died and become buried, until a recent flooding of the Swale apparently dislodged and uncovered the massive fragment of bone. In the Dales prehistory, antiquity, the Middle Ages and succeeding centuries have a seemingly timeless contemporaneity with the present. And if the material evidence of the prehistorical and historical periods is so abundantly visible in the dales, the impress of the past is similarly revealed in the language, customs and characters of present-day dalesmen. In a quite singular fashion these upland fastnesses have formed a locked-up repository in which has been stored and conserved much that is understandable only by references to what has gone before, to events momentous not only to dwellers in the Dales, but to the inhabitants of the island as a whole. In this lies the seeming paradox. The Yorkshire Dales constitute a region uniquely itself and at the same time present a microcosm of England.

About 8,000 to 10,000 years ago at the close of the Ice Age the first peoples wandered into the Dales. They were Palaeolithic or Mesolithic folk, who had trekked north in the milder summer months on hunting expeditions among the marshy valley-bottoms and wooded hills. Small flints and a bone harpoon fashioned by these Middle Stone Age hunters have been unearthed in Victoria Cave near Settle in Craven. From about 3,000 to 2,500 BC, as the climate became warmer, other groups of men moved into the Dales, bringing with them their more sophisticated Neolithic culture, still with the earlier, but improved Stone Age weapons and tools: flint axes, arrow-heads and cutting instruments. These men practised a primitive agriculture, cultivating wild grain (wheat and barley) and tending cattle, goats, sheep and pigs. Intermingling with the Mesolithic folk, these Neolithic peoples formed the first permanent settlers in the Dales, gaining their livelihood by hunting which supplemented their rudimentary farming. Traces of their settled existence are found in the places for the disposal of their dead: the burial-mounds or barrows, like the Giant's Grave to the east of Pen-y-ghent, or the raised rings and ditches, like those near Grassington in Wharfedale or around Ripon.

Some time after 2,000 BC, there arrived from the Rhine Valley and the Low Countries men who had learned from the East the use of copper and bronze for the manufacture of their artifacts: their weapons, tools and ornaments. They valued and traded in jet and amber, which they employed for their personal adornment. These Bronze Age peoples also had a life of the spirit as their religious observances and burial customs show. To them we owe the sacred circles of Yockenthwaite in Wharfedale and perhaps of Maiden Castle on Harkerside in Swaledale; also possibly those curious cup-and-ring stone carvings found on Rombalds Moor near Ilkley. Strange, too, was their habit of burying their dead, awkwardly crouched in round barrows, with beakers for the departed to drink from on his passage to the other world. Gradually the Age of Bronze gave way to the Iron Age, bringing with it upheaval, dislocation and migration among the continental tribes, the repercussions of their movements being felt in Britain. From the fifth and fourth centuries BC there crossed the sea from Germany men of the Hallstatt culture, workers in iron, which they fashioned into long-swords and spears and the husbandman's sickle. At Semer Water in Wensleydale, the little glacial lake charmingly enfolded between the fells, was found what may be described as a palimpsest of civilisations. In 1937 when the level of the lake was lowered by clearing away the accumulated silt that had blocked the outlet and caused the surface of the water to rise, artifacts of the Iron Age were discovered above what had been an earlier Bronze Age settlement and beneath this the remains of Neolithic habitation.

Across the North Sea and the narrow waters of the Channel in these later Iron Age migrations came from France the more aristocratic Celtic peoples of the La Tène culture, among them the Brigantes, who formed a loose confederacy covering much of northern Britain and embracing the Yorkshire Dales. These Celts buried their chieftains, both men and women, together with the chariots that had been their prerogative in life, in round barrows, like that discovered at Stanwick St John, north of Richmond. The Brigantes were, in the main, pastoralists, lovers of horses and of beautiful objects skilfully wrought in bronze and enamel; it is they whom we may look on as the first historical dalesmen. Their huge earthworks remain as witnesses of their political and military capacity—and of an extraordinary communal energy. It was the Brigantes who offered the main resistance to the Roman invasion and conquest of Britain in AD 43 and it was from the Dales that they marched under their leader Venutius to their irrevocable defeat; subsequently it was in the barely accessible fastnesses of the Dales that the survivors found their refuge. Chiefly as a measure to counter further military threats from the Brigantes, Agricola, the Roman governor of Britain, reorganised the Dales, setting up an integrated system of forts and camps for the legionaries and their auxiliaries, linked by that splendid network of roads which remains to this day. Evidence of the 350 years of Roman occupation can be seen at many points in the Dales.

Yet the blessings of the Romano-British civilisation enjoyed under the *pax romana* were threatened in the fourth century by raids of Picts and Scots from beyond Hadrian's Wall and, more ominous still, by the appearance in the rivers and inlets of the east coast of the longships of Germanic pirates, the *adventus Saxonum*. If the Anglo-Saxons arrived in hostility, they stayed as husbandmen. It was groups of Anglian farming folk who, venturing westwards up the river-valleys from the seventh century on, settled in the Dales. Since the valley-bottoms were mostly undrained marsh, they made their habitations on the more fertile lands of the hillsides, surrounding their hamlets with cultivated open fields. Outside the villages of Grinton, Fremington, Reeth and Healaugh in Swaledale, as in Wensleydale and elsewhere, may be seen today the grassed terraces of their strips, the lynchets or ranes, that they ploughed to grow those basic crops which provided their frugal fare:

> Oats, peas, beans and barley grow,
> Oats, peas, beans and barley grow,
> Do you or I or anyone know
> How oats, peas, beans and barley grow?
> Waiting for a partner . . .

Partners came to share with the Angles life in the Dales. Like their own ancestors they were sea-rovers, the Viking peoples from Scandinavia. After 876, when Halfdan, the leader of the Danish Great Army, 'portioned out the lands of the Northumbrians', his Danes settled, apparently peaceably enough, alongside the Angles, mostly in the eastern parts of the Dales. Then, in the following century they were joined by Norse Vikings, coming from their settlements in Ireland and taking up unoccupied land in Craven and at the western heads of the Richmondshire dales. It was these pastoralist Norsemen who have perhaps left the greatest racial impression on life in the Yorkshire Dales in the customs and especially the language. It is said that in the Narvik landing during the Second World War Yorkshire infantry—composed of men from the Dales—speaking their own dialect, could converse with the local Norwegians.

Over these centuries Christianity had spread among the dalesmen. The Northumbrian King Edwin and his court had been converted in 627, persuaded by his Christian wife and, according to his compatriot the Venerable Bede, by a moving speech from one of his attendant nobles, with its striking symbolism: 'Man is like a sparrow, mighty king.' Soon the Roman priest Paulinus, the assistant of St Augustine of Canterbury, was baptising converts in the waters of the Swale. If paganism died hard, the existence of early Saxon crosses, possibly on the sites of earlier 'field-churches', marks the progress of Christianity throughout the Dales.

With the eleventh-century Norman Conquest fully-fledged feudalism became established in the North with the creation of the marcher lords, one of whose principal functions was to protect the frontier against the persistent armed incursions of the Scots. In 1070 William the Conqueror presented what later became known as the Honour of Richmond to Alan Rufus, cousin of the Count of Brittany, as a reward for his martial services on the field of Hastings and in overcoming northern resistance to Norman rule. Part of the feudal dues of the tenants of the Honour was paid in service against the Scots; much later in 1513 it was the 'warlike wights' of Craven and Richmondshire who marched north to Flodden Field. The great feudal estates of the Fitz Hughs, Percies, Nevilles, Cliffords, Mowbrays, Scropes and lesser barons extended into the Dales. In the neighbourhood of their fortified castles arose the abbeys. The Normans were great benefactors of the monasteries; within a century and a half of the Conquest eight abbeys and priories had been founded in the Dales. The coming of the monks, particularly the Cistercians, gave an impetus to the development of the wool trade, the greatest single contribution to the nation's mediaeval wealth.

One of the dominating figures of the disastrous Wars of the Roses was Richard Neville, 'Warwick the Kingmaker', the head of the Nevilles of Middleham in Wensleydale. Yet the battles were not armed conflicts between Yorkshiremen and Lancashiremen: for the Yorkist cause were the Scropes and Mowbrays; Percies and Cliffords fought for the Lancastrians; Warwick for both. If the Wars of the Roses weakened this feudal economy, its eclipse arrived only with the Tudors. The Dissolution of the Monasteries under Henry VIII precipitated the Pilgrimage of Grace and the Rising of the North and the failure of both rebellions brought in their train savage reprisals and much misery to the undeserving commons of the Yorkshire Dales. The Tudor settlement occasioned the rise of the landed gentry, many of whom, Catholic and Protestant alike, had profited by the dispersal of the lands of the suppressed monasteries; and from their tenants, holding their farms by 'ancient birthright of title', descended the sturdy yeoman of the Dales. In the seventeenth century some of these men bought their lands and built, often on the site of a much earlier dwelling, the typical solid stone farmhouses with their mullioned windows and the yeoman owner's initials and the date proudly displayed carved on the lintel of the doorway.

In the eighteenth and early nineteenth centuries, as a supplement to the farming of the area, came the development of industrial ventures: a revival of the age-old lead-mining, coal-mining, home-knitting and the establishment of woollen and cotton mills, these last taking advantage of the plentiful water-power. Transport was facilitated by turnpike roads. Trade increased, every larger community had its own specialised craftsmen working locally and some their priests, parsons and ministers as well as their doctors and attorneys. Nonconformity in religion was in the air of the Dales; earlier there had been the Catholic recusants and Catholicism remained, particularly among old families of the landed gentry. Then came George Fox and John Wesley, Quakerism and Methodism finding a ready response in the religious consciousness of ordinary dalesmen. A series of Enclosure Acts dating from the late eighteenth century and the nineteenth radically changed the face of the Dales and the dry-stone walls came into being, parcelling out the land. These walls are caught up and echoed in the scars, screes and outcropping of rock, so that one is permanently aware in the landscape of the pervasive presence of stone.

With the advance of the nineteenth century the earlier prosperity faltered, dwindled and died. Lead came to be imported cheaper from abroad. Coal was more plentiful, of a superior quality and more easily mined elsewhere. Improved machinery and large-scale production put paid to the woollen and cotton mills in the Dales. Underemployment meant emigration; in the lonelier dales and on the fellsides houses, once teeming with vigorous life, became abandoned and derelict, haunted by owls and forlorn memories. What remained for a diminished population of dalesmen were the time-honoured livelihood farming and the new and growing tourist industry. For with the coming of the railways the beauties of the Dales, that had caught the imagination of the devotees of the Picturesque and delighted poets and painters alike became open to a wider public. By the second half of the twentieth century prosperity had returned to a Dales profoundly changed both economically and socially. What had not changed was their extraordinary natural beauty. To preserve this for the dalesmen as much as for the nation, by an Enabling Act of 1950 the Countryside Commission was set up. In 1954 it established the Yorkshire Dales National Park—680 square miles (1,761 square kilometres) of incomparable landscape of Pennine mountains, wild felltop moorlands and the intervening green river-valleys.

To delimit or even delineate the Yorkshire Dales is a somewhat arbitrary matter; and it is not made easier by the fact that changes in county administration have run counter to history. The Yorkshire Dales National Park embraces both the district historically known as Craven (with the wapentakes of Claro and Staincliffe and the Liberty of Ripon) in what was formerly the West Riding, and that of the historical Richmondshire (with its Honour embracing the wapentakes of Gilling West, Hang West and Hang East) in the North Riding. These two regions are central to any conception of the Dales. As a result of the Local Government Act of 1972 the ancient ridings of the Danish Vikings disappeared and portions of the traditional Yorkshire have been lost to neighbouring counties; for example, Dentdale, with Dent and Sedbergh, now form part of the new county of Cumbria, and Teesdale part of the old palatinate of County Durham. The Pennine massif, with its peaks of over 2,000 feet (608 metres), popularly considered as the backbone of England, is cleft by numerous river-valleys and these constitute the dales proper. The high fells around Mallerstang Common (historically part of York-shire, but now in Cumbria) form a watershed; within only a short distance of each other are the sources of streams or their tributary becks, some, like the Swale and the Ure, finding their outlets ulti-mately in the North Sea; others—the Eden and the Lune—dis-charging their waters into the Irish Sea. A downpour from the same cloud can thus achieve its haven in opposite oceans. East of the great hump of Whernside, which straddles the new border between North Yorkshire and Cumbria, rise the headwaters of the Ribble which also flows into the Irish Sea.

For present purposes the River Tees has been taken as the northern limit of the Yorkshire Dales—the old boundary of the North Riding and County Durham. South of the Tees the major dales have been formed by a fan-like system of rivers, which join the Ouse and enter the North Sea by the estuary of the Humber. From north to south, these are the Swale, the Ure, the Nidd, the Wharfe and the Aire. On the east the highlands descend to the Vale of York; the motorist travelling north on the A1 from Wetherby to Scotch Corner sees their outline continually on his left. For the southern boundary of the Yorkshire Dales I have followed an imaginary line drawn from a little east of Otley and passing through Ilkley, Skipton, Gargrave, Settle and Clapham, to Ingleton; the western frontier being formed by another imaginary line from Ingleton to the Howgill Fells, to the north-west, that is, of Sedbergh. In the present arrangement of county administration, then, the Yorkshire Dales are found for the most part in North and West Yorkshire, but also overspilling into Cumbria and County Durham. Old loyalties die hard, and it would be difficult to imagine an elderly inhabitant of Dentdale as anything other than a true Yorkshireman.

Geology is a difficult, exacting subject and many people, specialists apart, feel that it is better avoided altogether. However, the very beauty of the Yorkshire Dales is founded on rock; it is just this configuration and the physical composition of these features of the landscape that have contributed such an essential part of the Dales' arresting, dramatic quality. And in this drama it is not too fanciful to see the rocks as the *dramatis personae*. To gain the fullest enjoyment from the spectacle it is desirable to know something of the principal characters that compose it; but what is required is not a detailed knowledge, only a general understanding, whose relevance can be so rewarding in what it reveals.

Almost the whole of the Dales belongs to a single geological era, that known as the Carboniferous period, which occurred some 280–345 million years ago. The main exception to this is in the north-west, the region of the Howgill Fells, whose slates are of an earlier period, the Silurian, some 55 million years, or more, previously. In the Carboniferous period the present surface of the Dales lay resting on still older rocks—Pre-Cambrian, Ordovician and Silurian —deep beneath the limpid, tropical waters of a sea teeming with marine life. Petrified remains of maritime plants and creatures are found high on the hills of the Limestone country: crinoids (sea lilies), marine shells (among them *nautili* and *ammonididae*) and corals. On the sea-bottom was deposited the massive thickness of the Great Scar Limestone, that beautiful pearl-grey, grey-white stone (chameleon-like it changes its shades with changes of light and moisture), the stone that characterises much of the central and south-western dales and gives them their peculiar charm. As the volume of this sea became shallower, other deltaic sediments were deposited, consisting of layers of shales, sandstones and limestones—these three kinds of rock composing the triad that is known as the Yoredale Series (from their having been studied and identified by the geologist Phillips in Wensleydale, the dale of the River Ure or, formerly, Yore). Later still, in the equatorial swamps of the vast Pennine delta (whose giant forests have yielded our coal deposits) was laid down a coarse-grained sandstone, known as Millstone Grit. (From the Middle Ages millers used it as grinding stones since they found that it did not overheat the grain.) Millstone Grit forms much of the surface of the eastern dales today and caps such summits in Craven as Ingleborough and Whernside. Over the ages it has weathered considerably, leaving in places fantastically sculptured shapes such as those at Brimham Rocks, near Pateley Bridge in Nidderdale. The scenery is most striking when, travelling westwards from the dark walls and sombre building stone of the Millstone Grit country, you come out near Bolton Abbey into the light grace of the Great Scar Limestone of Craven. The beauty of the greys and whites is seen in the dry-stone walls around Clapham; in Wharfedale in such distinctive features as the mass of Kilnsey Crag; and in the 'pavements' above Malham, the precipitous face of Malham Cove and the tumbling rock formation and screes of Gordale Scar.

In Wensleydale the Great Scar Limestone is buried far below the surface of rocks of the Yoredale Series, only appearing in places; it is this alternation of shale, sandstone and limestone (different from that of the Great Scar) that has produced the stepped or terraced landscape of that dale. In Swaledale it is from rocks of the Yoredale Series and Millstone Grit that the grandeur of the landscape has been hewn and carved; in the upper dale, to avoid the hard rock of Kisdon the Swale switched its course to cut the beautiful chasm of Kisdon Force, with its overhanging woods and tumbling waterfalls; and downstream the Yoredale strata are clearly visible where the Swale is joined by the rushing waters of Gunnerside Beck.

Limestone, being chemically composed of calcium carbonate, is soluble in water. In the Great Scar country of Craven the erosive action of running water has been at work over thousands of years to create that silent, subterranean world, where potholes lead down to great cavernous cathedrals with their stilettoed stalagmites, glistening stalactites and shapely pillars, their underground rivers and mirrored pools; that mysterious dark (or when lit for visitors, scintillating) region, the earthbound elysium of the speleologists —Ingleborough Cave, the White Scar Caves and the Stump Cross Caverns. This water-weathered limestone can be seen everywhere above ground, not only in the dry-stone walls, but in the scars and screes, the scattered outcroppings and those remarkable pavements, like that above Malham Cove. Here water has penetrated between vertical and horizontal crevices in the rock and, dissolving the limestone, has enlarged the intervals between the planes, the vertical fissures being known as 'grikes', the corrugated surface of the pavement being divided into 'clints'. From a distance, in certain lights, the appearance of Malham limestone pavement is that of a freshly ploughed field, strangely man-made in the natural soft greensward of the moor.

It was at the end of the Carboniferous period, when the deposited rock strata of the seabed were forcibly uplifted by gigantic earth movements, that there occurred great fractures in the earth's surface, 'faults', when the landmass on one side of the dividing fault was dramatically raised or lowered. The two principal geological upheavals of this kind in the Dales are the Craven and the Dent faults. The Craven fault runs easterly through Ingleton towards Pateley Bridge, being revealed spectacularly in the abrupt cliff-faces of Giggleswick Scar and Malham Cove. The Dent fault, from west of

Ingleton, lies roughly north-easterly, marking the boundary between the rocks of the Carboniferous period of the Dales and those of the earlier Silurian of Cumbria. During this period minerals, molten at extreme temperatures, were forced from deep within the earth through these fractures to form veins containing ores valuable to man, such as the lead that was the source of much of the Dales' mining activity.

One of the chief formative agents of the present landscape of the Dales was active in the Quaternary Ice Age, which began about one million years ago, when the surface of the land was covered with an immense sheet of ice so thick that only some of the highest mountain summits showed above the enveloping ice-cap. The intervals between these four successive glacial periods were much warmer than today; and as the ice melted, the glaciers began that forward movement which carved out the present river-valleys, carrying with them débris of rock, gravel and alluvium, which formed the terminal moraines so often seen in the U-shaped valleys and, in the flatter places, those humpbacked drumlins that abound in Wensleydale and upper Ribblesdale. At times these moraines blocked the valleys, creating swamps and lakes. Semer Water and Malham Tarn are glacial lakes formed in this way, the latter lying on a bed of impervious boulder clay and slate.

In the Victoria Cave the remains of animals that lived and roamed the Pennine Dales in these inter-glacial interludes have been discovered. During one of the warmer periods conditions must have been such as we associate with tropical Africa, when there flourished in the heat the lion and the hyena, the elephant and the hippopotamus. Subsequently, when the climate became cooler, the woolly rhinoceros grazed these highland slopes. Still later, when tundral conditions reigned, as the last great ice-sheet retreated, reindeer found their summer feeding on these uplands, in company with the Arctic fox and hare, the lynx and the elk. As the last glacial ice withdrew and springtimes softened into a gentle thaw, lichens appeared and mosses, and with them Arctic and alpine plants; then the first hardy bushes and dwarf trees, of juniper, perhaps birch and willow. The increasing warmth brought grasses, heaths and sedges and taller trees—besides the birches, hazel and alder, pines, elm and oak—conditions ultimately suitable for the advent of man.

The difference in the nature of the original rocks and in the effects of erosion on them has effected the variety and richness of the Dales' countryside, its outward appearance and its characteristic flora and fauna. As a rule, the origin of soil is easy to recognise from the vegetation it produces and the use to which the land is put. In Millstone Grit country the soil, which is acidic and of a low fertility, may, if poorly drained, have developed deep thicknesses of peat, covered by mosses or rough cotton grass; the fells are boggy under-foot and studded with tarns, the haunts of black-headed gulls. Those regions where the rocks are predominantly of the Yoredale Series, may show wider differences of natural vegetation. Shales break down into a deep and heavy soil, rich in humus, which is well suited to woodland; yet this soil, which, being deficient in calcium, is naturally sour, can, if it is well limed and drained, provide pasture, valuable meadowland and even arable crops. The fells of the Great Scar Limestone are immediately identifiable from their emerald greensward, the light, lime-rich, well-drained soil producing in the springy turf those grasses so ideal for sheep-grazing.

When the earliest settlers penetrated the Dales, it seems that they mostly kept to the higher regions of the Great Scar Limestone country, avoiding the thick woodlands and the swamp-infested valley-bottoms. There, on those well-drained uplands, they pastured their animals and raised their few arable crops. The British who followed still considered the foot of the valleys uninhabitable on account of the marshes and lakes and the dense thickets of alder and willow, which were too difficult for them to drain and clear. The felltops they found did not differ greatly from what we see today: in regions of the Yoredales or Millstone Grit they are covered with cotton grass, moss, heather and bracken. Open woodland of oak and birch covered the hillsides between 300 and 900 feet (91 and 274 metres). It was below this, in natural clearings in the oakwoods or in those they cleared by dint of their own persevering labour, that the Angles and Danes chiefly found their homesteads and created their nucleated villages. Later still the Norse, more solitary in their social habits, reverted to the earlier pattern of settling on the unoccupied high ground, often in isolated farms. The constant cropping and treading of animals assisted man, who by axe and fire succeeded in gradually clearing the woodland that had once covered much of the hillsides and valleys of the Dales. A great deal of the deforestation, however, only came about from the seventeenth century on, when trees were felled for fuel, especially for the widespread smelting of lead.

At the time of the Norman Conquest the stag might almost have stood as the symbol of the feudal system; hunting the deer was a royal—or, at least, a baronial—pastime, and great tracts of forest (not necessarily woodland) were preserved in the Dales, where the severest forest laws were enforced by the king's, or the lords', verderers. Man-traps kept out the intruder; too often they left him maimed for life. In 1171 the monks of Jervaulx Abbey were granted free pasturage by Earl Conan of Richmond in his preserved New Forest in Arkengarthdale, with the strict stipulation that no hounds or mastiffs were to be kept; this, despite the perpetual menace of wolves. No commoner was allowed to keep a large dog at all, unless it had been correctly 'expediated'; that is, it had had three claws cut from each forefoot to prevent its hunting. To keep the deer away from their crops the peasants had to keep watch all night or sleep, wrapped in their cloaks, among the strips of their open fields. Venison was a valuable commodity; human life was cheap.

Although in modern times herds of deer have been kept at Studley Royal, in Bolton Park in Wensleydale, in the deer-park at Bolton Abbey and at Buckden in Wharfedale, the native deer were linked so closely with feudalism that they might be said to have disappeared with it. In Swaledale the Wharton family carefully protected their deer, which only died out early in the eighteenth century. In fact they did not vanish completely then; there are still wild native deer in Swaledale today, although their haunts are a well-guarded secret, known only to few dalesmen. As late as the Stuarts herds of deer still existed, particularly in the remoter dales, such as Arkengarthdale, Raydale and Cotterdale.

In Craven the Cliffords of Skipton Castle were, from earliest times, continually at loggerheads with their neighbours, clans like the Nortons, by reason of their highhanded way of hunting the deer almost where they willed in the forests of Skipton, Barden and Bolton. In the seventeenth century the hunters met their match in the Yorke family of Gouthwaite in Nidderdale. After the Dissolution of the Monasteries the Yorkes, although they remained Catholic in religion, acquired in Wharfedale the manors of Kilnsey, formerly the property of Fountains Abbey, and of Appletreewick, once owned by the prior and canons of Bolton Priory. The Protestant Cliffords of Skipton, by purchase and marriage with the great Percy family of Northumberland, had, after the Dissolution, gained possession of most of Littondale, which was well stocked with deer and game as was the other Percy property further to the north in Langstrothdale Chase. Between 1606 and 1633, encouraged or led by Sir John Yorke of Appletreewick, bands of marauders, 'notorious deer-stealers, men of mean estate and worse condition', hunted deer where they found them in Nidderdale, Ribblesdale, Langstrothdale and up Littondale. On a June day in 1607 one such band, equipped with greyhounds and armed with crossbows and guns, met at 'Haltongill Field' in Littondale, where they found a herd of thirty deer quietly grazing. Setting after them, they pursued them up on to Pen-y-ghent and then to Malham Moor, where they felled two hinds, and 'cawsed other two to breake their neckes from the toppe of a Great Rocke'. Despite protracted lawsuits the feud between the Cliffords and Yorkes continued, as did the killing of the deer, this usually taking place at night. At Appletreewick Fair in 1621 (perhaps the strong ale was the cause) words led to deeds. A stand-up fight broke out between Sir John's men and those of the Clifford faction and the feud reached its climax. But the issue was to all intents already solved since the contentious deer were virtually extinct.

If deer are mostly a thing of the past, other game is plentiful in the Dales: the red and black grouse that abound on the moors, the pheasants in the rich grasses and woodland of the valleys; partridges, snipe, wild duck and wood-pigeons. The playful hares, that used to come down from the fells and gambol in the meadows in the evening, seem largely to have perished in the harsh winter of 1980. Rabbits, though periodically ravaged by myxomatosis, still survive and multiply, appearing to find it healthier to leave the open ground and burrow under the dry-stone walls. Other wild creatures to be observed are the stoats (sometimes seen in their cream winter coat, attacking a rabbit in the snowdrifts), weasels, badgers, hedgehogs, and an occasional fox. From the Glorious Twelfth the moors are given over to the incomers—of all nations, although there has yet to be seen a Japanese businessman in a deer-stalker hat. Grouse-shooting is a rich man's pastime; the *Victoria County History* of 1907 gives an interesting commentary on the sport:

It was on a Yorkshire moor, Blubberhouses, that Lord Walsingham on 23 August 1872 shot 842 birds himself. On 30 August 1888 the same great marksman, by shooting for fourteen hours and eighteen minutes, and by firing an average of 108 shots an hour, succeeded in bringing down 1,058 birds.

We are not told of his lordship's other interests.

Those who live under the moors or walk them frequently hear the melancholy maniacal cackle of the grouse and the sad bleating of the black-faced gimmer separated from her ewe. They will hear, too, the curiously distanced cry of the curlew; and, on a summer's day on the fells, the high-up song of the skylark. In spring on the fellside the acrobatic aerial display of the lapwing or peewit can be enjoyed, as it climbs, plunges, whirls and gyrates in a flurry of feathers, with its wild call of 'p'weet-p'weet'. The golden plover is only found today on more remote moors or around Malham Tarn. In these moorland tarns the redshanks watch flotillas of moorhens and black-headed gulls from the water's edge; and in the high places, among the rocky crevices of the cliff-face, ravens nest. The dale-bottoms are filled with brightly coloured little birds, cheerful companions to the cottagers: great and blue tits, redstarts, wagtails, yellowhammers, the finches, robins, wrens and wheatears. Nor are the lively songbirds lacking, the thrushes and blackbirds. Little and barn owls, too, are common: and along the surface of the rivers flash brilliant kingfishers with submarine-searching dippers in their waters. At times, if rarely, the leisured, hovering flight of the kestrel, merlin and peregrine falcon can be seen; and, rarer still, in the high remote regions, the soaring buzzard. The sparrows, magpies, carrion crows, jackdaws, flocks of rooks, starlings and fieldfares are ubiquitous as is the springtime cuckoo. As well as for the specialised geologist then, the Dales hold much for the ornithologist and the ordinary bird-lover.

The same can be said for the botanist; but not for specialists alone:

> A primrose by the river's brim
> A *Dicotyledon* was to him,
> And it was nothing more.

The Yorkshire Dales are a paradise for all lovers of the wildflowers of field and wood. Fortunately the areas taken over by the Forestry Commission for its regimented plantations of larch and spruce are limited; and the woods of chiefly indigenous deciduous trees (with the occasional holly and yew)—woodland often the relic of the primaeval forests—are, with their undergrowth, filled with their freshness and natural beauty: oak, sycamore, hornbeam, lime, mountain ash, hawthorn, hazel and blackthorn, and, reflecting their greens in the streams' mirror, alder and willow. The fells are brown-purpled with heather, the hillsides mauve with willow-herb; and in autumn burnished with the flame of bracken. Spring comes late in the Dales and snowdrops and primroses by the roadside are its harbingers, while wild garlic (that poor relation of lily-of-the-valley) throws its confetti over the green of the woodland clearings. In the sheltered summers of the woods bloom foxgloves, the giant bell-flower, bluebells, violets and orchids; beside them, the fields are carpeted with yellow heart's-ease and gay with the blues and mauves of scabious and meadow cranesbill; the lanes are lined with dog-roses, marguerites, forget-me-nots, and with that northern rarity the water aven, with its miniature Japanese-lantern flowers, crimson sepalled. The autumnal splendour of the woods, like those around Bolton Abbey, blaze in their reds, russets and brilliant yellows. In winter the trees, isolated in dun or white fields, stand spectrally gaunt, their branches outlined in Rembrandt-etched lineaments in the blackest of Indian ink.

These are the woods and wild flowers for all to see; other plants are more unobtrusive. Hidden away in the grikes of the limestone pavements of Craven grow discreetly such varieties as hart's tongue fern, herb Robert, black and green spleenwort, wood anemone, bloody cranesbill, brittle bladder fern, the globe flower and lily-of-the-valley. Just north of Grassington in Wharfedale is the privately owned property of Grass Wood, which is botanically famous for the number of uncommon plants growing there among its velvet carpet of lilies-of-the-valley: rare orchids, including the fly orchid and the dark-red helleborine, the rare milkwort, bird's-eye primrose, meadow saxifrage, butterwort, the blue moorgrass and Jacob's Ladder. In high sheltered spots are found Arctic or alpine plants, leftovers from the glacial ages, varieties not commonly found in England.

From their geological origins, their climatic weathering and their man-made history the Yorkshire Dales bear a strong family likeness; even Great Scar Limestone and Millstone Grit differ no more radically than blonde and brunette and both can occur in the same family. Each dale, however, has its marked individuality, its particular physiognomy; each wears its view with a difference. Teesdale has a boldness about it, from the source of the Tees on Cross Fell in Cumbria, the highest peak in the Pennines (2,893 feet, 880 metres), past its falls at Caldron Snout and the majestic High Force. (Its majesty is somewhat tarnished when the river is not in its awesome spate by the colour of the water below the falls which resembles Newcastle Brown Ale!) This boldness and strength remains, where the river carves its beetling cliff, on which rises Barnard Castle, and flows in its deep chasm downstream. Below Eggleston Abbey the Tees enters the beautiful wooded country of Walter Scott's *Rokeby*, to the point where it is joined by the River Greta and the woods of Brignal:

> O, Brignal banks are wild and fair
> And Greta woods are green.

And there, by Greta's fine eighteenth-century bridge (painted by Cotman and Girtin), it truly ends as a dale. Swaledale is perhaps the grandest of the dales; in its upper reaches, embraced by the high fells of the Pennines, it has a wildness, a rugged austerity; but as the Swale descends and the valley widens, the woods and the trees that often follow the line of the walls soften any severity. Beyond Marrick and Ellerton Priories it becomes increasingly sylvan, so that from among the age-old yews below Willance's Leap it seems that Richmond and its castle, raised on their bluff, are encompassed by woods. As a contrast, it is the pastoral, parklike quality that distinguishes tranquil Wensleydale; Wharfedale has a similar suavity, its trees and copses a foil to that lightness of tone that derives from the limestone of the Craven country. Great Scar Limestone is again very much in evidence in Ribblesdale, with its scattered screes, scars and labyrinthine caves. The Aire and the Ribble, here in their Dales' sources and headwaters, retain their purity, not yet contaminated by modern industry, still as they were in Carlyle's time: 'The Ribble and the Aire roll down, as yet unpolluted by dyers' chemistry; tenanted by merry trouts and piscatory otters.'

All of the larger dales are joined by subsidiary dales, each with its distinctive quality, its individuality hidden in the folds of the fells, there for the discovering. Perhaps as good an impression as any of the variety and beauty of the Yorkshire Dales is gained from the mountain road that climbs up from Dentdale to descend by the western flank of Whernside into Kingsdale and to Ingleton. From Dent and its cobbled streets the road up Deepdale, bordered by hazel hedges and wild roses, leads through the green lushness of an alpine valley, to climb—with gates to be opened and shut—to the head of the pass at White Shaw Moss (1,385 feet, 422 metres). At this height Whernside, on the left, seems hardly impressive, just another hill, despite its 2,414 feet (736 metres). Before one stretches Kingsdale, as far as the eye can see, bare save for the occasional copse or clump of firs, its beck appearing as a narrow ribbon of silver, the dale-end lost in a mist that merges with an anonymous skyline.

CHAPTER 2

Resistance to Rome: the Brigantes

ABOVE THE HAMLET of High Fremington in Swaledale and beneath the grey Limestone scar of Fremington Edge stands Intake Wood. This stretch of dense woodland is the relic perhaps, a reminder at least, of the ancient royal forests that once clothed the mid-hillsides of upper Swaledale and of the neighbouring Arkengarthdale. In the brilliance and heat of a summer's day, to enter the wood is like passing straight from a sunlit terrace into a close-shuttered room; cool and dark. The depth of this sudden obscurity is unexpected; no less a contrast is the tenebrous freshness of the trees and thick undergrowth. The silence seems almost tangible, so uncanny as to suggest some actual bodily presence and a conscious withholding of all sound. Ash, hornbeam, sycamore, beech for the most part, with the occasional larch or a holly among evergreens: the trees with their canopy of brances provide shelter for tall creamy white and carmine foxgloves and for that secluded native of the North Country, the beautiful giant bellflower, whose mauve petals show up spectrally white in the half-light. In the spring the edges of the wood are full of primroses and dog violets; in the lane up to it, which is bordered with clumps of pink wild roses, grows the early purple orchid. Later, under the dry-stone walls that enclose both wood and fields, appear the pale blue of scabious and the deeper blues of meadow cranesbill and harebells, those smallest of the campanulas. In the creation of the quiet beauty of this spot nature has required no adjunct from the work of man.

Immediately to the south of the wood and visible from the lane, the grassed surface of the field, here as smooth and immaculate as a bowling green, rises to form what is seemingly a man-made earthwork, to all appearances a defensive rampart. That this was its purpose is borne out by a closer view, since the straight line of the bank falls away abruptly to a broad *vallum* or ditch, in places as much as 20 feet (6 metres) below the level of the rampart. A little to the south, the lane cuts through this massive earthwork, which from that point can be observed continuing down the hillside and through the trees in the grounds of Draycott Hall. Nor does it end there; beyond the houses on the Richmond road it will be seen crossing the water-meadows in the direction of the Swale. Over the river its prolongation can be discerned running up the other side of the dale to the east of Swale Hall. Further to the west, towards the prehistoric site of Maiden Castle on Harkerside, is a second line of earthworks. This can be picked out best from High Fremington in the evening light, when the westering sun casts a strong shadow from the rampart and the wall which surmounts it. These earthworks, so formidable as to defy the passage of centuries, may seem a fit and enduring monument to the earliest historical inhabitants of the Yorkshire Dales, the Brigantes.

To the question: Who were the Brigantes? near-contemporary literary sources, supported by the recent findings of archaeology, have provided an answer. Some time in the third century BC, in the general movement of peoples on the Continent, a group or groups detached themselves from their homelands around Lake Constance and, moving north, crossed the Channel into these islands, bringing with them their La Tène culture. Characteristic of these La Tène Celts were the practice of a pastoral economy, with the breeding of livestock, particularly horses and cattle, and a highly developed aesthetic sense, revealed in their skill in metalwork. These early Britons achieved a hegemony over the tribes already inhabiting North Yorkshire, whose primitive agriculture and grave-objects suggest that their culture was of the type known as Iron Age A or even that more rudimentary still of the Late Bronze Age. The Brigantes, the hillmen, appear to have carried their name with them, possibly from the locality in Switzerland from whence they came, and it was by this name that they were known to the Romans. To the east of the Vale of York they had as neighbours the tribe of Parisii, a people of a similar La Tène culture, who had migrated from the Seine Valley and whose name is perpetuated in that of the city of Paris. When they emerged in history, in the first century AD, the Brigantes headed a monarchical confederacy of tribes, extending over a vast territory roughly from the Calder to the Solway–Tyne and even beyond.

If the aristocracy of the Brigantes, the chiefs of these warrior pastoralists and horse-copers, lived, as it has been said, with a 'certain barbaric splendour', others of the possibly subjected tribesmen maintained a precarious existence, dwelling in the highlands outside the towns in small villages, isolated farmsteads or even in single huts, with just one or two tilled fields and enclosures for livestock. Some trade there undoubtedly was, since the Brigantes possessed a gold and silver coinage of their own, embossed with the names of their kings and queens: Volisios, Dumnoveros (or Dumnocoveros) and Cartimandua. Hoards of these coins have been found, and alongside them numbers of Roman silver coins dated between 209 and 41 BC, such as were commonly used by both Roman and British traders before the Claudian conquest of AD 43. It is likely that the trade with the more agriculturally advanced South was chiefly in horses, sheep and cattle. It may be that the charioteers of Cassivellaunus, so admired by Julius Caesar in his earlier invasion some hundred years before Claudius, obtained many of their horses, and even their knowledge of cavalry tactics, from the horse-breeding Brigantes. Like other Celts they possessed an innate artistic flair. The skill of their artificers in metals is proved by the beautiful bronze torque or necklet discovered a century ago at Embsay and the decorated swords and scabbards found at Flasby and in the neighbourhood of Ripon—the celebrated swastika rock carving at Ilkley is also thought to be the work of Brigantian artists. In 1844, outside the great earthworks at Stanwick St John, six miles (9.6 kilometres) north of Richmond, was unearthed a magnificent collection of grave-objects of the first century AD, representing a chariot-burial characteristic of La Tène culture. The grave was probably that of one of the ruling dynasty of the Brigantes. This collection is preserved in the British Museum, where it provided the original nucleus of the Department of British and Mediaeval Antiquities.

Some time before 1833 a buried hoard of Roman military equipment was discovered on Fremington Edge, consisting of pieces of the harness of cavalry horses—pendants, roundels, flat strips and studs. The items became separated and are to be seen today in the British and York Museums. The handbook of 1852 of the York Museum describes them as, 'several specimens of silvered bronze horse-furniture, ornamented with slightly-engraved patterns. Found on

Fremington Hagg, near Reeth, in Swaledale.' The precise site of their discovery is not known: West Hagg (hagg is Old Norse for 'a cutting down of trees') is about 500 yards (457 metres) east of Intake Wood. It has been conjectured that this was a cache of booty captured by the Brigantes in an engagement with the Romans, then buried and forgotten since it was never recovered. To link this find with that made at Stanwick goes far to explain the earthworks on Fremington Edge and to unfold the story of the heroic resistance to the Roman conquest of Britain put up by these remote ancestors of present dalesmen, the Early Britons of Brigantia.

In 55 BC Julius Caesar, provoked by the help given by the Britons to the Gallic peoples, crossed the Channel to carry out what was in effect a reconnaissance of the southern coast of this island. This achieved, he withdrew. The following year he returned and penetrating north of the Thames defeated the Belgic tribe of Catuvellauni under their king, Cassivellaunus. Having secured the submission of the neighbouring native tribes and coming to terms with Cassivellaunus, he once more withdrew. For almost a century the relations of the Britons with the Continent were chiefly the pacific ones of trade. It was not until the time of the Emperor Claudius that the Romans attempted a full-scale invasion and conquest of Britain.

It is from the fortunate preservation of Latin and Greek texts and the patient work of archaeologists that there can be built up—if the fragmentary evidence is pieced together—a peculiarly vivid picture of events at that time and of the actual men and women who shaped them, here in these northern regions so far from the centre of the then known world. From the pages of the historians Tacitus and Dio Cassius and the satirist Juvenal, among others, it can be seen how seriously these happenings in this remote frontier of the empire were viewed in Rome and how the names and characters of prominent personalities among the Britons were familiar there even to the ordinary man in the street. And where literary sources are silent, stones and potsherds, when interpreted by archaeologists, can speak instead.

In AD 43 an army of some 30,000–40,000 well-seasoned troops, composed of four legions with auxiliary regiments, landed in Kent under the command of the experienced general Aulus Plautius. Roman imperial frontier policy took two forms: either subjugation by the sword or the formation of alliances with those native rulers willing to accept some kind of clientship to the empire. In the former kingdom of Cassivellaunus the main opposition to Aulus Plautius came from Caratacus, a younger son of the recently deceased King Cunobelinus (Shakespeare's Cymbeline). However, when his army suffered a major defeat on the Medway, Caratacus sought refuge in south Wales, where he counted on raising the tribe of Silures so that he could continue the war against the Romans. The Emperor Claudius in person took possession of the capital of the kingdom at Colchester. There, before he retired to the Continent, submission was made by two important native kingdoms: the Regni of Sussex and the Iceni of East Anglia. Some while after, but still in the time of the first governor, Aulus Plautius, the Brigantes under their queen, Cartimandua, described by Tacitus as the largest and most powerful of the British tribes, resigned themselves to becoming a Roman protectorate.

The first hero of the British resistance was Caratacus. Accepted as leader by the warlike Silures in Wales, he was in contact with already disaffected elements among the Brigantes further to the north; and both peoples made raids into the lands of tribes under Roman protection. The extensive northern kingdom of the Brigantes has been described as a 'coalition of isolated groups in an uneasy balance, united by the marriage connections of the great families', recognising the rule of Queen Cartimandua, who herself, according to Tacitus, owed her position 'to the influence that belongs to high birth' (*pollens nobilitate*). Among these leading families opinions on the desirability of the Roman alliance differed from the beginning; the queen appeared from the outset to be pro-Roman, and in her policy she was at first supported by her consort Venutius, although he may have had some reservations that in time hardened into opposition and at length into open enmity.

The second Roman governor, Publius Ostorius Scapula, on taking office found active hostility from the tribes on the borders of Roman-occupied territory and disaffection within. First he had to put down a rebellion of the Iceni of East Anglia, whom he disarmed, before marching towards north Wales, in order to drive a wedge between the troublesome Silures and the ambiguous Brigantes. When, as Tacitus puts it, 'he was within measurable distance of the sea that looks towards Ireland', he had to abandon the operation to go to the rescue of Queen Cartimandua, some of whose Brigantian tribes had risen in revolt. Although it appears that the queen was assisted by her husband in suppressing the rebels, the kingdom was virtually in a state of civil war and it required the restraining presence of Scapula himself to restore order 'by the execution of a handful of men and the pardon of the rest'. Cartimandua was left in power but without doubt she was warned by the governor that its continuance depended upon her ability to repress any future insubordination.

However, Tacitus assures us, 'neither severity nor clemency had any effect on the Silures', among whom the influence of Caratacus was paramount. Realising the formidable nature of his task, Scapula placed a colony of hardened veterans at Colchester so that he could release the legion stationed there; then he advanced against the Silures, 'the native prowess of whom was heightened by their confidence in Caratacus, whose many successes had raised him to a pinnacle above the other British leaders'. At first Caratacus eluded the legions, skilfully retreating into the mountain fastnesses of north Wales. But in AD 51, rallying about him 'all those who feared a Roman peace'—'they make a wilderness and call it peace'—he resolved to accept a decisive battle on a site of his own choosing, where the terrain and the fortifications he had raised gave him the advantage. The result was an overwhelming victory for the disciplined legionaries. The wife and daughters of Caratacus were captured, his brothers surrendered; but Caratacus himself for the second time escaped his enemies.

In the kingdom of Queen Cartimandua opposition among the chiefs to her pro-Roman policy and her dependence on Roman arms was growing so that Caratacus in escaping after his defeat might have thought to find shelter and active support among the leaders of the Brigantes. In this he was disappointed; the queen was too committed to Rome for the security of her throne. She threw Caratacus into chains and, as proof of her loyalty to the empire, had him conveyed to Ostorius Scapula. As Tacitus admits, however, 'even in Rome the name of Caratacus was not without honour'. Sent there to grace the Emperor Claudius' triumph over his countrymen, he behaved with grave dignity, when paraded with his family before the emperor and the Roman people; and he ended his days in Rome in honourable captivity.

The infamy of the betrayal of such an outstanding leader as Caratacus was not lost on Venutius. With the years the political dissensions within Brigantia continued, until in about AD 56 domestic discord between Queen Cartimandua and her husband brought the matter to a crisis. Materially her pro-Roman policy had profited the queen. As Tacitus explains:

> From this came her wealth and the wanton spirit that success breeds. She grew to despise her husband Venutius and took as her consort his armour-bearer Vellocatus, whom she admitted to share the throne with her. Her house was at once shaken by this scandalous act. Her husband was favoured by the feelings of the people; the adulterer was supported by the queen's passion for him and her fierce spirit.

Venutius, retiring among his own relatives and followers in the north of the country, became the recognised leader of the discontented elements in the kingdom, who sought to dethrone the queen and break off relations with the Romans. Again Cartimandua appealed to Rome for help, and in AD 57 the governor, Aulus Didius Gallus sent a force of auxiliaries to her assistance and succeeded in maintaining her on the throne—but not without difficulty, for Tacitus says that the fighting was so serious as to require support for the auxiliaries from a legion.

The events of these years are graphically recounted by Tacitus from the Roman side (*Annals*, xii, 40):

> Since the capture of Caratacus, however, the Briton with the best knowledge of the art of war was Venutius. He had long been loyal, and had received the protection of Roman arms during his married life with Queen Cartimandua: then had come the divorce, followed by immediate war, and he had extended his hostility to ourselves. At first, however, the struggle was confined to the two; and Cartimandua by underhand means got hold of Venutius' brother and close relations. Furious at her action and smarting under the ignominy of submitting to the domination of a woman, the enemy—a powerful body of young and picked warriors—invaded her kingdom. The event had been foreseen by us, and the cohorts sent to the rescue fought a sharp engagement, with doubtful results at first but a happier sequel.

Thenceforth the territory of Brigantia was torn in two; Cartimandua, relying heavily on Roman arms, managed to support herself precariously in the south of the country, possibly from Almondbury; while in the north Venutius, in command of the anti-Roman forces, established his headquarters in the fort on top of Ingleborough and, encouraging the most vigorous of the native youth to armed resistance, carried out sporadic attacks on the territories under Roman protection.

Elsewhere the Britons were not accepting Roman supremacy with docile passivity. In AD 61 the Iceni of East Anglia rose in revolt under their queen Boudicca. It is curious that in British folk-history it is Boadicea (Boudicca) who holds pride of place, not the heroic figures of Caratacus and Venutius. To Victorian romanticists Boadicea was a heroine; to a sixth-century Briton, Gildas, she was an 'unclean lioness'. The revolt quickly spread; Scapula's disarmament of the tribesmen had been carelessly carried out. The seemingly peaceful towns and countryside had been denuded of troops in order to concentrate them on the frontiers, unsettled by forays from the Silures and Brigantes. The veterans of the colony of Colchester, with their women and children, were overwhelmed and massacred. Boudicca then moved on London, where the massacre and conflagration of Colchester were repeated; next it was the turn of Verulamium. To this day excavations in the city of London reveal the layer of ashes, all that remained after Boudicca's army had done its work.

The governor, C. Suetonius Paulinus, was 230 miles (368 kilometres) away in Anglesey, when news of the revolt reached him. He marched east at the head of the legions. It was the reckless audacity of Boudicca's army that proved its undoing. Accompanied in the rear by their women and children conveyed in wagons, the Britons moved to attack the carefully disposed ranks of the legions in an unwieldy and undisciplined mass, trusting in the superiority of their numbers. Suetonius Paulinus did not wait until they had formed but, ordering a charge, he swept them back against the confused barrier of their wagons. There was no hope of escape; men, women and children, even the horses, were cut down as they stood. The massacres of Colchester, London and Verulamium were avenged. As the last act amid the indescribable horror of all this carnage, Queen Boudicca took poison.

The tenure of the next two governors was largely devoted to the pacification and rehabilitation of southern Britain after the Boudiccan revolt. In the North, Venutius and his Brigantian followers had not felt themselves strong enough to take up arms in support of the Iceni and their neighbours. Their opportunity presented itself in AD 69, the 'Year of the Four Emperors'. In the civil wars that followed the suicide of Nero in the autumn of 68, no fewer than four emperors (Galba, Otho, Vitellius and Vespasian) had been raised to the purple within twelve months. The victorious survivor was Vespasian, the founder of the Flavian dynasty, who had commanded a legion in Britain at the time of Claudius. After some vacillation the legions of Britain, under the new governor, Vettius Bolanus, following the lead of the emperor's old corps of the Second Legion, recognised Vespasian. Tacitus takes up the account of this fateful year:

> Inspired by these differences between the Roman forces and by the many rumours of civil war that reached them, the Britons plucked up courage under the leadership of Venutius, who, in addition to his native spirit and hatred of the Roman name, was fired by his natural resentment towards Queen Cartimandua.

From Ingleborough and Stanwick Venutius mustered his Brigantian tribesmen and calling on aid from outside his territories he attacked those southern regions held by the queen under Roman protection. The fighting is admitted by Tacitus to have been severe, since the cavalry and infantry sent by Bolanus at Cartimandua's urgent request only got the upper hand, 'after meeting with indifferent success in a number of engagements'. Finally, however, the Romans succeeded in extricating the queen from her dangerous position and removing her to safety. The events are summed up by Tacitus in one of the most pithy of his lapidary phrases: 'the kingdom was left to Venutius, the war to us'.

The new emperor Vespasian, with his first-hand knowledge of Britain, took stock of the serious state of affairs in the province: the whole of the North beyond the Humber and Trent, the lands of the Brigantes, was threateningly hostile to Rome, and its leading spirit, the able and experienced Venutius, was in command of its formidable forces; a further threat was posed in the west from the still unconquered Silures. The response of the emperor was to recall Vettius Bolanus and to replace him by the capable Q. Petillius Cerialis, the legate who had been active in opposing Boudicca and who had recently played a distinguished part in quelling the rebellion of Julius Civilis in the Rhineland. With the new governor was sent a further legion.

One of Cerialis' first actions in furtherance of his object of disposing once and for all of the power of the Brigantes was to advance the Ninth Legion from Lincoln to York. The choice of York for a legionary centre revealed his intention. As R. G. Collingwood expressed it: 'the ridge on which York stands . . . is the true centre for all offensive strategy in north-eastern England. It is not a defensive position; it is not a position to block the movements of an invading enemy; it is a position from which to strike.' About the same time, as archaeologists have revealed, he advanced another legion north to Chester. His intention was not so much to hem in the Brigantes in the Pennines, but, if possible, to bring Venutius to a decisive engagement. The latter was well aware of this and for his part had not been idle; rather he had made his own careful dispositions, effecting such extensive and well-planned counter-measures that their magnitude surprises and impresses us today. From Ingleborough he moved the main body of his troops east to a site that he had selected for strategic reasons; not for nothing had Tacitus described Venutius as 'pre-eminent in military skill'. Stanwick St John lies within the angle formed by two later Roman roads, today the meeting-point of the A1 and the A66 at Scotch Corner. If the Ninth Legion would almost certainly march north up the Vale of York, avoiding the Brigantian-held Dales' country, so the Brigantes and their auxiliary tribesmen from the north and the north-west could readily converge upon the Stanwick neighbourhood to join their compatriots from the Dales and, by way of the Stainmore gap, from Lancashire and Cumbria.

Stanwick, Venutius' Brigantian stronghold, must be one of the most imposing achievements of the early inhabitants of this country, rivalling in its conception and construction that of Maiden Castle in Dorset. Perhaps in AD 57, after his decisive break with Cartimandua —if not earlier, in AD 51, at the time of her treachery in the betrayal of Caratacus—Venutius, moving north out of reach of the Roman presence, had seen the possibility of constructing a fort here on the hill known as The Tofts. The defences are typical of those Brigantian hill-forts mentioned by Juvenal in his Fourteenth Satire: the 17-acre (7-hectare) site is enclosed by a bank or rampart and ditch, the bank being 24 feet (7 metres) high on the west side. Shortly after, but not later than AD 60, the initial hill-fort was added to by a new enclosure, more than 130 acres (52 hectares) in extent, bringing within its circuit the water from the Mary Wild Beck, and this too was defended by ramparts of earth, revetted by dry-stone walls and by ditches. Then, some time about AD 70, when he saw that a Roman attack was inevitable, probably imminent, and in preparation to meet it, Venutius enlarged again the surrounding defences to enclose a further 600 acres (242 hectares), thus providing a vast circuit of ramparts and ditches extending for some 6 miles (9.6 kilometres). The reason for this extensive enclosure lies in the fact that the Brigantes, a predominantly pastoral people, could muster within these defensive works their herds and flocks, thereby safeguarding their food supplies in case of siege. It was not necessary to mount guard on the ramparts at all points—despite the extraordinary demands on manpower necessary to construct these huge earthworks, the armed forces of the Brigantes and their allies would have been insufficient to cover and defend the circuit in depth. Militarily their main strength lay in their cavalry; from the central fort on The Tofts a lookout could observe the direction of the enemy's advance and the cavalry be deployed to oppose them.

Venutius' military provision against the anticipated Roman attack did not end here in the great fortress of Stanwick. Many, perhaps the bulk, of the Brigantes inhabited the hills and valleys of the Pennines, the Yorkshire Dales, and their commander foresaw a possible enemy penetration of their homelands from the south by way of the river-valleys. In addition to the building of the stone hill-fort at Ingleborough in the west, and those near Gregory Scar (north of Grassington in Wharfedale) and on Addleborough in Wensleydale, he set his people to the construction of a secondary line of defence of banks and ditches. Again in Wharfedale, on Great Hunters Sleets, north of Kettlewell, they excavated the deep ditch of Tor Dyke and fortified it with a rampart and enclosures on its northern side. And on Fremingtone Edge, possibly as a defensive position to fall back on in necessity—on the loss of Stanwick, for example—they undertook the digging and raising of another of those monumental earthworks that bear witness to the efforts and stubborn perseverance of the Brigantes under the heroic leadership of Venutius. The evidence of these widespread labours is there for all to see in the Dales: on Ingleborough, exposed in winter to the bitter winds from the north-east; at Tor Dyke, below Great Whernside on the moors so dun and desolate in autumn rains; on Fremington Edge, in the vernal serenity of the overhanging woods; and at Stanwick St John—above all, at Stanwick. Here, just to the east of the church and few houses of the village of Forcett, a tree-topped mound separates the wheatfields. In late August the wheat stands ripe for cutting, so saturated with sunlight that, rather than honey-coloured, it is bleached to a shade of palest straw. In 1951 archaeologists cut a clearing in the trees on a short section of this ridge and excavated and repaired the fortifications raised there by Venutius. The sun catches the top of the dry-stone wall above the lofty rampart; beneath the stone-faced revetment and in deep shadow the ditch was dug far down until it reached the level of the huge natural flags of the limestone bed. It is only with difficulty that we can imagine today the superhuman expense of manual labour this required. The grandeur of Venutius' undertaking, and the vastness of its scale, evoke our astonishment and compel our admiration.

Tacitus in his *Agricola*, which is best seen as a eulogy of his father-in-law, the governor of Britain from AD 78–85, gives a passage, significant for what it says and does not say:

> But when Vespasian, in the course of his general triumph, recovered Britain, there came a succession of great generals and splendid armies, and the hopes of our enemies dwindled. Petillius Cerealis at once struck terror into their hearts by attacking the state of the Brigantes, which is said to be the most populous in the province. After a series of battles, some not uncostly, Petillius had operated, if not actually triumphed over, the major part of their territory.

We do not know the precise date of the final catastrophe, or of the death of Venutius—(Petillius Cerealis was recalled in AD 74); but the power of the Brigantes was broken. The 1951 excavations at Stanwick St John, carried out by Sir Mortimer Wheeler for the Ministry of Works under the provisions of the Ancient Monuments Act, have disclosed that the main gateway on the outer perimeter was never completed. It seems that Petillius struck before the Brigantes had put the finishing touches to their great defensive system. It was here that the calamity befell them. As Sir Mortimer says, 'We can almost see the tribesmen toiling vainly at their gate, almost hear the Ninth Legion tramping up from its new fortress at York to one of its rare victories.' And with its victory, which for him was final defeat, Venutius vanishes from history.

With the back of Brigantian resistance broken and its leading spirit removed the first task of the Roman governor was the administrative one of policing the Dales so as to forestall any resurgence of active hostility from the survivors of Stanwick who had sought refuge there. This was begun by Petillius Cerealis and continued by his successor, Sextus Julius Frontinus, the conqueror of the Silures in Wales; but the main credit for the Roman settlement of the North Country is usually given to Tactitus' father-in-law, Gnaeus Julius Agricola. Agricola had seen his entire military service in Britain. As a young man he served as military tribune under Suetonius Paulinus; appointed by Vespasian to command the Twentieth Legion, he distinguished himself under Cerealis in the defeat of the Brigantes; then, after governing Aquitaine and a brief consulship, he returned to Britain as governor in AD 78. The Agricolan system was based on the permanent stationing of two legions, their headquarters at York and Chester, and the establishment in the Pennines of a series of forts, manned by auxiliaries. These were connected by a network of military roads, along which patrols moved, and at any sign of Brigantian insurrection signals could be passed for reinforcements from the legionary headquarters. Ultimately the territory of the Brigantes was to be thoroughly enmeshed within this framework of Roman surveillance.

After the visit to Britain in AD 121 of the Emperor Hadrian and the construction of his great wall from the Solway Firth to the Tyne, the Brigantes were cut off in their rear from the assistance of more northern tribes. From York the military road north ran through Aldborough to the Roman camp at Catterick, the remains of this being partly covered by the present racecourse. This road became known as Leeming Lane. From Catterick it continued as Dere Street past Scotch Corner to Piercebridge on the Tees, then via Lanchester to Corbridge on the Tyne, south of Hadrian's Wall. At Scotch Corner a branch led off to the west through the Stainmore gap to Carlisle. Here the sites of the Roman camps can be seen at Greta Bridge, Bowes (*Lavatrae*) and Rey Cross. Between the last two, almost opposite the Bowes Moor Hotel on Spital, are the remains of one of the Roman signal stations. Two miles to the west of Rey Cross the modern A66 leaves the course of the Roman road, which it has followed hitherto, and the ancient road can be seen for a stretch, continuing with typical Roman directness. If the Brigantes found themselves thus contained to the north and east, they were no less so on the west, by the Roman roads from Chester, through Ribchester, to Carlisle, and on the south by the road through the Pennines to the fort on Castleshaw Moor and thence to Chester. Another road crossed the Pennines from York and Aldborough, through Skipton and the fort at Elslack to Ribchester. Ilkley (*Olicana*) was the meeting-place, the focus from all directions of no fewer than five Roman military roads. One of these went north over the moors to the fort at Bainbridge (*Virosidum*) in Wensleydale.

This Roman camp, which is situated on a hilltop just to the east of Bainbridge village, within sight of the River Ure, is right in the heartland of the Brigantes. Curiously enough no traces of road-building by the Romans are to be found down the dale in the direction of the important camp, and later civilian town, at Catterick. However, from Bainbridge their road may be followed today, running south-west as straight as a die across the flank of Wether Fell and over Cam Pastures; this would have joined the legionary roads from Chester to Carlisle. From the height of this road or from the grassed remains of the ramparts of the Bainbridge fort, amid the tranquillity and pastoral beauty of Wensleydale, we can appreciate the thoroughness of Roman measures to control the fierce tribesmen of the Brigantes. There is evidence that in this they were not always successful; Brigantian enmity persisted for a long time.

Beyond Fremington Edge, on Hurst Moor, the lead-mines (now worked out) were certainly known to the Brigantes; excavations have discovered many leaden objects on known sites of their habitations. It was the Roman custom to employ prisoners-of-war as slaves in working the mines; within a few years of the conquest of southern Britain the Romans were exploiting conscript slave labour in the lead-mines in the Mendips. From the circumstances of the places of discovery of pigs of Roman lead in the Dales, it appears certain that the Brigantes were cheating their masters in purloining the property of the imperial treasury. One such leaden pig, with the inscription HADRIAN (that is, of AD 117–38), was discovered buried in the ground at Hurst. Of the three other pigs of lead recovered in the Dales, two were unearthed on an ancient track-way on Hayshaw Bank in the parish of Dacre. They came to light in 1733, when a traveller felt his horse stumble with its foot in the hole where they were buried. On one side of the pigs was the inscription: IMP.CAES. DOMITIANO.AUG.COS.VII; on the other simply BRIG. The seventh year of the consulship of the Emperor Domitian was AD 81; the abbreviation BRIG. conveys the lead's origin, meaning 'from the territory of the Brigantes'.

That the warlike activities of the tribesmen continued into the second century is attested by a cryptic reference in the Greek geographer Pausanias' *Description of Greece* (viii, 43): the Emperor Antoninus Pius 'took away from the Brigantes in Britain the greater part of the territory, because they made an attack on the Gerunian district, whose inhabitants were Roman subjects'. This may have been about AD 154, under the governor C. Julius Verus. The passage tells us little more, however, since it is not known who the Gerunians were nor what territory remained with the Brigantes. (Some writers have attributed the mysterious disappearance of the Ninth Legion at York to its defeat and annihilation at the hands of the Brigantes, but this is unlikely.) For much of the succeeding centuries of the Roman occupation of this island—it is not always borne in mind how long this lasted: some 350 years, comparable to the centuries between the two Elizabeths—it seems that the Brigantes like the other peoples of Britain enjoyed the blessings of the *pax romana*.

This can perhaps more truly be said of the upper classes. After his victory at Stanwick, Petillius Cerealis established the tribal capital at *Isurium Brigantum*, Aldborough, under the watchful eye of the Roman northern military headquarters at York; and with time this grew into a thriving centre of civilian life and nascent culture. The remains here—the solid city walls, enclosing an area of 74 acres (30 hectares): the tessellated pavements and hypocausts of town houses, the foundations and pavement of a basilica and public baths and the wealth of precious objects—all are evidence of a high material civilisation in this Romano-British town, in the third and fourth centuries possibly one of the largest in the country. The standard of life and comfort here is matched by that of the owners of country villas in the Dales, such as those at Well, Middleham in Wensleydale and Gargrave in Craven—not many of them, it is true. There these Romanised Britons had the best of both worlds; with the amenities of the town within reach, they lived on their estates the cultivated life of country gentlemen, like their Gallic contemporary, Ausonius of Bordeaux, who in his relaxed verses tells how:

> Not far from town I live
> Yet not hard by . . .
> I change around,

And get the best of town
And country, turn and turn about.

It has been said of these Romano-British landowners, living in their sumptuous villas, with their central heating, patterned mosaics and wall-paintings, like those unearthed at Pompeii and Herculaneum, that the texture of their lives was more spacious than that of their successors until the days of the Tudors or Stuarts—or even of the Georges. Very different was the condition of the mass of Brigantian dwellers in the Dales. In their small villages or isolated homesteads they carried on an existence that their dalesmen successors would have recognised—hard, comfortless, precarious, with only their own exertions to serve their frugal needs and secure their survival.

CHAPTER 3

Place-Names

PLACE-NAMES FASCINATED Marcel Proust. In *Cities of the Plain* the Narrator, as a young man, is seated beside Albertine in the Little Train that puffed its way through the Norman countryside on a summer's evening, bound for one of Mme Verdurin's 'Wednesdays' at La Raspalière. Hearing that Mme Cambremer was to be a guest at dinner, the Narrator expresses his delight at the prospect of meeting her again, 'because she has promised me a book by the former curé of Combray about the place-names of this district . . . I am interested in that priest, and also in etymologies.' He is taken up by the Academician Brichot, 'Don't put any faith in the ones he gives . . . it is a mass of error.' The researches undertaken by Proust that form the basis for Brichot's brilliant refutation of the poor curé's etymologies which follows began in 1919 in a correspondence with the great authorities on French place-names, Louis Dimier and Henri Longnon. Proust's fascination for the study of the names of these Norman towns and villages reflects the instinctive direction of his probing, prehensile mind, for encapsulated in place-names remains so much of the remembrance of things past. Similar research in this country in deciphering topographical nomenclature has disclosed the origins of the present inhabitants of the Dales of Yorkshire, revealing the admixture of races that composed their ancestry and the regions of their first settlements.

In Britain there was no evacuation of the Romans, no ultimate withdrawal of the legions: like the old soldier, the Roman administration did not die, it simply faded away. From the second half of the third century and increasingly in the fourth the frontiers of the province were threatened by incursions from barbarians: by the Picts from the north of Hadrian's Wall, by the Irish from the west, and in the east by bands of sea-rovers, whom it is convenient to group together as Saxons. So perilous was the position of the northern command in AD 367 that the Emperor Valentinian, despite the pressure of the Germanic tribes at other points on the far-stretched frontiers of the empire, despatched Count Theodosius to its relief, reinforced by three crack regiments. After Theodosius had expelled the intruders, we learn from a contemporary Roman historian that, 'he protected the frontier with lookouts and garrisons, recovering a province that had yielded to enemy control'. These lookouts were the signal stations that he erected on the Yorkshire coast from the mouth of the Tees to Bridlington Bay; they were served by roads that radiated from the Roman camp at Malton, which he garrisoned with special commando units named the 'Anticipators'. Furthermore Theodosius initiated a northern frontier policy, whose effects were to be lasting: on both sides of the Wall he placed Roman *praefecti gentium*, prefects to rule over the native tribes. At this time York was the capital of one of the four provinces of Britain, administered by governors, under the vicar of the British Diocese, who was responsible to the praetorian prefect of the Gauls. Subordinate to the military commander-in-chief, the *magister militum*, was the Count of the Saxon Shore (a string of coastal forts from Portsmouth to the Wash, built for protection from Saxon raids) and the Commander of the Britains (*dux Britanniarum*), responsible at York for the northern frontier and for the policing of the Pennines.

In AD 403 the successful Roman general Stilicho, in the face of the threat to Italy from Alaric and his Visigoths, recalled the Twentieth Legion from Chester, the legion 'deployed in far-off Britain, that curbs the savage Irish and reads the marks tattooed upon the bodies of dying Picts', in the words of the poet Claudian. With Stilicho's victories the Roman world stood seemingly secure within its frontiers. Then, on 24 August 410, the unimaginable happened: Rome fell to Alaric. In the dissolution of the empire, the military and administrative bonds that bound Britain to Rome were loosened. Of the state of affairs there we hear little, save the laconic half-sentence of a Roman historian: 'Honorius dealt with the states of Britain by letter, telling them to look to their own defence . . . and remained inactive.' For nearly 400 years the states (*civitates*) of Britain had administered their own internal affairs under the control of a governor appointed by the emperor, to whose universal authority the legions also owed obedience. One of these states was Brigantia, whose territory embraced the Dales. In the period that followed the British were unable to re-establish, except for brief interludes, the controlling authority—a recognised central government; and their failure paved the way for the ultimate supremacy of the Anglo-Saxons.

Hints of the political arrangements in the North upon the demise of the empire are given by the genealogies of its later kings, whose names were celebrated in the old poetry of Wales at the end of the sixth century. The several dynasties of kings in the Pennines trace their descent from a common ancestor, Coel Hen, Coel the Old. As in other cases in the disintegrating empire, so perhaps here, the last imperially appointed commander of the northern forces at York, the *dux Britanniarum*, converted his command into a kingdom and, like Aegidius, his opposite number in Gaul, bequeathed it to his son. Temporary office was succeeded by inheritable rule. It was an early tradition that Coel's kingdom covered the whole of the North but that in later generations his rule became divided into a number of independent kingdoms. If a Roman *dux* named Coelius (or Coelestius) has provided a certain show of legitimacy to his successors' titles to their little states, he has furnished a well-loved figure for posterity: the 'merry old soul' of English nurseries is no other than Old King Cole of the Pennines. These same traditions place Coel, the northern king, as the older contemporary of Vortigern, the southerner with claims to the over-kingship of Britain at the time of the *adventus Saxonum*, the coming of the Saxons.

'Anglo-Saxons' is the hybrid term which, since the nineteenth century, has prevailed to name the Germanic tribesmen—Angles, Jutes, Saxons, Frisians, Franks and others—who crossed the North Sea in their longships, at first bent on plunder but later, in the fifth century, to settle in those lands, which subsequently became known, after just one of these several tribal elements, as England. The impact of these Germanic invaders was felt most strongly in the South of England and the Midlands; in the Dales of Yorkshire their effect was not so overriding. Here, further invasions of Scandinavians in the ninth and tenth centuries have left their distinguishing mark on the population, place-names, customs, dialect and local administration. The ridings—the 'thirds' into which Yorkshire was administratively divided—and the further division into wapentakes instead of the Anglo-Saxon hundreds, are both Danish terms. In the Yorkshire Dales a glance at the map will reveal how widespread is the Viking presence, clearly visible in the number of Danish and Norse among the Anglo-Saxon place-names. What is immediately significant is the paucity of topographical evidence that these dales were ever lived in by the British.

The horror felt by the cultivated Romano-British at the ferocity and the devastation caused by the invasion of these pagan barbarians from over the sea is shown in the pages of the British monk Gildas, who wrote his *De Excidio Britanniae* (*On the Ruin and Conquest of Britain*), a fervent denunciation of contemporary princes and bishops, about the year 547. Although the Saxons had been raiding and perhaps even settling for some time before, historians now consider that their first permanent settlement, under their leaders Hengist and Horsa, was about 428, some twenty years earlier than the traditional date of 449, given by the *Anglo-Saxon Chronicle*.

Since Honorius had told the Britons that it was up to themselves to see to their own defences, this task had been undertaken by the *magister militum* and the military *duces* in consultation with a council, constituted by the leading representatives of the cities and tribal *civitates*. Their acknowledged leader is known by the name of Vortigern: this, however, is not a personal name but signifies 'over-king' thus pointing to his status. Against the continual attacks of Irish and Picts, the British employed the expedient, common in the decaying empire, of enlisting barbarian 'federates', on the principle that dog best eats dog. Gildas, after a tirade against the sins and failures of the British rulers, both lay and ecclesiastic, and especially 'the proud tyrant' Vortigern, gives a highly colourful account of the settling of Hengist and Horsa on the Island of Thanet:

> The time drew nigh, when the iniquities of Britain should be fulfilled, as with the Ammorites of old. A Council was convened, to decide upon the best and soundest means of withstanding the frequent brutal invasions and raids of the aforesaid peoples [the Irish and Picts]. All the members of the Council, and the proud tyrant, were struck blind. . . . To hold back the northern peoples, they introduced into the island the vile unspeakable Saxons, hated of God and man alike. Nothing more frightful had ever happened to this island, nothing more bitter. The utter blindness of their wits! Of their own free will, they invited in under the same roof the enemy they feared worse than death. . . . So the brood

of cubs burst from the lair of the barbarian lioness, in three 'keels', as
they call warships in their language. . . . At the orders of the ill-fated
tyrant, they first fixed their fearful claws upon the eastern part of the
island, as though to defend it. . . . Their dam, learning of the success of
the first contingent, sent over a larger draft of satellite dogs. . . . Thus
were the barbarians introduced . . . in the guise of soldiers running great
risks for their kind 'hosts', as the liars asserted. They demanded supplies
which were granted and for a long time 'shut the dog's mouth'.

Nevertheless, Vortigern's strategy was at first successful; the Picts
were contained beyond the Wall. Then, acting on Hengist's advice,
Vortigern invited Octha and Ebissa, the Saxon chief's 'son and his
cousin', with federates from among their compatriots, and despatched them aboard forty keels to the North, as a permanent protection
against the Picts; and there they founded settlements astride the wall,
in territory later to form the kingdom of Bernicia (from Briganticia).
It is noteworthy that the other important northern Saxon settlement,
Deira, has a Celtic name, derived from *deifr*, 'waters', signifying the
Ouse and its affluents which converge on the Humber. By the early
430s it seems that the Saxons had a firm foothold in Kent and East
Anglia. Yet it was not until in or about 442 that, reinforced from
home, Hengist felt strong enough to break out and to threaten the
entire country. On the excuse that the agreed British supplies were
not forthcoming, the Saxons rose in revolt. A century later, Gildas
could still experience the horror that followed:

[The fire] once lit, did not die down. When it had wasted town and
country in that area, it burnt up almost the whole surface of this island,
until the red and savage tongue licked the western ocean. . . . All the
great towns fell to the enemy's battering rams; all their inhabitants,
bishops, priests and peoples, were mown down together, while swords
flashed and flames crackled. Horrible it was to see the foundation stones
of towers and high walls thrown down bottom upwards in the squares,
mixing with holy altars and fragments of human bodies, as though they
were covered with a purple crust of clotted blood, as in some fantastic
wine-press. There was no burial save in the ruins of houses, or in the
bellies of beasts and birds.

The Saxon rebellion began a long struggle that shattered the
political cohesion and the economy of Roman Britain but it did not
bring with it the conquest of the country. In 446 the Britons wrote to
Aëtius, the Roman commander in Gaul, with the moving plea for

help: 'The barbarians push us into the sea, the sea pushes us to the barbarians; between the two kinds of death we are either slain or drowned.' The tide of war ebbed and flowed; the British had some successes but the Saxons were strongly reinforced from their homelands. At length, some time after 455, feelers were put out for peace and a conference was convened; but no settlement followed. By an act of barbarous treachery, Hengist massacred the entire Council of the Diocese, 300 representatives of the cities and states, the most eminent and cultivated leaders among the British. From southern Britain there was a mass exodus, a migration of all those who had most to lose, to Normandy and Brittany. Some 12,000 fighting men were said to have migrated. This meant the extinction of Roman Britain.

All, however, was not yet lost for the remaining British; in the 460s they rallied under the leadership of Ambrosius Aurelianus. Then, with his successor in command, they found their true hero in the historical Arthur. The figure of Arthur is buried beneath such a weight of later legend that it is difficult to visualise the man. The ninth-century Welsh compiler known as Nennius credits him with twelve battles in which he was victorious, the most outstanding being the last, at Badon Hill, probably fought about 500, when the Saxons were decisively defeated and their eventual conquest of Britain delayed for more than two generations. Some of the sites of Arthur's battles given by Nennius are in the North but so widespread is the hero's fame that the name of Arthur has long been attached throughout this island to prominent physical landmarks (for example Arthur's Seat and Arthur's Leap) and to places, like Cadbury Castle in Somerset and Richmond Castle in the Yorkshire Dales—and abroad, under Mount Etna, in Savoy and southern Italy, even in Arabia. Legends gathered and far outstripped the historical personage, to form the Arthurian romances that, like those of the paladins of Charlemagne, are part of the literary heritage of Western Europe. In France 'the matter of Britain' was teased out and embroidered into the tales of King Arthur and his knights of the Round Table. Brought back to their native land, these romances stirred the imagination of Norman and Plantagenet courtly circles, whose chivalric ideals are embodied in the classical English version of Malory's *La morte d'Arthur* written at the end of the Wars of the Roses.

Memories of King Arthur are strong in the Dales. In Mallerstang are the ruins of Pendragon Castle. Local legend has it that here dwelt

Uther, Arthur's father, and that it was on this spot that the hero was born. And if the Dales may claim, as do several parts of Britain, the place of Arthur's birth, it may lay claim also to his final resting-place. In the folk-memory of other countries the legend persists of a national hero who has not died but lies sleeping, until his country's danger shall awaken him from his slumber, once more to lead his people to victory—as the German Emperor Barbarossa is said to sleep beneath the Harz Mountains. According to one British legend King Arthur lies buried below Richmond Castle in a cave deep in the bowels of the lofty spur on which the castle stands in a bend of the River Swale. And that he does indeed sleep there—at least, in local imagination—may be vouched for by an eighteenth-century story. One day an inhabitant of Richmond, a potter by the name of Thompson, was scrambling among the rocks in the cliff below the castle, when he came upon the entrance to a cave. Cautiously entering, he groped his way forward in the darkness, until suddenly, rounding a bend, he saw before him a chamber filled with light and suffused with the splendour from gleaming steel and the brilliance of silver and gold. In the centre of a circle of mailed knights, on a bier lay the recumbent figure of Arthur, majestic in armour, a royal chaplet on his head, and beside him, mysteriously refulgent, shone the sword Excalibur. After breathlessly taking in the scene, potter Thompson hastily retraced his steps to inform the town of his unbelievable discovery. Accompanied by an incredulous crowd, he returned to the mouth of the cave. But it was not there, where he had found it. And search as he might, he could never afterwards rediscover it.

It is usually thought that the Germanic peoples who settled north of the Humber were predominantly Angles. So long as their numbers were small they remained, separated in Bernicia and Deira, as tiny enclaves among the British. The newcomers, as settlers, did not favour the occupation of towns but preferred to group themselves as family nuclei in their farms and villages. Nevertheless, grave-objects found in York (the Romano-British name of *Eboracum* becoming changed to the Anglo-Saxon *Eoforwick*), suggest that, by around 500, the English were living alongside the British inhabitants within or in the proximity of the city walls. Historically the first known King of Bernicia was Ida, who came to the throne in 547, with his capital at Bamburgh. Of the first King of the Deirans, Aelle, little or nothing is known. It was not until the two kingdoms coalesced that, as Northumbria, they found the strength to expand. It has been said that, 'The continuous history of Northumbria, and indeed of England, begins with the reign of Ethelfrith, son of Ethelric, son of Ida, King of Bernicia.' Ethelfrith, who reigned from 593 to 616, married Aelle's daughter and occupied Deira, driving out the rightful heir, his brother-in-law Edwin. Bede, in his *Ecclesiastical History of the English Nation*, has this to say of his fellow-Northumbrian: 'Ethelfrith . . . ravaged the Britons more than any great man of the English . . . for he conquered more territories from the Britons, either making them tributary or driving the inhabitants clean out, and planting English in their places.' Ethelfrith consolidated English power in the whole North of England, penetrating the Pennines both in the north and the south and reaching the western sea. The Deirans had found their expansion to the west partly blocked by the British kingdom of Loidis Elmet, until this was conquered in the reign of Edwin, who succeeded Ethelfrith in the united Bernicia and Deira—that is, Northumbria, with its capital now at York. Place-names in the Dales reveal the early English settlements along the river-valleys: the Aire, Wharfe, Nidd, Ure, Swale and Tees. This suggests a very considerable increase in their numbers, augmented most probably from their homelands in Schleswig-Holstein, which Bede in the eighth century reported as remaining empty of inhabitants in his day.

It is the cause of some surprise that the Romans and the British should have left so few traces of their presence in the nomenclature of the Dales. The names of prominent natural features—mountains, hills, rivers, lakes—and of important towns or villages might be thought to survive successive waves of newcomers and to perpetuate the memory of those who first named them. Five thousand miles (8,000 kilometres) of excellent roads in Britain outlived the Romans, several important ones passing through the Dales or close to their borders, and the English who used them have signified their existence by the references to 'Street' (from the Old English *strait*, their name for 'road'), as in Dere and Watling Streets. In the higher ground of the Dales the Britons are remembered in the element *pen* ('summit', 'top'), as in Penhill in Wensleydale; and in Craven, in the beautiful name of Pen-y-ghent ('hill of the winds'?). It is by the names of rivers that the British are chiefly recalled: by the Aire, Wharfe, Cover, Nidd, Tees, and perhaps the Ure; in other British-named streams the memory remains of the Leeming, in Leeming Lane and the village of

Leeming, and of the Dacre ('the trickle') in the village of that name. The region of Craven retains its British name, although its origin is obscure; also the name of The Chevin, which signifies 'the ridge'; Dent and Catterick appear alone in bearing the names of original British settlements. The survival of British localities among a population increasingly English is suggested by names derived from the Old English *weala* ('foreigner', 'Welsh', 'British', 'slave'), such as Walden in Wensleydale and Walburn in Swaledale. We are told that Bishop Wilfred of York in the late seventh century was granted lands 'in the regions of Ribble, Yeadon, Dent and Catlow', the estates of British monasteries whose monks had fled—presumably at the coming of the English. Yet the absence of British place-names must not be thought of as pointing to the extermination of the race, since the British survived, if in a subordinate, frequently servile perhaps, status. It indicates rather the thorough-going settlement of the Pennines by the English and, after them, by the Scandinavian peoples. It is chiefly the English and the Norse Vikings who have left their mark in the place-names of the Yorkshire Dales.

There are aspects of the Anglo-Saxon peoples, the conquerors of Roman Britain, which popular history has often confused. There is no doubt as to the horror of the invasions, the bloodshed and destruction, the devastation of a fair civilisation, whose equal was not to be seen in England for more than a thousand years. This was most severely felt in the South. The Northumbrian Bede, writing in 731, could affirm that, 'the cities, temples, bridges and paved roads there made, testify to this day' to the legacy of Rome still remaining long after the first fury of the English invasions had been spent. In northern England there is evidence that, despite recurrent outbreaks of violence, the English and the British did settle down pacifically, often within hail of each other. Furthermore there is strong evidence for the survival of important groups of the British, since their administration and land tenure lasted until the twelfth century. Early English society was characteristically both free and aristocratic. Free in the sense that there was little economic dependence of the poorer members on the rich, the free churls farming their own lands with the help of their families and perhaps a few British slaves. Aristocratic in it being accepted that the thegns, the local chiefs (ealdormen) and the kings constituted a superior hierarchy, based largely on wealth, on land, but more especially on their military prowess. Loyalty was the key-note of this society—the churl to his thegn, the thegn to the ealdormen and both to their king; disloyalty meant degradation and dishonour. It must be stressed, however, that the English were above all an agricultural people, land-hungry, and where they settled they peaceably cleared, ploughed and sowed, pastured their flocks and herds and raised their families. If they were fighting men, instinctively warlike (and they were), nevertheless, it is seeing them in a false light when this is remembered to the exclusion of the fact that they were also the pioneers, who cleared the forests and tilled the fields of much of what was, until their coming, uncultivated England.

The *mores* of the English upper class, the thegns and ealdormen, were only partly shared by the churl. Yet it had been the sea-borne warriors who had led the way, first for loot, for the tip-and-run raid, to carry off unearned riches, leaving behind them their tracks strewn with slaughtered bodies and smoking ruins. These men gloried in their physical strength, boasted of their bravery, and felt only valid in their virtues as fighters; they were sea-rovers before they were settlers. The mood in which the English pushed out to sea in their longships is caught by the anonymous poet who wrote *The Seafarer*:

> My heart's thoughts constrain me to venture on the deep seas, on the tumult of the salt waves; at all times my heart's desire urges my spirit to travel, that I may seek the land of foreigners afar off; because there is no man on earth so high-hearted, nor so liberal with his gifts, nor so bold in his youth, nor so daring in his deeds, nor having so gracious a lord, that he will not always feel anxiety over his voyage, as to what is the Lord's purpose for him. He will have no mind for the harp, nor for the receiving of rings, no pleasure in women nor delight in the world nor mind for anything else, except the tossing of the waves, but he who puts out to sea has always yearning. The groves blossom, cities grow fair, the fields become beautiful, the world's astir. All these things urge on to his journey the man eager of heart, urge on the spirit of him who thus intends to depart far on the paths of the sea.

Behind all his loyalty to his lord, whose company and generosity he shared, with the receiving of gifts, the deep drinking, the poetry and the love of women; behind his wanderlust, his spirit of fearless adventure, his desire for easy gain, noticeable in the Early English, there is a pervading sense of the presence of an inexorable fate and of an unassuageable melancholy. For some of this leaden load of the pagan world was to be lifted by the acceptance of Christianity; with conversion could be born hope. The contemplative side of the Early English character was subsequently to bear fruit.

In the pleasant tale told by Bede it was the appearance of two young Deiran boys displayed for sale in the slave-market in Rome —'their bodies white, their countenances beautiful, and their hair very fine'—that first set the mind of Gregory, not then pope, to contemplating the converstion of the pagan English. In 597, as pope, he sent Augustine to England to the court of Ethelbert of Kent and there he inaugurated the sees of Canterbury, Rochester and London. When King Edwin of Northumbria married Ethelburga, the Christian daughter of Ethelbert of Kent, he had agreed that she might practise her own faith. The Roman priest Paulinus, first consecrated bishop, accompanied the princess north, on an evangelising mission. But it was only after some initial hesitation, and spurred on by letters from the Pope himself, that Edwin and his court were baptised in 627. Before the king took this step, he had called a meeting of his great council, at which an unknown noble spoke with persuasive effect, as reported by Bede in a celebrated passage:

> Thus, Your Majesty, the present life of men on earth, in comparison with that time which is unknown to us, appears to me to be as if, when you are sitting at supper in the winter with your ealdormen and thegns, and a fire is lighted in the midst and the hall warmed, but everywhere outside the storms of wintry rain and snow are raging, a sparrow should come and fly rapidly through the hall, coming in at one door and immediately out of the other. While it is inside, it is not touched by the storm of winter, but yet, that tiny space of calm gone in a moment, from winter at once returning to winter, it is lost to your sight. Thus this life of men appears for a little while; but of what is to follow, or of what went before, we are entirely ignorant. Hence, if this new teaching brings greater certainty, it seems fit to be followed.

The final act in the rejection of paganism in the North was that of the high priest Coifi, who, seizing a sword and spear and mounting a stallion (actions unheard of in a priest), galloped to Godmunding-ham, 'where he profaned and destroyed the altars which he had himself consecrated'. Paulinus was indefatigable, catechising and baptising; and we have a glimpse of him among the dalesmen, baptising in the Swale above Catterick. In those early days of Christianity there were few or no churches but priests would meet their flocks in the Dales to preach and perform Mass at known spots, which came to be marked with wooden, and later stone, crosses —the so-called 'field-churches'. As the new religion moved west over the Pennines with the English settlers, they erected their typical Saxon crosses at such places as Stanwick St John, Easby, Masham, Otley, Ilkley, Burnsall and elsewhere. The most beautiful of these crosses, however, carved by the skill of craftsmen schooled in English Northumbria, are perhaps to be seen further afield at Bewcastle in Cumbria or Ruthwell in Dumfrieshire.

As the Early English thrust westward from the Vale of York along the rivers and into the lower dales, we can follow them in their place-names and almost watch them as they clear the dense forest, set up their primitive wooden farmsteads and cultivate their small strips of arable land. Their progress in clearing the woodland that covered so much of the middle-hillsides of the valleys is shown by the prevalence of the place-name termination in *leah* (ley), which signifies 'a forest clearing'—Wensley, Ripley, Pateley, Bewerley, Ilkley, Otley and many others. An indication of an earliest settlement is the place-name ending in or containing *ing* (*ingas*), which denotes 'lands belonging to a tribe or family'. This will be prefixed by the chief's name and it may end in *ham*, 'homestead' or *tun* (ton), 'an enclosed farmstead or village'—as seen in Gilling, 'the settlement of the followers of Getla', Barningham, 'the homestead of the people of Beorna', or Easington, 'the enclosed farmstead of Esa's people'. These English settlements are disclosed in such place-name endings and others, of which the most common are *thorpe*, 'a hamlet or outlying farm'; *fold*, 'an enclosed pasture'; *cote*, 'a cottage or humble dwelling'; *worth*, 'an enclosure'; *wudu* (wood), 'a wood'; *wella*, 'a spring or well; *wic* (wick), 'a dwelling, building', or more specifically, 'a dairy farm'; and *croft*, 'a small enclosure, croft.'

The archaic tribal name of *in Hrypum*, by which the English knew Ripon, suggests that they were there perhaps as early as the beginning of the sixth century. Avoiding the low-lying marshland and seeking the most favourable sites for their settlements, they moved with their families and stock into Wensleydale up the River Ure (the name possibly derived from the Romano-British *Isurium*) to East Tansfield ('Tona's field'), to Masham ('Maessa's homestead'), to the Wittons ('the farms in the woods'), to Middleham ('the middle homestead'), to Leyburn ('the stream by the forest clearing') and to Wensley ('Waendel's clearing in the woods'). Where the River Cover joins the Ure they made their way into Coverdale to Coverham ('the farm on the River Cover'), to Agglethorpe ('Aculf's hamlet') and the Scraftons ('village on the lower lying ground'). Unlike their Saxon cousins in the South of England, the Yorkshire English made good use of the Roman roads; from Leeming Lane they advanced westwards into the foothills of the Dales: to Bedale ('Beda's corner of land'), Gilling and Barningham.

At Catterick the River Swale opened for the Early English the beautiful wooded valley to the west. From Brompton-on-Swale ('the enclosed land overgrown with broom') they do not appear to have settled on the site of the later Richmond but instead penetrated further westward to Hudswell ('Hudel's well') and Downholme ('the farm among the hills'). Here they had for neighbours the earlier dwellers in the British locality of Walburn. If some English settled on the low-lying land by the Swale at Ellerton ('the enclosure among the alders'), others climbed north into the forested hills at Hurst ('the wooded upland'). Further up the dale they founded three nearby settlements: at Grinton ('the green enclosure'), Fremington ('the farmstead of Fram's people') and Reeth ('at the stream'). Beyond Reeth the thick woodland of the upper dale seems to have halted their further progress at Healaugh ('the high forest clearing').

As they advanced westwards and then to the north-west along the course of the River Wharfe the English are traced in their many settlements: in Otley ('Otta's forest clearing'), Ilkley ('the clearing in the forest around the Romano-British Olicana'), Addingham ('Adda's people's farmstead'), Burnsall ('Bryni's corner of land') and Grassington ('the pasture farm'). In Littondale they took up their abode at Litton ('the farm on the slope'). In the valley formed by the River Aire their habitations are found at Skipton ('the sheep farm') and at Kildwick ('the dairy farm of the young men'); and, further west still, on the River Ribble are Settle ('the dwelling place') and nearby Giggleswick ('Gikel's dairy farm'). Although dating is difficult (and precise dating impossible), it would appear that the English settlement of the Dales had its main impetus from Ethelfrith's victory over the British at Chester in about 616 and perhaps was largely completed by the close of the century.

Six years after his conversion in 633 Edwin was defeated and slain in battle against the pagan King Penda of Mercia in alliance with the British Cadwallon of Wales. War continued to be endemic in English society with its upper class of warrior thegns whose chief *raison d'être* lay in their fighting qualities. Of the states which formed the Heptarchy, first one then another gained the ascendancy, its king being looked on as the *Bretwalda*, the ruler of Britain: initially Kent, then Northumbria under Edwin, to be followed by the Mercia of Offa and finally Alfred the Great's Wessex. In the North, it was the accession of Oswald, Edwin's nephew, that ushered in the Golden Age of Northumbria. During his childhood Oswald had spent some time among the monastic community on Iona, that source of enlightenment in a dark period, the monastery which had been founded in 565 by the Irish prince, priest and saint, Columba. Oswald's settlement of Aidan and his Irish monks from Iona on the island of Lindisfarne had a momentous significance in the civilising of the North; from it there grew that wonderful flowering of religious art that is the source of what may be called the Lindisfarne–Gospel culture.

In the manuscript illumination practised by these monks Anglo-Saxon art reached an early maturity, a splendour which, of its kind, has perhaps never been surpassed. The vellum pages of the *Lindisfarne Gospels* are aglow with the purest of colours—red, green, blue, bright yellow, pink, purple, brown and gold. In their delight in formal abstract decoration, whole pages—the 'carpet-pages'—are given over to the artists' unfettered development of the fullest possibilities of curvilinear design, in an exquisitely intricate interweaving of colourful arabesques. With their poets (like Caedmon and the authors of *Beowulf, The Seafarer* and *The Battle of Maldon*), their illuminators, the architects of their churches and the carvers of their crosses, the crudest barbarities of the Early English seem to have been softened, mellowed and transformed. How far the dalesmen felt these civilising influences we cannot know; but there were among them these conventual oases of culture; we know of English or Irish monks in their monastery in Dentdale.

For the year 787 there is an ominous entry in the *Anglo-Saxon Chronicle*:

> This year King Bertric took Edburga the daughter of Offa to wife. And in his days came first three ships of the Northmen from the land of robbers. The reeve rode to the spot, and would drive them to the king's town; for he did not know who they were; and there he was slain. These were the first ships of the Danish men that sought the land of the English nation.

Henceforth, the Christian English were to suffer in their turn the ravages that the British had undergone at their hands; they were now to be repaid in their own coin by the heathen Vikings. Six years after their first appearance off these coasts the Vikings returned, to sack and destroy, extinguishing that light of northern learning, the monastery of Lindisfarne. The fear, the terror they evoked among a settled workaday people comes through the pages of the *Anglo-Saxon Chronicle*:

> AD 793. These year came dire portents over the land of the Northumbrians, sorely terrifying the people: these were immense flashes of lightning and whirlwinds, and fiery dragons were seen flying in the air. These tremendous signs were followed by a great famine; and not long after . . . in the same year, the ravages of the heathen men miserably destroyed God's church on Holy Island, with plunder and slaughter.

The term Viking, which can mean 'bay men', 'fighting men' or 'settling men', refers to those Scandinavian sea-rovers—Danes, Norwegians and Swedes—who, like their fifth-century Germanic precursors, were impelled by shortage of land, sheer love of adventure, and in their case political feuds, to take to the sea. In their beautiful clinker-built ships, they sailed to all points of the compass, to plunder, discover, trade, colonise and conquer. Fearlessly they pushed out on the trackless ocean; west, past the Orkneys, to Iceland, Greenland and North America; south, to the coasts of France and the Mediterranean; east, partly by the rivers and partly overland through Russia, to the Black Sea and Constantinople, where Vikings formed the Varangian bodyguard to the Byzantine emperors. For the next eighty years along the coasts of the British Isles the appearance of their dragon-prowed ships with their brightly coloured sails brought terror to the inhabitants. In northern France and England their coming added a new plea to the Christian litany: *A furore Normanorum libera nos Domine.* A highly cultivated northern Englishman, Alcuin, the counsellor and confidant of the Emperor Charlemagne, summed up the feelings of his fellow-countrymen: 'It is some 350 years that we and our forefathers have lived in this land, and never before in Britain has such a terror appeared as this we have now suffered at the hands of the heathen.' In 794 the Vikings destroyed Bede's monastery at Jarrow; the following year it was the turn of that of St Columba on Iona. Continuing their raids around the north of Scotland and into the Irish Sea, the Northmen took the Isle of Man and landed at Dublin, Wexford and Waterford, where their settlements later were to form an Irish–Norse kingdom centred on Dublin.

In 866 there was a sinister departure from the hit-and-run tactics of earlier years. In that year the *Anglo-Saxon Chronicle* reports that, 'a great heathen army came into England and took up winter quarters in East Anglia, and there they were supplied with horses; and the inhabitants made peace with them.' This was the Great Army, led by Halfdan and Ivar the Boneless, the sons of the Danish Viking, Ragnar Lothbrok. The following year these Danes, moving north, destroyed a Northumbrian army 'with immense slaughter' at York. For years the Vikings marauded at will throughout much of England, until they were at length checked by the foresight and energy of the Wessex king, Alfred the Great. After having extracted what they could in booty, ransom and bribes, after having removed everything that was there for the taking and virtually stripping the land, the leaders of the Danes resolved to settle in the territory they controlled. The *Chronicle* states that in the year 876: 'Halfdan portioned out the lands of the Northumbrians, and his men afterwards tilled them and made their livelihood by them.' Of these Danish settlements, so important for the future history of Yorkshire, most were in the richer lands of the East Riding and in the Vale of York, their western limits extending only in a few places into the lower reaches of the Dales. Again the place-names disclose the Danish presence. In Hang East wapentake of the North Riding the characteristic Scandinavian termination of *by* ('farmstead' or 'village'), coupled with a Danish personal name, are found in the villages of Exelby, Firby and Hornby, each within an easy distance of the others, and point to the original farmsteads of the Danes Eskel, Frithi and Horni. A few miles to the west, Danby on the Ure marks the existence of Danish settlers among a population predominantly English. In Swaledale, Easby ('Esi's farm') may possibly be Danish. The Danes do not appear to have occupied lands further west, deeper in the Dales.

Of greater significance for the Scandinavian element in the peopling of the Yorkshire Dales was the coming of the Norse Vikings, principally by way of their Irish kingdom. In the first years of the tenth century a fleet of Norsemen, under their chief Ingemund, expelled by the Irish, landed on the west coast of England and succeeded in gaining a foothold in the Wirral. These Vikings were only forestalled from capturing Chester in 907 by the prompt action of Alfred's formidable daughter Ethelfled, the Lady of Mercia. In the first decades of the century the Irish–Norse were firmly established from the mouth of the Mersey to the Solway Firth. Being primarily a pastoral people, the Norse were often content to take up unoccupied lands on the higher ground, grazing their flocks and herds on upland pastures in the summer and descending to pass the winter in their frequently isolated farmsteads in the valleys. Attracted by the high fells and the natural grasslands of the lower slopes, numbers of them moved eastwards into the Pennines, into the heartlands of the Yorkshire Dales.

From Waterford in 918 the Viking chief Ragnald assembled a great expedition against the Scots and Northumbrians. According to an Ulster source, the armies 'met on the banks of the Tyne in the lands of the North Saxons'. Victorious in the battle, Ragnald wintered in the country; then, in the following year, he attacked and captured York from the Danes and established himself as King of Northumbria. The threat of a permanent Norse kingdom extending from Dublin to York was only removed by the death of King Eric Bloodaxe, the hero of Scandinavian sagas, who was treacherously slain by Earl Maccus 'on a waste place called Steinmoor' in the Yorkshire Dales in 954. It has been said that the battle of Stainmoor closed a period of northern history that opened with the granting of lands to the Danish followers of Halfdan in 876. During this period the Scandinavian settlement of Yorkshire took place, with its profound effects on the future of the county. Of the two racial elements in the Viking migration, the Danes and the Norse, it is the latter, almost entirely, who, with the English, are the forebears of present-day dalesmen.

Here again it is the place-names that reveal the coming of the Norse from the west, from Lancashire and Cumbria, into the

Pennine dales, which they began to inhabit in the tenth century. The sites on which they settled are shown by the Scandinavian elements in the names—some are specifically Norse, others they shared with the Danes. Their habitations are again discerned from their use of *by* and also *skali* (scale), 'a temporary dwelling, hut or shieling'; *topt* (toft), 'an enclosure'; *thorp*, 'an outlying farm'; topographical features are marked by *bekkr* (beck), 'a stream'; *gil*, 'a ravine'; *kelda*, 'a spring'; *thwaite*, 'a clearing'; *kirjka* (kirk), 'a church'; *eng*, 'a meadow'; *gartha* (garth), 'an enclosure'; *holmr* (holme), 'a water-meadow'; and *saetr* (sett), 'an upland pasture or shieling'.

Place-names which incorporate these elements are thick on the ground in the Dales. As an instance, in Ewcross wapentake, around Sedburgh, as many as 65 per cent of the topographical names are Scandinavian. In the Settle area and on Malham Moor it seems that many farmsteads originated as Norse settlements—in fact, the absence of older English names suggests that Malham Moor was originally settled entirely by the Norse. The incomers, however, in the main occupied lands among the existing English inhabitants, often on the higher ground, particularly that at the heads of the dales. In the upper reaches of both Wharfedale and Airedale the place-names are predominantly English, with only a scattering of Norse —in Flasby ('Flat's farmstead'), Thorlby ('Thorald's farmstead'), Cracoe ('crows' hill'), Scosthrop ('Skott's outlying farm'), Hawkswick ('Hauk's dairy farm') and Thorpe ('the outlying farm'—that is, from the nearby English Burnsall). In the name Kirkby Malham, Kirkby signifies 'the farmstead near the church', but the origin of Malham, although it is almost certainly Norse, is obscure. Again in upper Wharfedale there is a reminder of the Irish–Viking kingdom, from whence these Norse settlers principally came, in the Old Irish personal name of Eogan that appears in the curious village name of Yockenthwaite ('Yoghan's clearing in the wood').

The presence of Norse in the three northern dales is all-pervasive. If in Teesdale English and Norse place-names are fairly equally distributed, in Hang West wapentake, which includes much of the upper valleys of the Rivers Ure and Swale, the Norse quite outnumber the English. At the eastern approach to Teesdale in the vicinity of the ancient Brigantian stronghold at Stanwick Park, the names of three villages point to a cluster of Norse settlements in Stanwick ('stone walls', probably a reference to Venutius' earthworks), Forcett ('the pasture by the waterfall') and Eppleby ('the farm with the apple tree'). Farther up the dale, near where the Greta ('the stony') joins the Tees, are Rokeby ('Hroca's farm'), Scargill ('Skakari's ravine') and Boldron ('the forest clearing where steers, *boli*, are kept'). The Roman road, now the A66, crosses Stainmoor ('rocky moor'), passing the site of what was once Gilman's farm (Gilmonby) and Bowes, on the banks of the winding River Greta, (the name possibly deriving from the Old Norse *bogr*, 'the river-bends') to Rey Cross ('the cross at the boundary'). This old cross once marked the boundary between Yorkshire and Westmorland, and its naming recalls the Northmen's sojourn in Ireland in the use of the Old Irish *cros*.

From Barnard Castle in Teesdale the road south to Swaledale climbs through the Stang Forest (the Old Norse name for 'pole' aptly recalled in the Forestry Commission's plantation there), to Hope Moor and then drops down into the 'valley of Arkil's enclosure', Arkengarthdale, to Reeth in Swaledale. The English occupation of the valley of the Swale extended no further west than Healaugh; from there to the head of the dale the settlements appear to have been almost uninterruptedly Norse, as the names of both villages and farms indicate: Feetham ('the meadowland'), Crackpot ('the hollow of the crows'), Smarber ('butter-hill'), Gunnerside ('Gunnar's upland pasture'), Satron ('the wood cleared for grazing'), Muker ('the small cultivated field'), Thwaite ('the clearing' or 'meadow') and Keld ('at the spring').

In like manner the Norse occupied the upper reaches of Wensleydale, and the evidence of their presence is everywhere in the names of the natural features and villages. Of the former there are found Mossdale ('bog-valley'), Fossdale ('waterfall valley') and Raydale ('roe-buck valley'); Snaizeholme ('the water-meadow with twigs', from Old Norse *sneiss*); the prominent hill of Addleborough ('Authulf's earthworks'); and the stream, reputedly the shortest river in England, the Bain, from Old Norse *beinn* ('short', 'quick'). Of villages whose names are derived from 'upland pastures' (*saetr*) there are four in close proximity: Appersett ('that by the apple tree'), Burtersett, ('by the alder tree'), Countersett ('that belonging to Constans') and Marsett ('the pasture belonging to the Ant', possibly a nickname). Other village names are varied and distinctive: Aysgarth ('the gap among the oaks'), Carperby (again designating a farmstead by an Old Irish personal name, Caipre), Stalling Busk (possibly 'the stallion's bush'), Askrigg ('the ash-ridge'), Thoresby,

Bellerby and Harmby (referring to farms owned by Thor, Belg and Hiaerne respectively).

These Norse–Viking settlers of the Dales, differing from the more gregarious English in their villages, appear by nature to have been independent and solitary, often building their longhouses in the wilder, less accessible localities. Their characteristic longhouse—the living quarters, byres and barns all on the same axis under one roof—is reflected in the design of the stone seventeenth-century farmhouses that are so much a feature of Dales' architecture. As late as the seventeenth century a farmhouse in areas of Viking occupation was known as a 'seat house' (*saetr hus*), the summer house of these settling Norsemen—like the summer lodge of today. Sea-rovers turned sheep farmers. They have left their strong Scandinavian imprint on the nomenclature and on the living language of the Yorkshire Dales. Similarities of language facilitated communication between the Scandinavians and the English and, although the language of the latter ultimately prevailed, the Norse terms for natural features have survived in such words as 'beck', 'gill', 'tarn', 'mire', 'moss' and 'fell'. The last-named is interesting as the Norse word 'fell' denotes 'a place where trees have been felled, a forest clearing, an enclosure from woodland'. Obviously it refers to the wooded nature of the countryside which the Norsemen found and which was gradually denuded, partly by the constant cropping of young plants by their sheep and goats.

The Norse influence is most strongly evident in the local dialect of the dalesman. The well-known authority on Yorkshire matters, the late H. J. Scott, quoted the Rev. M. C. Morris on the origins of the Yorkshire dialect, and the assertions he makes about the county apply with even more aptness to the usage in the Dales: 'Speaking roughly I should say that at least three-fourths of our Yorkshire words may be traced either directly or indirectly to Scandinavian origin.' In the Dales it is, however, Old Norse rather than Old Danish that predominates. This linguistic survival will not perhaps be seen as so surprising when it is considered how many of the commonest words of contemporary English are of Scandinavian origin. 'Get', 'take', 'call', 'thrive', 'die', 'sky', 'husband', 'cross', 'window', 'egg', 'anger', 'slow', 'loose', 'ugly', 'happy', 'wrong', 'ill', 'hence' and 'though'—all these most English of words are etymologically Scandinavian. Despite his origins, modified and modifying as he was in the past, the dalesman is today, like the language, unquestionably, unequivocally English.

What his position might have been after September 1066, had the great invasion of England by Harald Hardrada, King of Norway, been successful, is another question. The ships of King Harold of England had retreated before the invaders to shelter in the Wharfe when Harald Hardrada landed his troops on the Ouse near Riccall. By a series of forced marches the army of Harold of England hastened north to meet him. At the battle of Stamford Bridge, fought on 25 September, the Norse army was shattered and their king slain. But the immediate future of the country was to lie with another band of Northmen, the Gallicised Vikings of Normandy. It was at York that King Harold heard of the landing of Duke William at Pevensey on the morning of 28 September. Moving with such speed that the mustering of the national *fyrd* was not possible, Harold returned to the South to repel the second invasion. At Hastings the defeat of the English army and the death of King Harold on 14 October 1066 was followed by the reluctant acceptance of William as king and thenceforth the military and administrative supremacy of the Normans.

CHAPTER 4

The Harrying of the North

THE TRADITIONAL TERM, 'the Harrying of the North', has something innocuous about it, almost a sporting ring. In reality it represents the consequences of political events which were in no way inevitable in themselves, with social consequences which were tragic for York-shire and the Dales. To understand something of the reasons behind the extreme severity of William the Conqueror's actions in the winter of 1069–70, it is necessary to look back on happenings in the North at least a generation before the defeat of King Harold on the field of Hastings in October 1066. Englishmen of that time had not our own advantage of hindsight. Then, and for some time afterwards, until the Normans were securely in the saddle, no one could be sure that there would not be a northern kingdom, centred on York, with native or Scottish or, perhaps, Scandinavian (either Danish or Norwegian) rulers.

In 1042, when Edward the Confessor came to the English throne, Siward the Dane was Earl of Yorkshire and, possibly in the same year, he conquered Northumberland, after murdering Eadulf, its Anglo-Saxon earl. The sea threat to the peace of these north-eastern lands, with their predominantly Anglo-Scandinavian inhabitants, came from the restless Viking kingdoms of Denmark and Norway; the landward threat came from the Scottish kingdom directly to the north and from the ancient Cumbrian kingdom of Strathclyde to the west and north-west over the Pennines. By Earl Siward's time the Scots were in control of at least the eastern portion of Strathclyde —later to be Westmorland; in about 1045 Siward annexed this territory, from which Galwegian raiders had constantly molested his lands. Then in 1054, with the help of a body of Edward the

Confessor's house carls, he defeated King Macbeth of Scotland and placed his own protégé Malcolm Canmore on the Scottish throne. In the following year Earl Siward died, leaving no adult male heir. Hitherto, with one exception, the rulers of the North had been local men, Anglo-Saxons or Scandinavians. Now both Siward's young son, Waltheof, and Cospatric of the Anglo-Saxon family of Bamburgh were overlooked when Edward the Confessor appointed the southerner Tostig, son of Earl Godwin of Wessex, brother of King Edward's queen and of Earl Harold to the Yorkshire earldom. It was this unfortunate choice that set the train for the breakdown of royal government north of the Humber and the slope down which the northern nobility slid to political destruction in the Harrying of the North.

In 1061 when Tostig, with Aldred, the new Archbishop of York, were absent on a visit to Rome, Malcolm Canmore combined a frontal attack over the Tweed with a western invasion of Cumbrian Strathclyde and as far south as Lancashire. The *Domesday Book* shows that in 1066 lands possessed by Tostig in Craven were still derelict and depopulated as a result of this Scottish invasion. The fact that Tostig attempted no reprisals against Malcolm after 1061 —that, in fact, he journeyed to Scotland and made peace with him—reflects the powerlessness he felt within his own earldom. This insecurity was further demonstrated by his subsequent murder of three Northumbrian nobles, Gamel, Ulf and Cospatric—this last in 1064 at the Christmas court of King Edward—a murder planned, it is said, by the queen, Tostig's sister, in his interest. To control the unrest among the northern nobility required armed strength and this in turn demanded resources which could only be met by increases in taxation in cash and kind beyond the customary dues of the North. In October 1065, after the harvest was in, the Northumbrians rose in rebellion and a group of insurgent thegns entered York in Tostig's absence to be joined by the men of York in killing his house carls and robbing the contents of the earl's treasury and armoury. The two racial elements of the North united in banishing Tostig and furthermore in their choice as Earl of Morcar, the younger brother of Earl Edwin of Mercia. This was a compromise since the Northumbrians would not willingly accept the Scandinavian Waltheof, nor the Yorkshireman Osulf, son of the murdered Anglo-Saxon Earl Eadulf. Edward the Confessor and Earl Harold, Tostig's brother, could only acquiesce in the results of the revolt of the northern thegns and the subsequent uneasy settlement. Harold himself was popular: 'tall and stalwart, comely and gentle, he drew men's eyes and hearts towards him'.

Earl Tostig, who had found refuge on the Continent, had failed in his two principal tasks: to defend the border against the Scots and to govern his earldom in face of native northern resistance; and his failure was serious in its long-term effects. In both northern races, among Anglo-Saxons and Scandinavians alike, it sowed a deep distrust of the interference of southerners in the accepted customary administration of the North. The death of Edward the Confessor in January 1066 and the accession of King Harold was followed by the Norwegian invasion of King Harald Hardrada with Earl Tostig in his train. Their defeat and deaths at Stamford Bridge and King Harold's at Hastings bequeathed to William of Normandy the unresolved problems of the North. These were in reality no different from the time-honoured ones: the security of the border and coast and, more especially, the internal divisions among the northern nobility, who united chiefly against what they thought to be threats to their almost autonomous status.

After receiving the submission of the national leaders at Berkhamstead, William was crowned as the successor of the Anglo-Saxon kings by Archbishop Aldred of York in Westminster Abbey on Christmas Day 1066. Among the English notables present was Earl Morcar. The following March the king returned to Normandy, accompanied by Morcar, but before departing he committed his first blunder in dealing with the North by appointing Earl of Northumbria one Copsig, an associate of Tostig. Copsig crossed the Tees to take possession of his earldom but he was surprised at a banquet by the existing earl, Osulf of Bamburgh, and murdered. Within the year Osulf was himself killed while attempting to assert his authority. The king then sold the earldom of Northumbria to Cospatric, who was related both to the Scottish king and the house of Bamburgh. When in the spring of 1068 the king ordered the levy of fresh taxation, Earls Edwin and Morcar rose in revolt and they were joined by Cospatric and the northern thegns. Coming north in person at the head of a Norman army, King William received the submission of Earls Edwin and Morcar. After he had fortified the Midlands with castles and garrisoned them with Norman troops, he advanced into Yorkshire and on his approach the rebellion collapsed. Without fighting a single battle, unopposed he entered York where he raised a castle. The leaders of the North, including Cospatric and Edgar the Atheling, had fled to the court of King Malcolm of Scotland.

William the Conqueror had been unsuccessful in securing the North through its native leaders, who in fact had led the insurrection against his authority. He was left with no alternative but to replace them with loyal Normans, appointing the barons William Malet, Robert fitz Richard and Robert de Comines to key positions in command of Norman troops. The last-named, with a body of 700 men, advanced over the Tees in January 1069 but fell into an ambush laid by the Northumbrians near Durham and the Normans were slaughtered almost to a man. This defeat signalled a general rising of the North. A band of rebels caught the governor of York, Robert fitz Richard, outside the city walls and killed him and his men. Cospatric and the leaders who had sought refuge in Scotland returned and they were joined by Archil, the most powerful of the Yorkshire thegns. A united northern army marched on York and laid siege to the Norman-held castle. It seemed as if William Malet was to suffer the fate of Robert de Comines and Robert fitz Richard, but timely word was sent to the king. William acted with decisive speed. His troops relieved the York garrison, setting fire to the city in the course of the fighting, when the churches were plundered. Before he left York after a brief stay, King William built a second castle and placed one of his most trusted subordinates, William fitz Osbern, in command. The rebels had retired to the Yorkshire Dales, awaiting the king's departure. When this occurred and they issued from the Pennines in order to renew the siege of the York castles, they were brought to battle in the open field by fitz Osbern and sharply defeated.

It was known to the rebel leaders that King Swein of Denmark was planning to send an expedition to England in the autumn. In the meantime they occupied the Dales and bided their time. On 8 September 1069 a Danish fleet of 240 ships entered the Humber. The Danes were met by the ships of Edgar the Atheling and Waltheof, the late Earl Siward's son. On landing, they waited until they were joined by Cospatric and his Northumbrians together with Archil and the Yorkshire thegns; then they moved to York. The Norman garrison, however, in setting fire to some houses that might have been useful to the enemy, had done their work only too well; the fire spread to envelop the whole city. Surrounded in the burning streets, the entire Norman force was killed or taken prisoner.

It appears that the Danes had wished to winter in York but its destruction frustrated their plans. Winter was approaching and with it King William, who had put paid to a secondary revolt in Staffordshire. The Danish army, unwilling to fight and unable because of the season to return home, came to an agreement with the king and retreated to their ships. William had gained a respite by separating the forces of his enemies. As before the rebels sought refuge in the Pennine fastnesses of the Dales. There they may have counted on the king's rebuilding and garrisoning of York castles, before he returned to the South, when they could resume their tried tactics of isolating bodies of Normans and destroying them before awaiting the spring and with it the possible return of the Danes. They had fatally misjudged their man. By one stroke of calculated brutality King William determined to 'solve' the northern problem once and for all. From York, where he established his court in its burnt-out shell, he set detachments of soldiers to rebuild the castles, others he sent to watch the movements of the Danes, but the main body he reserved to hunt down and exterminate the rebels. Some recent historians have considered it unlikely that William would have sent soldiers into the Dales in the depth of winter, but this is to fly in the face of the evidence of the well-informed and usually impartial Oderic Vitalis in his *Ecclesiastical History*. There, referring to King William, he states unequivocally, 'He himself continued to comb the forests and remote mountainous places, stopping at nothing to hunt out the enemy there.'

For the year 1069 the *Anglo-Saxon Chronicle* is brief and to the point: of Yorkshire it relates that the king 'laid waste all the shire'. The Vale of York and the major river-valleys at the heads of the dales were devastated and depopulated by French troops. King William struck at the base from which the rebels derived their power—the peasants. The thegns and their fighting men might have escaped to the more inaccessible places of the Dales, but the unprotected peasants on whom they depended for their subsistence were butchered by the Normans. If the unfortunates survived the massacre, they returned to find their homesteads burned, their ploughs and implements smashed, their livestock slaughtered, their grain (including the seed for the following year) removed or burnt. Long after the destruction wrought by William's soldiers, nature completed what he had begun, with the winter cold and famine. When the survivors had eaten those domestic animals that remained they faced starvation. Some joined the rebels and brigands who ranged in the 'free zone', the 'no-go area' of the Dales; others roamed the countryside, attacking settlements not despoiled by the Normans. Ultimately many sold themselves and their families into slavery to avoid starving to death; others simply perished. Symeon of Durham relates how the huts and roads of Yorkshire were littered with the decaying bodies that spread contagion among the living. Wolves came down from the fells to enjoy the Conqueror's bounty of human flesh. Those regions of the Dales which as parts of the Danelaw or with their Anglo-Saxon hamlets had been populous and even prosperous were left a scarred scene of frozen desolation.

Oderic Vitalis, a not unfavourable judge of William the Conqueror, laid the blame for this enormity fully on the king:

> Nowhere else had William shown such cruelty. Shamefully he succumbed to this vice, for he made no effort to restrain his fury and punished the innocent with the guilty. In his anger he commanded that all crops and herds, chattels and food of every kind should be brought together and burned to ashes with consuming fire, so that the whole region north of the Humber might be stripped of all means of sustenance. In consequence so serious a scarcity was felt in England, and so terrible a famine fell upon the humble and defenceless populace, that more than 100,000 Christian folk of both sexes, young and old alike, perished of hunger. My narrative has frequently had occasion to praise William, but for this act which condemned the innocent and guilty alike to die by slow starvation I cannot commend him.

Statistics yield only a coldly factual survey of the universal misery and horror. The compilation of the *Domesday Book* reveals that some seventeen years later in 1086 the upper reaches of the Tees, Swale, Ure, Nidd and Wharfe—the Yorkshire Dales—were almost entirely depopulated. Entry after entry records the impoverishment of Yorkshire from, as it expresses it, 'T.R.E' (*tempore regis Eduardis* —the time of King Edward the Confessor) to the year of the composition of *Domesday*; the success of the Conqueror's harrying is measured by the decline in the value of the county, which in 1086 stood at only one-third of its former worth. Of some 1,900 villages mentioned in the survey, about 850 were without a single inhabitant, and in another 300 there is explicit reference to waste, *Wasta est*. If the Dales suffered in the common destruction of life and property, the dalesmen had not the monasteries to turn to in their distress, as did the inhabitants of the richer parts of Mercia, where the English Abbot Aethelwig of Evesham succoured his compatriots, the victims of the Conqueror's calculated cruelty. As a contemporary monastic chronicler relates:

> A vast number of men old and young, and of women with their little ones, came to Evesham in their distress, fleeing from famine; all these Aethelwig supported as best he could. Many, who had long been starving, died after eating ravenously, and the wretches lay throughout the town, indoors and without and even in our cemetery, starving, and dying when they ate.

King William left York at the beginning of 1070, despite the winter, to carry terror and destruction through the Pennines on his way to Chester. Upper Teesdale appears to have escaped the attention of the Normans. However, in the summer, taking advantage of the undefended border, the Scots, with the wild Galwegian tribesmen from Strathclyde, crossed through Stainmore, carrying devastation down the dale and into Cleveland. From there they returned, driving before them the captured cattle and English slaves. The historian W. E. Kapelle has recently (in 1979) assessed the consequences of William the Conqueror's inhuman Harrying of the North: 'These conditions ensured that the North could never again threaten William's control of England. He had solved the political problem of the North by destroying native society in Yorkshire. . . .'

As with so much of the highlands of the Pennines, the Yorkshire Dales were long denied the Normans. While these regions were still held by the Anglo-Scandinavian survivors, William had not fully solved the problem of the North. If his control of England was not threatened from this unconquered territory, his control of the North was. A more valid solution was to be found only at the time of his grandson Henry I. The assault on the free zone was not attempted by the Conqueror, but he took the first steps in cordoning it off and blocking the exits by the formation of a series of great feuds and strong castellanies. Attackers from the Dales—'brigands' to the Normans—made it necessary in the seventies for the sheriff of

Yorkshire, Hugh fitz Baldric, to move about his business in the company of a small army. To the south of the unsubjugated area William bestowed on Ilbert de Lacy a compact fee at Pontefract, stretching to the foothills of the Pennines and commanding the Aire gap. Further north, in order to control from the east the passages through the mountains by the valleys of the Ure and Swale and, more especially, over Stainmore, he granted his distant relative Count Alan of Brittany the great estate of some 199 manors, which became known as the Honour of Richmond. Further north still, to block the Tyne gap and to defend the Scottish border, he constructed a castle, which was to become Newcastle, and created the Norman, Robert de Mowbray, Earl of Northumberland. West of the Pennines Roger de Poitou held the upper waters of the Ribble, thus guarding the western approaches to the highlands and to the Aire gap.

After 1087 William Rufus carried on his father's policy. In the castellany of Skipton at the head of the Aire he placed Robert de Rumilly and before 1092 to the north of this he created a frontier lordship analogous in the west to the Honour of Richmond in the east, which he granted to Ivo Taillebois. Ivo's estates here occupied much of Ewecross wapentake and later were to constitute the nucleus of the barony of Burton-in-Lonsdale. But Rufus' main contribution to the settlement of the North was his annexation of Cumbria in 1092 and the building of a castle at Carlisle. Here the Norman Ranulf Meschin performed the services of a marcher lord, containing both the Galwegians and the Scots. In order to ensure Ranulf's supplies for an adequate body of armed retainers, William Rufus planted around Carlisle a colony of peasants, with their livestock, moved from the South. Furthermore the king felt strong enough to penetrate deep into the free zone, granting lands to Guy de Baliol in upper Teesdale, where he built Barnard Castle on the River Tees. This process of infeudation and sub-infeudation continued, Henry I bestowing estates both on Normans and on individual English, some of whom were younger sons like himself and willing to swallow their pride, to forego the wheat bread of the richer baronies and eat the humbler oatcake of the Pennines. By 1135 a line of manned outposts stretched across the highlands from Carlisle to Richmond with the founding of the castellanies of Appleby, Brough and Bowes.

The extensive feudal estate, later to be known as the Liberty, Honour or Earldom of Richmond, created by William the Conqueror for Count Alan of Brittany, made him one of the largest landowners in the county, since, in addition to the compact holding of 199 manors in 'Richmondshire', with a further forty-nine outlying Yorkshire manors—much of it the forfeited property of Earl Edwin of Mercia —Count Alan held lands in no fewer than nine other English counties. In all he held 440 manors, yielding an annual rent of £1,200, a princely sum in those days. If the grant was a reward for the Count's military services—he had been present in command of the important Breton contingent at Hastings and had taken part in William's Harrying of the North—the king had other ends in mind, both defensive and offensive. Militarily this was a frontier outpost, its concern the defence of the northern and north-western borders against external enemies, as well as to counter the internal threat from the yet unconquered uplands of the free zone; but, above all, it provided a policing and administrative region, for there remained the urgent necessity of rehabilitation, the peaceful resettlement and repopulating of the areas devastated in the Harrying. The feudal economy depended *au fond* on a productive peasantry.

Alan Rufus, the first lord of Richmond, was a younger son of Eudes Count of Penthièvre and second cousin to the Duke of Brittany; through his maternal grandmother he was related to William the Conqueror. '*Terra comitis Alanis*', 'the land of Count Alan', as his holding is described in the *Domesday Book*, had as its nucleus the former Anglo-Saxon manors of Gilling and Catterick, but it extended far and wide into the plain and on the foothills of the Pennines, as well as into Teesdale, Swaledale and Wensleydale. As if making a symbolic break with the past and with an eye to the future Count Alan shifted his feudal centre deeper into the Dales, selecting for his castle a site of great natural strength on high ground which falls away sharply in a curve of the River Swale. The romantic grandeur of Richmond Castle—dressed stone upon solid rock, seeming to rest on the summer foliage of the trees at the water's edge—caught the imagination of the painter Turner. Even today in its tidied-up state under the care of the Ministry of the Environment it impresses by the sweep of its curtain walls and the massive mid-twelfth-century keep. From the marketplace the keep dominates the town. Work was begun on building the castle early, soon after the grant of the fief, which was possibly made by King William at York in the winter of 1069–70; and the construction shows some remarkable features for the period in which it was built. Firstly the material was stone, when the earliest Norman castles were more often of the motte-and-bailey type of raised earthworks and timber. Further, the living quarters were an innovation; the building known as Scolland's Hall, a two-storeyed, four-roomed edifice, was the first castle hall to be built in England, if not in Europe. Again the herringbone masonry of the curtain wall is architecturally interesting, as are, from the point of view of fortification, its intermittent towers. All this is Count Alan's eleventh-century work; the great keep belongs to the next century. It was raised by his great-nephew Earl Conan in about 1150, incorporating a portion of the original gateway, which then led into the barbican, now built over with houses. This differs from other Norman keeps in its position in the circuit of the curtain wall (not isolated in the bailey) and in the severity of its purely military, defensive function—it possesses no kitchen, fireplaces or lavatories and no domestic amenities at all. The garrison, which was originally Breton (the French presence in the town of Richmond is recalled today in Frenchgate and the street name of Maison Dieu), was provided by a feudal service, that of castle-guard, which was owed by all the principal mesne tenants. The military responsibilities of Count Alan as tenant-in-chief, holding directly of the king, demanded that he should develop the full feudal potentialities of his Honour of Richmond.

As the foundation of the feudal system was service based on the possession of land, it was doubly requisite, after the Conqueror's only too successful Harrying, that Count Alan of Richmond should bring order into the cultivation of his manors. By 1086, at the time of *Domesday*, the process of sub-infeudation was well under way, many of his Breton knights having been rewarded as sub-tenants with grants of land. We hear of only one English tenant-in-chief in Yorkshire, Cospatric, who (whichever one of that name he was) must have made his peace with the king. He died soon after and, although his lands were divided among his sons, it seems that for the future they held them as sub-tenants to the conquering race. This would have been usual with any natives who continued to possess estates after the Conquest. From *Domesday* and early charters there appear three rather shadowy relations of Count Alan, who may possibly have been bastard half-brothers: Bodin, Ribald and Bardolf. All three were enriched by the acquisition of confiscated lands.

Manors in Teesdale, formerly owned before the Conquest by Torphin, were granted by Count Alan to Bodin, among them Ravensworth, Romaldkirk and Cotherstone. Torphin must have been a large landowner, since another manor of his at Bedale in Wensleydale was also given to Bodin. These mesne lordships afterwards descended to the celebrated families of Fitz Alan and Fitz Hugh. The Fitz Hughs, as lords of the manor of Ravensworth, began the building of their castle there at an early date.

The manor of Middleham in Wensleydale, held at the time of Edward the Confessor by Ghilpatric, and subsequently laid waste, was bestowed on Ribald. It was his grandson Robert who, at the time of Count Conan, began the castle. It does not appear from *Domesday* that the third brother, Bardolf, held lands in 1086—perhaps he was a late arrival from Brittany. However, it is reported that Bodin in his old age, 'moved by a desire to serve God and renounce the world', left all his vast estates to Bardolf, while he and his brother Ribald, the lord of Middleham, retired to become monks in St Mary's Abbey, York. This Bardolf was the ancestor of the Fitz Hughs.

It seems that peasants from the depopulated parts of the Dales were brought by the Norman landlords to work on their manors in the richer regions at the eastern entrances to the river-valleys. At the time of *Domesday* Count Alan's lands between the Swale and the Ure were some of the most productive in Yorkshire. With the accession of Henry I in 1100 the reopening of the Dales had begun and the first stages of the Norman resettlement been completed. As it has been said, if Yorkshire was thus laid open to 'the exploitation of the Norman barbarian', it was also open to the glorious French civilisation of the twelfth century, 'to the architecture and the sculpture, to the Cistercians and all they meant to Yorkshire'.

CHAPTER 5

The Fleeces of Fountains

THE EARLY MONASTICISM in the North—so much of it of Celtic inspiration—that stirring of intellectual life, which in its golden age had produced the *Lindisfarne Gospels* and scholars like Bede and Alcuin, did not survive the invasions of Danish and Norwegian Vikings. Within a hundred years of the first arrival of the Northmen in 787 the light, which had spread its illumination from Iona with such incandescent brilliance, was utterly extinguished. The tenth-century rekindling of the monastic flame in the South, associated with the names of Dunstan, Aethelwold and Oswald (the last a Dane by extraction), brought no warmth to the North. At the time of the Conqueror's Harrying northerners looked in vain for an Abbot Aetheling to offer relief to the starving survivors at the gates of his monastery. Yet within the century succeeding that of the Conquest the limited area of the Yorkshire Dales alone possessed no fewer than eight flourishing abbeys or priories. It was the labour of monks that did so much to resuscitate the shattered economy of the Dales. The future lay with the Cistercian fleece.

Western monasticism claims as its founder St Benedict of Nursia (*c*.480–*c*.547), who, as abbot of Monte Cassino, composed his Rule for the guidance of his monks, regulations which have formed the basis for the communal life of the Benedictine Order and for those monastic orders that have subsequently arisen from it. In the course of the centuries relaxations in the Rule and the rigour of its observance have constantly brought about movements of reform on the part of those monks who wished to follow Benedict's ordinances in all their primitive purity. One such attempt at reform took place in the tenth century at Cluny in Burgundy, where a century later the great abbey, in the splendour of its architecture and liturgical observances, reached a height of influence and celebrity throughout Europe. In Normandy the ducal house, as a matter of intelligent policy, favoured the monasteries, so that Bec, Caen, Jumièges, Fécamp and Saint-Evroul became centres of literary and philosophical enlightenment and leaders in an efflorescence of ecclesiastical architecture second to none in the West. It was another Burgundian movement of reform, however, the Cistercian, and the vigorous call from that inspired propagator of Cistercian ideas, St Bernard of Clairvaux, that were to have the most lasting influence on the Yorkshire Dales.

The abbey of Cîteaux, which lies a short distance south of Dijon, was founded in 1098 by a group of monks from Molesmes, who wished to revivify the Rule by observing to the letter the practices laid down by St Benedict. In Benedictine houses which followed the observances of Cluny, with the many accretions to the canonical offices in the magnificence of their liturgy, had come curtailment in other matters, so that the choir monks had ceased to perform any manual labour. The acceptance by the Pope in 1119 of the *Carta Caritatis*, the Charter of Charity, a body of rules drawn up at Cîteaux under its abbot, the Englishman Stephen Harding, marks the beginning of the Cistercian Order of reformed Benedictines, the White as distinct from the Black monks—the latter being a collective term for the Benedictines, Cluniacs and Augustinian canons. The *Nomasticon Cisterciense* lays down that: 'In cities, castles, villas no monasteries of ours shall be built, but in places far removed from the conversation of men.' *Ora et labora*, by prayer and work, the *opus Dei* supplemented by labour in the fields, the Cistercians were to create a revolution in the farming methods of Europe. A severe critic of the order, the Welsh historian Giraldus Cambrensis, could but acknowledge: 'Give the Cistercian a wilderness or a forest, and in the matter of a few years you will find a dignified abbey in the midst of smiling plenty.' The monasteries of the Black monks were endowed and enriched by the gifts or rents, leases, tithes and church dues of all kinds; the White monks, although they accepted gifts of land, possessed no source of income other than that which they earned with the labour of their hands. A century later a fresh wave of reformers, the Franciscan friars, would look critically on the Benedictines of their day as somewhat effete epicureans and the

Cistercians as little more than uneducated farm labourers, 'consecrated peasants'.

Living a life of severe austerity, in accordance with the *Carta Caritatis*, the Cistercian choir monks, even when they reduced the hours spent in church to the bare canonical observance, found by experience that there was insufficient time to achieve the manual work that was required of them. Early on, therefore, they introduced an innovation that was to contribute greatly to their remarkable success. This was the system of lay-brothers (*conversi*), men who were not priests but who lived together under the same monastic vows of poverty, chastity and obedience and performed the material tasks, particularly of building and farming, on which the monastery depended for its existence. Another innovation of far-reaching consequence was the creation of outlying sub-stations, known as granges; and, since the choir monks were not permitted (except on occasion) to be absent overnight from the monastery, these were lived in and run by the *conversi*, with the seasonal help of hired labourers. The famous Burgundian vineyards of Meursault and Clos de Vougeot were granges of Cîteaux and were cultivated by the lay-brothers. A further French reforming order, which was to have important Yorkshire offshoots, was modelled on this Cistercian farming way of life, although it followed the Rule of the Augustinian canons. This was the Premonstratensian, founded in 1120 by St Norbert at Prémontré, near Laon.

The extraordinary impetus that spread the Cistercian movement throughout Europe, so that a contemporary could with some justification declare that all the world was becoming Cistercian, came from the lifework of St Bernard of Clairvaux. Bernard's powers of persuasion were prodigious. It was under his leadership, moved by the spell of his words and the clarity of his faith, that a band of men, of noble birth like himself, presented themselves as postulants at the gates of the abbey of Cîteaux at Easter 1112. Bernard was twenty-two. Just three years later, he was sent, with twelve monks as companions, to found a daughter abbey at Clairvaux, in a remote and desolate spot on the borders of Burgundy and Champagne. Within fifteen years of Bernard's quitting Cîteaux, although he seldom left his monastery, his fame had spread from Burgundy to the whole of France—indeed throughout Western Christendom. His advice was sought from all quarters, high and low, secular as well as ecclesiastic. When in 1145 a Cistercian ascended the papal throne in the person of Eugenius III, Bernard wrote to him: 'They are saying that it is not you but I who am Pope, and from all sides they are flocking to me with their suits'. This was the man who was so intimately connected with the religious life in the Yorkshire Dales.

The first revival of monasticism in the Dales came about 1100 with the establishment in Richmond of a Benedictine priory, dedicated to St Martin. In or about 1113 a priory of Augustinian canons was founded at Bridlington on the coast by Walter de Gaunt, lord of the manor of Healaugh in Swaledale, and a few years later the priory received from Walter's wife Maud, the daughter of Count Stephen of Brittany, lord of the Honour of Richmond, the grant of the tithes of the Healaugh manor, as well as the church of St Andrew at Grinton. Subsequently further grants of land in Swaledale were made to the priory by the Gaunt family. Another priory of Black monks— Augustinian canons from Huntingdon—was founded in 1120 at Embsay in Craven by the Norman lord and lady of Skipton, William Meschin and his wife Cicely de Rumilly. In 1157 the priory was moved to a most beautiful site among the woods at Bolton on the banks of the River Wharfe. The move to Bolton was effected, it is said, at the wish of Alice de Rumilly, in memory of her son the boy Egremond, who was supposedly drowned while crossing the Wharfe at the nearby Strid. Bolton Priory and the historical associations of the spot were to fascinate the poet Wordsworth (see page 172).

It was at the personal wish of St Bernard himself that his English secretary, William, led twelve monks directly from Clairvaux to found a monastery in Yorkshire in 1131. On lands beside the River Rye granted them by the Norman Walter Espec, lord of Helmsley, they built Rievaulx Abbey. The success of the venture was contagious; the arrival of the Cistercians provoked a crisis among the Black monks of St Mary's Abbey, York, which led to the foundation of one of the most famous and most beautiful of all English abbeys —Fountains.

St Mary's Abbey came into being in 1078 as a daughter-house of the Benedictine community of Whitby. As in many Benedictine foundations, the increase of material riches at St Mary's had brought a relaxation in the Rule. Caught up in the Cistercian enthusiasm, a group of monks sought out the prior, Richard, to ask that he approach the aged Abbot Geoffrey with a request for reform. When the abbot temporised, putting difficulties in the way, Richard appealed to the Archbishop of York, Thurstan, who appointed a day on which to visit the abbey, to hear and adjudicate the matter. On his arrival at St Mary's, there was uproar in the chapter-house, and the archbishop was obliged to barricade himself in the church. Finally he left, placing the abbey under interdict and taking with him Richard and his twelve fellow-monks. Abbot Geoffrey wrote, seeking assistance and advice from the king and from notables in Church and State, among the other abbots whom he addressed being Bernard of Clairvaux. Bernard answered Geoffrey in two letters supporting the actions of Richard and his reformers; he also wrote to Thurstan, warmly thanking him for taking them under his protection. From York the archbishop invited the seceding monks to spend Christmas with him at Ripon, where he had extensive estates. There on 27 December 1132 he bestowed on them some wild, uncultivated land not far distant in Skelldale. From these beginnings arose the magnificent abbey dedicated, as was customary with Cistercian houses, to the Virgin Mary, Sancta Maria de Fontibus—Fountains—named from the abundance of springs of pure water in the narrow valley through which runs the River Skell.

Those who visit Fountains Abbey today in the mellow sunlight of an English summer afternoon and approach over the smooth lawns the ruined church and monastic buildings, their pale-coloured masonry set against the variegated green background of magnificent trees, find difficulty in imagining the desolate wintry scene, when Richard, having been duly elected abbot, led his troop of monks to their inhospitable refuge. This unpropitious site was typical of the 'waste howling wilderness' that Cistercian labour so often turned into blossoming plenty. Between the river and the steep side of the valley, beneath an ancient elm, they built their huts and a timbered church and around them they began to cultivate a garden. First, they applied to the Abbot of Clairvaux, requesting that they be accepted into the Cistercian Order. Bernard replied, congratulating them on their actions and sending a trusted monk, one Geoffrey de Amayo, to instruct them in the Cistercian Rule. Without lay-brothers to assist them, the going was hard for the monks; so hard that after two years Abbot Richard journeyed to Clairvaux to beg of Bernard the asylum of a grange in France. This request he acceded to, but meanwhile in Skelldale the tide had turned. Hugh, the Dean of York, a man of means and culture, offered himself as a novice at Fountains, bringing with him money, lands and the nucleus of a library. He was followed by two rich canons of York; benefactions of land to Fountains had begun, and with them came recruits. Expansion rapidly followed. Between 1138 and 1150, a brief period of twelve years, some ninety professed monks passed through Fountains to found six new abbeys in England and one in Norway.

In 1151 Roald, the constable of Richmond Castle, chose a beautiful position on the north bank of the River Swale, something under a mile downstream from Richmond, for the foundation of a house of Premonstratensian canons. It seems that there may have been an earlier *monasterium* on the spot. Easby Abbey, dedicated to St Agatha, had an abbot and twelve choir monks, the number (imitating Christ and His twelve apostles) usual both with Cistercians and Premonstratensians, when an offshoot was colonised from the mother-house—in the case of Easby from Newsham, the first house of the Order of White canons to be established in England. Like the Cistercians the Premonstratensians engaged, through their lay-brothers, in sheep-farming; and they too prospered. About the year 1190 Easby in turn sent out a colony to found a daughter-house at Eggleston in Teesdale, a mile east of Barnard Castle. Eggleston Abbey, which was dedicated to St Mary and St John by its founder Ralph de Moulton, stands high on the banks overlooking the River Tees, again in a serenely beautiful pastoral and wooded setting. It is an undeniable fact, and the reasons for it are bound up with the causes of the early success of the monastic movement, that all the abbeys and priories in the Yorkshire Dales are found in situations of quite extraordinary natural beauty. Even if this was the result of hard persistent labour by the monks, the sites did possess the possibility of such development. The choice of locality was often fortuitous, however, and more often than not consisted of unprepossessing wasteland.

Second thoughts played a part in the foundation of Jervaulx Abbey in Wensleydale. In 1145 Peter de Quinciaco and a group of monks of the Savigniac Order from Normandy were granted lands at Fors, near Askrigg, by the Norman Acarius fitz Bardolf, lord of Ravensworth. Two years later the Order of Savigny joined that of Cîteaux; so that, when the land at Fors from its poverty proved unable to support the community, it was as Cistercians that in 1156 the monks moved lower down the dale to the richer and more attractive site of Jervaulx, to lands given them by Conan, son of Alan Earl of Richmond. The activities of the abbey came to embrace coal- and lead-mining and horse-rearing, as well as sheep-farming. From Normandy the Savigniac monks brought with them the secret of making cheese by a particular method; later, when ewes' milk had been replaced by that from cows, this was to become the celebrated Wensleydale cheese.

In the same dale, 4 miles (6.4 kilometres) west of Jervaulx, on a secluded site by the River Cover, a tributary of the Ure, arose the abbey of Coverham, dedicated to St Mary of Charity. Here again the first choice of locality had proved unsuitable. This Premonstratensian house was founded, in or before 1187, at nearby Swainby by Helewisia, daughter of Ranulf de Glanville, the Justiciar of England. The monks were transferred to Coverham at some time between 1196 and 1202 by the son of the foundress, Ranulf fitz Robert, lord of Middleham.

However, it was not only the menfolk of the Yorkshire Dales who responded to the monastic call and sought the seclusion of conventual life; in the second half of the twelfth century two nunneries were established, both beside the River Swale, within a mile of each other. Marrick Priory, a house for Benedictine nuns, was founded by Robert de Aske, some time between 1154 and 1158. Although it was originally endowed with adequate lands in Swaledale, as early as 1252 the revenues were barely enough to sustain the community, and it was therefore ordained that visitors to the guest-house should stay for one night only. The hospital at Rey Cross on Stainmore was dependent on the nuns of the priory. Downstream and on the opposite, south, bank of the Swale was Ellerton Priory, a house of Cistercian nuns. Its origin is uncertain—Scottish raiders after Bannockburn violated the convent and destroyed its documents—but it may have been founded by a shadowy figure named Wimerus in the reign of Henry II, or could it have been by Wymar, steward of the Honour of Richmond at the time of William II?

Although they were not situated in the Dales, other monastic houses besides Bridlington possessed lands there. In upper Swaledale the Cistercians of Rievaulx were given extensive rights of pasture and enclosure by Gilbert de Gaunt, some time before his death in 1241. In Craven also the Cistercian abbeys of Sawley and Furness were in possession of large tracts of summer grazing on the fells.

Of the utmost importance in the economic development of the Dales is the fact that in the course of time all these religious communities, including those of the nuns, became engaged in the wool trade. Marrick (referred to by the Italians as *Marriche in Chosta Ricciamont*) and Ellerton (*Elertana*) Priories both had business dealings with Florentine merchants.

From the foundation of Fountains the interest of St Bernard of Clairvaux in the affairs of the abbey was particularly intimate. On the death of Richard, the first abbot, in 1138, Bernard advised the monks to choose as his successor another Richard, who had been the sacrist of St Mary's, York; and at his death five years later Bernard virtually appointed as abbot one of his most trusted followers, the Yorkshireman Henry Murdac, at that time the Abbot of Vauclair. But it was in the long-drawn-out dispute over the canonicity of the election of William fitz Herbert to the see of York, in succession to the remarkable Archbishop Thurstan, that Bernard of Clairvaux brought all the resources of his powerful pen to the aid of his beloved Dales' Cistercians. In a letter to the Pope himself he vented the full force of his indignation at the alleged simony of the election, denouncing fitz Herbert as 'weak and feeble, and I hear it on the authority of truthful men that he is rotten from the soles of his feet to the crown of his head', and referring to the archbishop's supporter, Bishop Henry de Blois, in scarcely canonical style, as 'that old whore of Winchester'. It seems that the 'truthful men' were the monks of Fountains under their abbot Henry Murdac (or that fitz Herbert's partisans thought them the main stumbling block to the ratification of his election), for in 1147 an armed band broke down the abbey gates and ransacked and set fire to church and monastic buildings. If their intention was to kill Abbot Murdac, they failed, since he was unrecognised and left unharmed as he lay prostrate before the high altar.

In Archbishop Thurstan's original grant to Fountains had been the lands in the immediate vicinity of the future abbey buildings and others to the north, at Sutton, within a day's journey from the monastery, as was allowed by the Cistercian Rule. Gifts of land flowed in: at How Hill, Cayton, Marton-le-Moore, Warsill and Morker. The coming of the monks must have caused hardship to the existing occupiers of the lands, since these were, according to the habit of the Cistercians, 'reduced to granges' (*redactae in grangias*) by evicting the inhabitants and pulling down their dwellings, before the fields were taken over for cultivation by the lay-brothers. In 1151 Fountains was given estates further afield: at Cowton (by Earl Alan of Richmond) and at Kilnsey-in-Craven, in the parish of Burnsall. The latter grant was made by the second founders of Bolton Priory, William fitz Duncan, nephew of David King of Scotland, and Alice de Rumilly, the lady of Skipton Castle. At Kilnsey a grange was established, which became important as the headquarters for the great sheep runs on Fountains Fell north of Malham Tarn. In the summer months the sheep grazed on the breezy uplands of the fells, the shepherds (hired men for the most part) living in shielings and milking the ewes in the open; there cheese was made and the sheep were dipped and shorn. In the autumn the flocks were brought down to the granges to crop the stubble or fog and to be folded for the winter. Over the fells the flocks would be driven along the ancient green roads, like that of Mastiles Lane from Malham to Kilnsey. It was at the grange there that the *conversi* resided, supervising the shepherds and collecting the cheese and the wool to be conveyed by pack-horses to the huge storehouse at Fountains Abbey.

At Fountains Abbey the monastic day began between one and two in the morning (according to the summer or winter *horarium*), when the choir monks rose and descended in their night shoes from their dorter in the eastern range and, by way of the cloister, processed to the church. There the winter's cold and the darkness were dispelled in a communion of abnegation, petition and praise; sublimated in the male unison of recited prayer and the rich sonority of the Gregorian chant. In the course of the day the choir monks would follow the canonical hours—matins, lauds, prime, tierce (Mass), sext, none, vespers and compline. Even though the Cistercians had dispensed with the ritual elaboration of Cluny (St Bernard, however, was insistent in demanding the most faultless and harmonious performance of the liturgy), still up to seven hours might be spent in church. Such devotional observances were not demanded of the *conversi*, who for the most part were illiterate—it was one of the attractions of the Cistercian movement that it allowed these uneducated men to share in the communal life. At Fountains their dorter was in the western range of buildings above the magnificent vaulted twelfth-century cellar, where, along with the abbey's domestic requirements, the wool was stored. The *conversi* visited the church before beginning work and again before retiring. Their religious practices were simple; they had learned by heart the Pater, Gloria, Credo, Miserere and other short prayers, which they repeated in observance of the canonical hours. They were required to communicate only seven times in the course of the year. For them the period of sleep was longer than that of choir monks; their food in the monastery was similar in quality but slightly more liberal in quantity; it was more abundant when they were in residence at the granges. It was there that they spent much of the year, returning to the monastery at certain intervals and for prescribed feast days.

The Cistercians, from their connection with their Burgundian mother-house, had experience of sheep-farming, and in Yorkshire they found conditions ready made for the successful development of the large-scale production of wool: an abundance of excellent pasturage and two hardy breeds of native sheep. William the Conqueror's harrying in the preceding century had left vast tracts of the Dales under-populated and open to extensive exploitation; much was first-rate grassland of the limestone country. Dr Whitaker the historian of Craven estimated that Fountains possessed more than a million acres (404,694 hectares) in estates stretching westwards from around Ripon and Kirkby Malzeard up the river-valleys of the Nidd, Wharfe and Ribble to their headwaters in the north, and south to the Malham and Kilnsey districts. Of the two varieties of indigenous sheep which the monks found in the Dales, one was extremely hardy, capable of thriving on the rough mountain or moorland herbage and yielding a coarse wool; this was the progenitor of the black-faced Scotch sheep and the celebrated Swaledales of today. The other, a larger animal of more delicate habit, which with improvements in breeding developed into the modern Wensleydale, produced the long fine wool that formed the basis of the mediaeval English wool trade, the source of the national wealth.

Although at the time of *Domesday* great abbeys like Peterborough, Winchester and Ely had considerable flocks of sheep, it was not until the coming of the Cistercians that large-scale sheep-farming and an organised trade in wool for the export market, chiefly to Flanders and Italy, developed. From about 1170 onwards the Cistercians were selling the bulk of the finest wool in the country and until the fourteenth century the White monks were economically, in the words of Professor David Knowles: 'the most powerful group and producers of the finest fleeces'. Wool was carded, spun and woven at

Fountains for the monks' own use—it was laid down that their habit was to be made from natural undyed wool—but their production was almost entirely for export. Where the Cistercians gained a rewarding advantage over other producers for export was in their practice of carefully grading their wool. In consequence the representative of one of their regular customers, like the well-known firms of Bardi or Frescobaldi of Florence, could visit Fountains, inspect a sample and place their order, knowing in advance what they were buying. They knew also that at the due time the wool, as specified, and done up in sacks, would be delivered.

The cellarer at Fountains was responsible not only for the work on the granges, the whole process of intensive sheep-farming, but for the commercial disposal of the wool. In this last operation his zeal might get the better of him and lead to the dangerous practice of forward sales; in reality, this entailed a loan to the abbey on the security of future wool. Interest, too, might be paid in the form of a reduced price being quoted for the wool or the delivery of additional sacks. Although this form of dealing in futures was prohibited in 1157 by the Cistercian general chapter, it nevertheless continued. In 1214 the abbot of Fountains was deputed to look into the conduct of *conversi* who were buying up wool from other sources to sell at a higher price; this also was condemned but the profitable practice went on. Between 1220 and 1247, under Abbot John of Kent, were built the magnificent presbytery and the eastern transept of the Nine Altars, one of the glories of Early English architecture; and in addition a new infirmary was raised. To meet the great cost incurred, in 1276 Fountains found itself obliged to mortgage the abbey on the receipt from Italian bankers of four years' advance payment for the wool clip. Despite the subsequent problems the abbey had in meeting its obligations, the Italians did realise that it was impracticable to sell up the foremost Yorkshire abbey; it became necessary, however, for the king to step in. In the event it was the Italian houses and not Fountains that went bankrupt.

By the fourteenth century the wool trade in monastic hands had become invaluable to the country as a whole, being the greatest single element in the national wealth. To this wealth the Yorkshire Dales had made a significant contribution. The wool clip of Fountains topped the list of the production of English monasteries, with an annual output of seventy-six sacks (27,664 lb, 12,547 kg). It also received the highest price in Yorkshire for the best quality wool

—£14 (in the money of the time) per sack. Rievaulx was high up the list, its production amounting to sixty sacks, although its wool was not of Fountains' quality. Jervaulx and Bridlington each produced some fifty sacks a year, yielding a steady income, even if their wool was not so highly priced as that of Fountains. Easby, Eggleston and the nuns of Ellerton had individually an annual production of ten sacks, and here again the quality of their wool was somewhat inferior. One of the highest prices paid by the foreign purchasers of English wool was for that from Tintern Abbey—£18.66, but the clip was comparatively small, a mere fifteen sacks. The architectural excellence of the abbeys and priories of the Dales, buildings that wealth made possible—and with them the beauty of their settings —had come then from monastic purses richly lined with the golden fleece.

CHAPTER 6

The Court of the North: Middleham

THE MANOR OF Middleham in Wensleydale had been granted in 1086 by the lord of Richmondshire, Count Alan of Brittany, to his younger brother Ribald. The present castle, which supersedes an earlier one of the motte-and-bailey type, whose ruins are visible on the skyline about a quarter of a mile to the south, seems to have been begun by Ribald's grandson Robert, to command the road through Coverdale from Richmond to Skipton. In 1270, on the death of his descendant Ralph, possession of the manor and castle passed to the latter's daughter, known as the 'Lady of Middleham', who was married to Robert Neville, the son of the lord of Raby in Teesdale, some 20 miles (32 kilometres) as the crow flies to the north, in County Durham. Of all the great feudal houses of mediaeval England these Nevilles of Raby would seem to have merited C. W. Oman's description as 'incontestably the toughest and the most prolific'. A succession of rich marriages had made the Nevilles among the most powerful lords in the North, rivals to the Percies of Northumberland. King Richard II, after his successful suppression of baronial resistance in 1397, sought to reconcile the head of the Nevilles, Ralph, by raising him to the dignity of an earldom. The Percies had twenty years earlier been created Earls of Northumberland; the titles of York and Richmond were for royal holders; King Richard created Ralph Neville Earl of Westmorland, though he seems to have held not a single manor in that county.

The Nevilles' claim to toughness and prolificacy was well illustrated in the new earl. When Henry of Bolingbroke landed at Ravenspur in 1399 to claim Richard's throne, Ralph Neville was one of the first to join him; and in the rebellions of Northumberland and his son Hotspur and the subsequent revolt of the Scropes and Mowbrays against the House of Lancaster, he and the Neville arms were prompt in their aid to Henry IV. Earl Ralph's prowess extended beyond the field of battle; by his first wife he had nine children; his second, Joan Beaufort, daughter of John of Gaunt, bore him another fourteen. The Countess Joan, who was step-sister to Henry IV, was a strong personality and she saw to it that the offspring of the first marriage did not gain at the expense of her own children. The nominal seniority and the title became appanages of the Nevilles of Raby and Brancepeth; but the real head of the family was her eldest son Richard Neville, who acquired by a judicious marriage the title of Earl of Salisbury and it was to him that the Yorkshire estates went, with his headquarters at Middleham and Sheriff Hutton.

Successful both in the field and in the bed, Ralph Neville, first Earl of Westmorland, was no less successful in the marriage market. There followed what John Gillingham has described as 'probably the most amazing series of child marriages in English history'. No fewer than thirteen of the partners in eleven marriages were under sixteen when they were joined as husband and wife. The Nevilles thus became allied to the noblest and the richest of the great English families. It was not thought unbecoming that the Earl of Salisbury's eldest son, another Richard, should, when six years of age, marry the heiress Anne Beauchamp, three years his senior. Through her young Richard Neville became Earl of Warwick, with an income of £4,000 a year, which made him one of the richest barons in the land. Perhaps the greatest of the matrimonial prizes in Earl Ralph's estimation was won by his youngest daughter Cicely, from her beauty known as the 'Rose of Raby', who at the age of about nine was betrothed to the eleven-year-old Richard Duke of York.

Richard Plantagenet was a landless orphan, four years of age, when on 25 October 1415 his elder brother's death in the thick of the fighting on the victorious field of Agincourt left him the royal duchy of York. The Lancastrian sympathies of Ralph Earl of Westmorland now stood him in good stead; for the sum of £2,000 the wardship of the young Duke of York was granted to him by King Henry V and the boy journeyed north to be brought up with a horde of young Nevilles at Raby and Middleham. There he spent his boyhood and adolescence as one of the family. In 1425 old Ralph, first Earl of Westmorland, died, leaving his title and Durham estates including Raby and Brancepeth to his heir, his Neville grandson, also called Ralph.

Middleham and his Yorkshire lands he left as a jointure to his wife the Countess Joan Beaufort. It was she who arranged that these estates should pass to her own children, so that this alienation of lands brought with it an alienation of minds between the senior and junior branches of the Nevilles—a breach which would later have serious political consequences for the family on the outbreak of the Wars of the Roses. In 1430 when he was nineteen, his Middleham wardship behind him, Richard Duke of York was present at the hollow ceremony in which the boy sovereign Henry VI was crowned King of France in Notre Dame de Paris.

In this age of livery and maintenance the dun bull and the 'saltire argent on a field gules', the badges of the Nevilles, were borne by what was indeed an army of retainers. In 1449, at the very time Henry VI and the Earl of Somerset were losing Normandy, the Neville Earl of Salisbury was entering into a contract with a knight from Westmorland, a neighbour to his own great holding around Middleham:

> The indenture made between Richard Earl of Salisbury, on the one part, and Walter Strykelande knight, on the other, beareth witness that the said Walter is retained and withholded to the same Earl for the term of his life, against all folk, saving his allegiance to the King. And the said Walter shall be well and conveniently horsed, armed and arrayed, and always ready to bide come and go with to and for the said Earl, at all times and places, as well in time of peace as time of war, at the wages of the same Earl.

It was by such means that these great marcher lords, Nevilles, Percies, Cliffords (and the lesser Scropes, Dacres and Mowbrays) built up their formidable armed strength. While thousands could shout for a Percy, as many could respond to the call of a Neville.

Middleham Castle had been the principal residence of Richard Earl of Salisbury and it became 'the favourite retreat' of Salisbury's famous son, Richard Neville Earl of Warwick, the 'Kingmaker'. Imposing today in its ruined splendour, it must have been of a solid sober magnificence in the Neville heyday, yet gay with the fluttering of flags and pennons, filled with the clangour and colour of a military establishment whose lords had shared so often with the Percies the onerous wardenship of the Marches against the Scots. The castle consists of a rectangular late twelfth-century keep, its main axis running north and south, with a chapel of a century later projecting from its eastern wall. This central keep stands within a fourteenth-century enclosure with corner towers, which is entered by a fine gateway at the north-eastern angle and comprises a range of domestic buildings on the north, west and south sides. The keep is of two storeys, the entrance stairway to the first, main floor being along its eastern wall. An internal wall partitions the building longitudinally; on the east was the great hall from which a doorway at the head of the stairs led to the chapel; on the west were situated the earl's presence chamber and the living rooms. Below, on the ground floor, were the kitchens, storerooms, cellars and other domestic offices and two wells. On the eastern side of the enceinte a guard tower protected a drawbridge which crossed the moat, giving access to an outer courtyard, where stood the stables, smithy, armourer's workshops and the slaughterhouse. What today in slow, old, racehorse-ridden Middleham is so difficult to revive, to recapture even in the imagination, is the clamour, the clatter, the clip-clop of iron on cobbles, the clanking of armour, the whole pulsating external living of a great mediaeval household, where the word 'privacy' applied most aptly perhaps only to the lord's own thoughts.

But amidst this seething chaos there was an order. The household of a feudal magnate, a nobleman of the rank of the Earl of Salisbury, resembled, indeed was modelled on the royal court with its hierarchy of greater and lesser officers, officials, attendants, guards, servants and pages. It was customary in these great houses for the children of other noble or knightly families to be accepted as one of the lord's household (sometimes as wards, as Henry V placed young Richard Duke of York at Middleham under the tutelage of Ralph Earl of Westmorland), to be accepted as apprentices in the forms of courtly conduct, to be schooled in 'the urbanity and nurture of England'. In direct contact with the earl were his chief officers, the steward, the comptroller of the household, treasurer and secretaries, who conducted the day-to-day life of the establishment according to a detailed code of duties and privileges. It was a highly formalised society, elaborate in its etiquette—it was the age of the magnificence of the court of Burgundy, a splendour highly sophisticated—more sophisticated perhaps than civilised. In the great hall, besides those closest to the earl, his personal friends, counsellors and captains, mingled officers of the Wardrobe, the Master of the Henchmen (the noble pages), squires of the household, chaplains and children of the chapel (choristers), ladies in waiting on the countess, heralds, musicians, ushers, grooms—the whole multitudinous ménage of Middleham.

Symptomatic of the anarchical condition of fifteenth-century England was an incident which occurred to a bridal party on Heworth Moor near York on 24 August 1453. The Earl and Countess of Salisbury with their son Sir John Neville and accompanied by a large retinue of knights and men-at-arms, were riding home from the marriage of their son Sir Thomas to Maud Stanhope, when they fell into an ambush prepared by Lord Egremont, the second son of Henry Percy Earl of Northumberland. The Nevilles fought off the Percies but men were wounded and slain on both sides. The old feud between the two families had broken out with a new virulence. A contemporary chronicler saw in this 'battle of Heworth' the beginning of a time of troubles, not only for the North but for the whole of England.

In the same year came the final loss of Gascony (Normandy had been recovered by the French three years previously), and the feeble Henry VI lapsed into one of his intermittent bouts of insanity. Despite the open hostility of the headstrong Queen Margaret of Anjou and her court party, Richard Duke of York, the former ward of Middleham, was proclaimed protector for the defence and rehabilitation of the realm. A few days later the Earl of Salisbury was appointed chancellor. Events, however, quickly proved the appositeness of the remark: 'If Henry's insanity had been a tragedy, his recovery was a national disaster.' York and Salisbury were superseded by the queen's supporter the Earl of Somerset, with the backing of the Percy family. It was now a struggle (literally to the death) of the Duke of York and the Nevilles against the court and the Percies. In May 1455 the Wars of the Roses began with the first battle of St Albans, when the Yorkists were victorious and the Percy Earl of Northumberland and Lord Clifford of Skipton were among the dead on the field. York was once more 'Protector and Defensor of this land', Richard Neville of Warwick was appointed to the commanding captaincy of Calais, and for the moment the Nevilles were in the ascendant. The indomitable Queen Margaret was not to be idle, however; on 12 October 1459 at Ludlow a newly raised Lancastrian army defeated the Yorkists, and the Duke of York, his sons Earls Edward of March and Edmund of Rutland, together with Salisbury and his son Warwick, had to seek refuge abroad. In June 1460 Salisbury's brother, Lord Fauconberg, crossed from Calais and seized Sandwich, where he was joined by Salisbury, Warwick and Edward of March. Later, reinforced by the retinues of the Duke of Norfolk and Lord Scrope of Bolton, they moved towards Northampton, where the Lancastrian army was assembled around Henry VI. On 10 July 1460, largely through the opportune treachery of Lord Grey of Ruthin, the victory lay with Warwick and the Yorkists, the hapless king becoming their prisoner.

At this point the Duke of York returned from his refuge in Ireland and in a parliament called for October 1460 he laid formal claim to the throne. In this he had no support from Warwick; instead, a compromise was reached whereby Henry VI retained the throne, but on condition that on his death he was to be succeeded by York and subsequently by York's heirs. With her young son disinherited, Margaret of Anjou roused Lancastrian resistance; in the North the Percies took up the cause and the Neville estates were laid waste; some of their tenants were forced, on pain of death, to forswear their allegiance. In December 1460 a strong Yorkist force under the command of the Duke of York and the Earl of Salisbury, who were accompanied by their sons Edmund of Rutland and Sir Thomas Neville, marched north and spent Christmas at York's castle of Sandal, near Wakefield. Warwick stayed in the South to guard London; Edmund of March, given his first independent command, was despatched to Wales. Possibly on account of the difficulty of obtaining supplies in winter, York decided precipitately to attack the numerically superior Lancastrian army. The result was a disastrous defeat. The Duke of York was killed on the battlefield as were Sir Thomas Neville and many of the leading knights. Later in the evening the ageing Earl of Salisbury was captured and executed the following day at Pontefract. Edmund of Rutland died in the pursuit, slain on Wakefield Bridge by Lord Clifford. (The Lancastrian leaders, Somerset, Northumberland and Clifford were all sons of men killed five years earlier at St Albans.) Shakespeare, often so inaccurate as regards the historical details in his *Henry VI* and *Richard III* plays, conveys powerfully the climate of vendetta, of ineluctable blood feud. Clifford addresses the doomed Rutland:

> The sight of any of the house of York
> Is as a fury to torment my soul:
> And till I root out their accursed line
> And leave not one alive, I live in hell

> Thy father slew my father; therefore, die.

This element of blood-spilling vindictiveness was carried to the extent of exposing (on the queen's orders) the severed heads of York and Salisbury on Micklegate Bar in York, the duke's adorned with the mockery of a tinsel crown. The brutal progress southwards of the queen's troops warned the Londoners, who closed and manned their gates against them. Despite Warwick's discomfiture at the second battle of St Albans, he joined the successful advance eastwards of Edward Earl of March and together they entered a welcoming London. On 4 March 1461 York's heir Edward of March was proclaimed King Edward IV of England. A contemporary, William Gregory, wrote of the general hopes engendered by the change of government: 'Let us walk in a new vineyard, and let us make a gay garden in the month of March with a fair white rose and herb, the Earl of March.'

On the eve of Palm Sunday, 29 March, in a blinding snowstorm, which favoured Edward IV's forces, the Lancastrian army was routed at Towton near Tadcaster. Fortunes were entirely reversed and it was the heads of the Lancastrian leaders that were now displayed for public derision and obloquy on Tower Bridge. The Earl of Northumberland had been fatally wounded, the Neville Earl of Westmorland, who had espoused the Lancastrian cause, had been killed; and with them perished Lords Dacre and Welles. In Yorkshire the Nevilles of Middleham were triumphant. Richard Neville, Earl of Warwick, was, next to King Edward IV, the most powerful man in the land; his brothers were high in the king's favour: the valiant John Lord Montagu and George Bishop of Exeter and chancellor; his sister Elizabeth was married to Lord Stanley, a strength in the Midlands. Warwick, centred on Middleham, 'his engine-room of power', was appointed in supreme command of the settlement of the North as warden of both the Eastern and Western Marches. At Easter following the victory of Towton King Edward was entertained at Middleham with such festivities as the house and tenants could provide after years of depredations at the hands of the

Lancastrian Percies, Cliffords and Dacres. There, in the specially furnished castle now dwelt most frequently the Countess of Warwick and her two young daughters, Isabel aged nine and Anne, some four years younger.

Edward IV was eighteen years of age when he assumed the crown. One of his first acts was to create his younger brother George, aged twelve, Duke of Clarence and the youngest Richard, only nine, Duke of Gloucester. Then in November 1461 the king despatched Richard, a frail boy appointed to the magniloquent office of Commissioner of Array for the North Parts, to Middleham, that he might enter the household of his Neville cousin, the Earl of Warwick. It has been said that Richard of Gloucester's education at Middleham was conducted in the company of 'moors, men-at-arms and monks'. It is unlikely that the boy, impressionable and introspective, remained unmoved by the grandeur and beauty of Wensleydale and Coverdale. The moors he had all about him, to gallop in the parks, to hunt the deer and wild boar and to practise the elaborate knightly art of falconry. He could ride over the hill to the south to visit the monks at Coverham Abbey or, further west down the dale, the Cistercians in their beautiful buildings and wooded site at Jervaulx. Up the dale, deeper into the Pennines—not far from where the River Ure plunged flashing over the falls at Aysgarth—stood the peel tower of Nappa Hall, where James Metcalfe, the veteran captain who had followed Lord Scrope to Agincourt, could talk of victories and not of defeats in France and of the inspiration of the leadership of a Henry V. Later Miles Metcalfe and other members of this vigorous and prolific clan were to be Richard's counsellors and supporters.

Midway between Middleham and Nappa Hall, built on the rising moors to the north of the Ure, stood Bolton Castle, which had only been completed in 1399 and had been erected in spite of the displeasure of the Nevilles. There resided Lord Scrope of Bolton; both he and Scrope of Masham were redoubtable fighters and consequently, with their retainers, valuable allies. The Scropes had originally made their mark as much as *noblesse de la robe* as *de l'épée*; since the time of Richard Scrope, chancellor to Richard II, they had held high position in Church and State. The 'Good' Archbishop Scrope of York had led a rebellion against Henry IV and had suffered for it with his life. The present Lord Scrope had fought with Warwick at Northampton. Just as were the moors, so were men-at-arms all around young Richard of Gloucester; it was on emulating their feats at arms that this not over-strong boy set his heart.

For special festivities, like Christmas and the spring feast of Corpus Christi, Richard would ride with the Countess of Warwick and her two daughters, escorted by the chief officers of the household and a troop of attendant soldiers and servants down the dale and across the plain to the metropolitan city of York. There they would be put up at one of the great religious houses and, between the services in the Minster and witnessing the mystery plays, they would be ceremoniously entertained and feasted by the mayor, aldermen and the Council of Twenty-Four, and presented with especially fine white milk loaves of 'demain' bread, fresh fish and the choicest of wines. The young duke early gained a respect for the solid bourgeois qualities of the good men of York and they in their turn retained a loyalty to him to the end.

Life for Richard of Gloucester at Middleham was both strenuous and studious. Sharing his regimen of courtly apprenticeship were other scions of noble families, two of whom, Sir Robert Percy and Francis, later Viscount Lovell, became his close friends and remained so. In the absence of the great Warwick himself, their welfare was looked after by his steward, Sir John Conyers. The boys lived a life in common, under the supervision of the master of henchmen, rising early and attending Mass, before breakfasting on meat, bread and ale. (Warwick was noted for the lavish hospitality of his table; in his London house it was said that each day six oxen were consumed at breakfast—anyone present, even the most menial, could take away as much meat as he could pierce with his dagger.) After breakfast there followed a period of study: Latin (possibly under one of the household chaplains), French, penmanship, some mathematics, history, the elements of law and music. Serious attention was paid to the science of chivalry, to feudal etiquette and deportment, the boys being instructed in possessing 'all courtesy in words, deeds and degrees; diligently to heed rules of goings and sittings'. Their reading was in Christian doctrine, treatises on chivalry, knighthood, arms, jousting and warfare; allegories such as *La Forteresse de Foy* and history as it was depicted by such authors as Froissart in his *Chronicles*. For lighter reading there were the French romances so popular at the time, many dealing with the exploits of King Arthur and his knights, 'the matter of Britain'. The culture of this renascent age reflected the light from the resplendent court of Burgundy.

After a meal eaten with the company in the great hall at about nine-thirty or ten, the boys prepared for the day's martial exercises. Clad in armour—their knightly 'harness'—they were drilled and practised in the use of arms: sword, battle-axe and dagger. Then, in the saddle they exercised in the control, balance and shock of the tiltyard, or galloped over the moors, their bodies becoming innured and strengthened under the weight of armour and the manoeuvring of their weapons and mounts. The artificial formalities of jousting never interested the serious-minded Richard; the management of conventional weapons did though and he became adept in their use. Back at Middleham they took their supper at four in the winter or five in the summer months; and then, in the company of the countess and her ladies-in-waiting and the girls Isabel and Anne, their education continued in the acquirement of the gentler courtly graces.

This was the great age of pre-Tudor English music, with masters of polyphony like John Dunstable and Robert Morton, who influenced the Netherlandish musicians and composers, chief among them Guillaume Dufay, Gilles Binchois, Okeghem and Josquin des Prez. It is to be presumed that the music at Middleham was of a high standard at the time of Richard of Gloucester's wardship, as it was at the contemporary pleasure-loving court of his brother Edward IV. In 1484 the Silesian nobleman Nicholas von Poppelau, with letters from the emperor, visited Richard (by now Richard III) at Middleham and praised the magnificence of the religious music he heard there. Richard's sister Margaret was to marry Duke Charles of Burgundy, a connoisseur at a court celebrated for the excellence of its music. The evenings at Middleham would be given over to conversation, the reading of chivalric romances, dancing, instrumental music and the singing of motets and madrigals and other accompanied or unaccompanied pieces, in which it seems likely that the youths' voices would be a welcome adjunct. Before retiring for the night, each boy would be given his 'livery', a bedtime snack of bread and ale; and, in the wintertime—between All-Hallows Day and Good Friday—in addition his 'winter livery' of firewood and candles. For Richard of Gloucester Middleham became his predilection, a place he later looked on as his home.

In the formative years that Richard spent at Middleham, before leaving for his brother the king's court in the spring of 1465, he would have seen much of his soldierly Neville cousins, Richard of Warwick and John Lord Montagu. After Towton the two commanders were almost continuously engaged in the North in suppressing the remnants of Lancastrian resistance, headed by the Percies and Cliffords and aided by the Scottish allies of Queen Margaret of Anjou. Fresh from his victories at Hedgeley Moor and Hexham in April–May 1464, and the execution of the Earl of Somerset and the chiefs among the captured Lancastrian leaders, Montagu arrived at Middleham, where the gruesome public spectacles were repeated with the beheading of Sir Philip Wentworth and six squires. King Edward had set out to reinforce Warwick and Montagu, delaying only at Stony Stratford on 1 May to celebrate his clandestine marriage with Elizabeth Woodville, the captivating widow of Lord Ferrers, who had died fighting in the Lancastrian interest at St Albans, and the daughter of the Lancastrian Lord Rivers. The king reached York, 'and kept his estate there solemnly in the palace', and there rewarded John Lord Montagu by the grant of the title and the great Percy estates of the attainted Earl of Northumberland. From York it is likely that the king stayed at Middleham on his way to the siege and capture of the Clifford stronghold of Skipton Castle in Craven. Although Edward IV had recompensed the Nevilles handsomely for their services in his gaining and retaining the crown, his surreptitious marriage into the Woodville family should have warned a wiser and less ambitious man than Warwick that thenceforth the king was determined to be master in his own house.

Warwick had favoured a French alliance in order to withhold from Queen Margaret and the Lancastrians the support they had received from Louis XI of France; and with a treaty he had linked the proposal of a French marriage for Edward IV. Now, gradually he saw his own ambitions crossed, his dominance in the king's council undermined, the position of the Nevilles at court replaced by a host of 'upstart' Woodvilles, on whom the king lavished titles, offices and rich estates. Warwick's *amour propre* outweighed his sounder judgement and he drew closer to the Duke of Clarence, the king's younger brother and heir-presumptive, Shakespeare's 'false, fleeting, perjur'd Clarence'. The king did not cease to smile on the Nevilles; he continued to employ Warwick on high business of state and he advanced his brother George, the chancellor, to the vacant archbishopric of York. But when Edward IV heard that Warwick had in mind the marriage of his elder daughter Isabel, now in her fifteenth year, to Clarence and that the eighteen-year-old youth favoured the match, he peremptorily forbade it.

In the summer of 1467, while Warwick was in France, ostensibly to arrange an alliance between the two countries, Edward IV received in London the Bastard of Burgundy and concluded a formal treaty with him in opposition to France, the terms including the betrothal of the king's sister, Margaret of York, with the Duke of Burgundy's son and heir, Charles of Charollais. Two days before Warwick's return from the court of Louis XI the king went in person to the house of the sick Archbishop of York and left, taking with him the chancellor's great seal of state. Feeling that he had been duped and slighted by his sovereign, Warwick retired to Middleham, where he was joined by his brothers, George the dismissed chancellor and John Earl of Northumberland. When at Christmas Edward IV summoned Warwick to court, he replied that 'never would he come again to council while all his mortal enemies, who were about the King's person, namely, Lord Rivers the Treasurer, and Lord Scales and Lord Herbert and Sir John Woodville remained there present'. Warwick and the Nevilles of Middleham were directly challenging the authority of the king's majesty. Edward IV continued to smile, to enjoy his pleasures, to act as if nothing untoward was happening; and to withhold his hand.

Throughout 1468–9 Warwick went on maturing his plans: whether these included placing his protégé Clarence on the throne or merely reasserting his ascendancy over a chastened Edward IV is impossible to tell. In the spring of 1469 there was a rising in Yorkshire, led by mysterious figures who adopted the names of Robin of Holderness and Robin of Redesdale. The rising, which was captained by the former and had as one of its aims the restoration of the Percies, was easily put down by John Neville Earl of Northumberland. Robin of Holderness was executed by his orders at York but Robin of Redesdale slipped through his fingers, only to turn up in Lancashire. Robin of Redesdale seems to have been the pseudonym of Sir William Conyers of Marske in Swaledale, a close relation of Sir John Conyers, the Nevilles' trusted steward at Middleham. Other prominent Neville supporters from the Conyers clan were with him, and several of Warwick's own kindred, among them his nephew Sir Henry Fitzhugh of Ravensburgh and a cousin, Sir Henry Neville, son of Lord Latimer. In the meanwhile Warwick himself, Clarence and Archbishop George Neville unobtrusively crossed the

Channel to Calais, where on 11 July the archbishop married Warwick's daughter Isabel to George Duke of Clarence. Edward IV was
at Northampton when he received the news of the advance of Robin
of Redesdale from the North and of Warwick's invasion and successful rousing of the South. Seeing the preponderance of the forces
arrayed against him, the king allowed himself to be taken prisoner by
Archbishop George Neville in late July 1469, and, after a brief
incarceration at Warwick Castle, he was brought in honourable
captivity to the Neville headquarters at Middleham. Warwick, too,
came north but he quickly realised that the North was not with him
in the matter of his capture of the king.

He was soon to discover more: that diplomatically he was no
match for Edward IV. By September the king had departed from
Middleham to appear at York and Pontefract, where he called a
meeting of his council, which was joined by Richard of Gloucester,
Lord Hastings (both with an armed retinue) and a good number of
the leading members of the nobility. Ceremoniously Edward was
escorted to London, where the city welcomed him. Outwardly the
king seemed on the best of terms with his former captors. John
Paston wrote: 'The King himself hath good language of the lords of
Clarence, of Warwick, and of my lords of York and Oxford, saying
that they be of his best friends.' He restored Henry Percy to his title
and estates of Northumberland and in compensation for the loss he
raised John Neville to the marquisate of Montagu. In March–April
1470, however, Warwick and Clarence attempted to take advantage
of an armed insurrection in Lincolnshire but, when it failed and they
saw that there was no active support forthcoming, they fled to
France.

There the wily Louis XI brought about the seemingly impossible: a
reconciliation between Queen Margaret of Anjou and Warwick,
whereby Warwick changed his political allegiance from the Yorkist
to the Lancastrian cause. His offer of playing the role of Kingmaker
by replacing Henry VI on his throne was rewarded by the betrothal
on 25 July 1470 in Angers Cathedral of his younger daughter Anne
Neville to Edward Prince of Wales. A rising in Yorkshire was
planned to draw King Edward to the North so that Warwick might
land on the south coast and join up with Lancastrian insurgents in
Wales and the West Country. Late in July Lord Fitzhugh of Ravensworth led a rebellion of Neville supporters in Richmondshire; at the
king's approach, however, their forces melted away. The king was

still in Yorkshire in mid-September when he heard of Warwick's landing. On his way south Edward IV halted at Doncaster to allow the northern forces under John Neville of Montagu to catch up. There he learned of Montagu's treachery. With two Neville-led armies in the field against him there was no safety except in headlong flight. In the company of Richard of Gloucester, Rivers, Hastings and a few other lords he escaped with difficulty to Holland, to the refuge of his brother-in-law, the Duke of Burgundy.

The Milanese ambassador wrote: 'It is a difficult matter to go out by the door and then try to come in by the windows.' This is precisely what Edward IV achieved. Landing on 14 March 1471 at Ravenspur on the Humber—where Bolingbroke had come ashore seventy-two years previously—Edward waged the short campaign, which included the victories of Barnet and Tewkesbury, that has won him the admiration of those versed in military matters. Both politically and militarily he outmatched his opponents. It seemed that with an uncanny tactical flair and no small share of luck he could not put a foot wrong. At Barnet on 14 April 1471, Easter Day, Richard Neville Earl of Warwick and John Neville Marquess of Montagu lost the battle and their lives; at Tewkesbury on 4 May perished Edward Prince of Wales, recently wedded to Anne Neville, and with him died the political hopes of the House of Lancaster.

> Now is the winter of our discontent
> Made glorious summer by this sun of York;
> And all the clouds that lour'd upon our house
> In the deep bosom of the ocean buried.

With these celebrated lines Shakespeare opens his *King Richard III*, the dramatic piece (rather, the melodrama) that has indelibly coloured all our thinking as regards the enigmatic personality of Richard of Gloucester. Another source of subsequent misconception of his character is the unfinished *History of King Richard III*, written by the revered Sir Thomas More. The Tudor case against Richard could hardly have two more brilliant protagonists. Nevertheless the figure they portray is most unsatisfactory; it does not square with known facts, so that the enigma remains today the matter of highly contentious debate. From Tudor times, then, Richard has had a bad press; even his appearance has been grossly distorted. More writes of him that he was 'little of stature, ill-featured of limbs, crook-backed, his left shoulder higher than his right, hard favoured of visage . . .'. The contemporary portrait of him hardly bears out this last remark: the clean-shaven face, with the well-shaped nose, wide-set eyes, the thin but finely drawn lips is that of a highly intelligent, controlled, pensive man. Cruel? It would be difficult to judge. In 1484 at Middleham the traveller Nicholas von Poppleau observed that: 'King Richard was three fingers taller [i.e. than himself] but a little thinner and not so thick set . . . ; he had delicate arms and legs, also a great heart.' There is no mention of physical deformity; this is undoubtedly part of what Tillyard calls the 'Tudor myth'. Thin, delicate-looking, perhaps stooped; but with 'a great heart'. His prowess on the battlefield proves the last—at Barnet, Tewkesbury, the numerous Scottish affrays and the scene of his heroic end at Bosworth.

Among the many conflicting assessments of the character of Richard of Gloucester, one attribute cannot fairly be denied him (although some have tried): his power to gain the respect, indeed among many the affection, of the people of Yorkshire. By adoption he became a denizen of Middleham; from the confidence placed in him as a young man by his brother Edward IV and the success with which he fulfilled his public offices he became known as the 'Man of the North'. His active career as Edward's trusted lieutenant ('*Loyaulté me lie*'—Loyalty binds me) might be said to have begun after the king's imprisonment at Middleham in the summer of 1469. He raised the troops which, joined with those of Lord Hastings, escorted Edward, with the ceremony due to the king, from Pontefract to London in September of that year. Richard was just seventeen. His reward (and the duties it entailed) was the office of Constable of England and the appointment to command in Wales. In August 1470 the king, fearing for the security of the North, entrusted Richard with the task, traditionally performed by Percies and Nevilles and now vacated by the *émigré* Warwick, of guarding the northern borders as warden of the West Marches. A month later, however, he and Hastings were the companions of King Edward in his hasty flight to the safety of Burgundy from the forces of the returned Warwick and the Nevilles. Then, in March 1471, came Edward IV's triumphant re-entry through the windows. The victories of Barnet, where he led the right wing, and of Tewkesbury, where he commanded the vanguard, owed much to the steadfastness and bravery of Richard of

Gloucester. The king was prompt in recognising Richard's merits and capacities: to the wardenship of the West Marches was now added that of the East and Middle Marches, with authority over the traditional holder, the Percy Earl of Northumberland. In the disposal of the dead Kingmaker's vast property, Clarence claimed the lion's share. But in the North Richard stepped into Warwick's shoes; not only was his the overall command as the king's lieutenant 'beyond the Trent', but the greater portion of the Neville property in Yorkshire was granted to him, including the castle of Middleham. Before he left London to take up his post he received the king's permission to marry the widowed Anne Neville, whom he had long known from their childhood spent together at Middleham Castle.

After the death of Edward Prince of Wales at Tewkesbury his widow Anne, now fifteen, had been placed with her sister Isabel Duchess of Clarence at the duke's London house. Clarence demanded, as part of Warwick's forfeited possessions, the estates of the Countess of Warwick and the wardship of her daughter Anne. When in September Richard hurried back to London from the North to claim his bride-to-be, his requests to Clarence concerning her were met with a studied refusal. The king, appealed to by Richard, ordered Clarence to cease his obstructions. However, on Richard's going to Clarence's house in search of Anne, he was informed that she was not there and furthermore, since she was not considered his ward, Clarence professed no knowledge of her present whereabouts. In fact she was located in the household of one of Clarence's dependants, 'disguised as a kitchen-maid'. From there Richard removed her to the sanctuary of St Martin le Grand. The evidence points to a genuine love-match. Without waiting for a papal dispensation, Richard of Gloucester and Anne Neville were quietly married in London and in the late spring of 1472 they settled in their home at Middleham. He was twenty and she four years his junior. In the following year Anne gave birth to a son, whom his parents named Edward after his uncle the king. The south-western tower of Middleham Castle is still known as the Prince's Tower, from the tradition that the child was born there. Next to it, in the western range of buildings was the Duchess Anne's rooms, and adjoining the corner tower, in the southern range, was the nursery ('Nursee') of the Neville children, for winter warmth well placed above the bakehouse.

If the career of Richard of Gloucester had been confined to his activities from Middleham Castle between the years 1472 and 1483, he would have been remembered for his military competence, his efficient administration and, perhaps above all, for his evenhanded dispensing of justice, worthy of the king's trust in him, as the beneficent and benevolent lord of the North. His task was a formidable one: to guard the frontier against the Scots, to reconcile the smouldering animosities of former Lancastrians, to work in harness with the resentful Percies and to protect the commons against the arbitrary and frequently illegal actions of their feudal superiors. In all he set his hand to he achieved a quite remarkable success.

He appointed the old Lancastrian Lord Dacre as his deputy in the West March; in the Middle and East Marches he supervised the wardenship of Henry Percy Earl of Northumberland. In his dealings with the earl he showed a political finesse which demanded great diplomatic tact. In May 1473 at a royal council held in Nottingham an accord was sworn in the king's presence, whereby Henry Percy acknowledged the superior authority of Richard of Gloucester, and by the same token the latter undertook to respect the traditional Percy rights and to act towards the earl as his 'good and gracious lord'. Their relationship was not an easy one, particularly because of ancient Percy claims upon the citizens of York. However, the compact on the defence of the borders held; the Scots were driven back and Edinburgh taken; the crowning of the work of pacification was the recapture of Berwick, which had been sold by Queen Margaret of Anjou. For Edward IV's fruitful invasion of France in 1475—fruitful in that Louis XI bought off the English king with an annuity of 50,000 crowns—Richard and his Blanc Sanglier Poursuivant called the northern contingents to his standard of the White Boar. The response was an eloquent pointer to Richard's reputation; the recruits came in in excess of the stipulated 120 men-at-arms and 1,000 archers. His recompense was the grant of the Cliffords' former castle of Skipton-in-Craven.

In the winter of 1477–8 Richard was recalled to London by the king; there he pleaded unsuccessfully for the life of his brother George of Clarence, who was executed for treason on 18 February. An unbiased foreign witness, Dominic Mancini, who was well placed to observe and report on current events, wrote to his patron Angelo Cato of Richard of Gloucester at the time of Clarence's death:

Thenceforth he came very rarely to court. He kept himself within his own lands and set out to acquire the loyalty of his people through favours and justice. The good reputation of his private life and public activities powerfully attracted the esteem of strangers. Such was his renown in warfare, that whenever a difficult and dangerous policy had to be undertaken, it would be entrusted to his discretion and his generalship. By these arts Richard acquired the favour of the people, and avoided the jealousy of the Queen.

At the partition of Clarence's estate both Richmond and Barnard Castles came to Richard. Three days after Clarence's death he obtained a licence to found two collegiate bodies of chantry priests and choristers at Middleham and Barnard Castle, to pray for the souls of the king and queen, of Anne, little Edward and himself and of the deceased members of his family—perhaps that of Clarence was foremost in his mind. From the king he successfully petitioned for the holding of two fairs annually in Middleham. His charity touched even nearer home. In 1473 he secured from Edward IV permission that his mother-in-law the widowed Countess of Warwick should leave the sanctuary of Beaulieu Abbey and that thenceforth she should live at his charge with her daughter Anne at Middleham. The following year he persuaded the king to release from prison the inveterate intriguer Archbishop George Neville. Furthermore, when the young son of John Neville Marquess of Montagu was deprived of his duchy of Bedford, the king acceded to Richard's request that he might be brought up at Middleham as his ward. His benevolence extended to the granting of an annuity to the Countess of Oxford, the Kingmaker's sister, although her husband was his enemy. At Sheriff Hutton he gave shelter to two young boys, safe from the malice of the Woodvilles: Clarence's son the Earl of Warwick and the son of his own sister Elizabeth, John Earl of Lincoln. If Richard of Gloucester owed a debt to the Neville family for his happy boyhood at Middleham, he amply repaid it.

The key to Richard's remarkable success in the administration of Yorkshire was his Council for the North, on which served such men as Lords Scrope of Bolton and of Upsale, Dacre, Greystoke and Lovell, Sir Richard Radcliffe, James and Miles Metcalfe and other leading Yorkshire figures of previously Lancastrian as well as Yorkist sympathies. Like the king's council its primary function was to govern but it developed into an important judicial body, a court both of requests and of appeal; Richard, it was said, 'offered good and indifferent justice to all who sought it, were they rich or poor, gentle or simple'. Particularly intimate were his relations with the city of York, then the second metropolis of the kingdom, where he was active in settling civic disputes and acting as intermediary between the city and the king. On his frequent visits from Middleham to York the municipal authorities showed their appreciation for what 'the high and mighty prince the Duke of Gloucester hath at all times done for the weal of the city'; on one occasion the city fathers voting that, 'the Duke of Gloucester shall, for his great labour now late made unto the King's good grace for the confirmation of the liberties of this City be presented, at his coming to the City, with six swans and six pikes'. So attentive was he to the rights and dignity of the mayor and aldermen that he sent under escort a servant of his own treasurer, one Thomas Redeheid, who had insulted a citizen of York while on a visit to Middleham, to be punished as the York civic authorities saw fit.

In the spring of 1477 on Corpus Christi Day, the Thursday after Trinity Sunday, Richard, accompanied by the Duchess Anne, was present at the great cycle of mystery plays performed by the guilds of York. On the following day the ducal couple, gorgeously arrayed, were inducted with the full panoply of mediaeval splendour into membership of the Corpus Christi Guild, twenty years after Richard's mother and Anne's great-aunt Cicely Neville, the 'Rose of Raby', had been enrolled in the same religious corporation. By the spring of 1483 it seemed that the lord of Middleham had achieved much in the difficult task set him by Edward IV: the reconciliation of the North to the rule of the House of York; by his own persevering work he had made good his title to the demanding lordship of the North.

On 9 April 1483 Edward IV died, naming in his will his brother Richard Duke of Gloucester protector to his heir, the twelve-year-old prince, now Edward V. The controversy that has arisen and continues unabated over the forcible seizure of the throne by Richard has obscured the undeniable value of his earlier northern achievement. What was gained as much by persuasion, example and equitable dealing was secured henceforth through force or by the threat of force. The capture of the young king, the executions of Rivers, Grey and Vaughan, the beheading without trial of Hastings, the removal of the prince from sanctuary and the murders of the princes in the

Tower—it was a bloody passage that led to the throne. In P. M. Kendall's sympathetic study *Richard the Third* it seems that the exculpation of his hero rests very heavily on the plea of not proven.

Richard was at Middleham in mid-April 1483 when messages from Lord Hastings informed him of the king's death, his own appointment as protector, and the attitude of the Woodvilles. To a realist of the time the question was a simple one: was it to be Richard of Gloucester or the Woodvilles? He struck first, and won. Anne came south from Middleham for the magnificent pageantry of the coronation performed by old Cardinal Bourchier on 6 July in Westminster Abbey. The progresses Richard III made through his realm, receiving petitions, listening to grievances and dispensing justice, were highly popular: 'He contents the people where he goes as well as ever did prince . . . God hath sent him for the weal of us all.' In August young Prince Edward, their only child, left Middleham to be present at the resplendent reception of his parents by the citizens of York and there in the Minster his investiture as Prince of Wales took place. From York the queen and her delicate son returned to Middleham. King Richard and Queen Anne were at Nottingham when in April 1484 news was brought to them of the death at Middleham of the Prince of Wales. The Croyland Chronicler vividly reports the parents' agony of mind: 'You might have seen his father and mother in a state bordering almost on madness, by reason of their sudden grief.' Queen Anne only survived her son by less than a year, dying in London on 16 March 1485 and being interred in Westminster Abbey. On 22 August of the same year her husband, Richard of Gloucester, King Richard III, perished on Bosworth Field.

'Loyalty binds me.' It did not bind others. Richard lost his crown to Henry Tudor through the disloyalty of two of his leading subjects: the treachery of Sir William Stanley and that of Henry Percy Earl of Northumberland. The second, actively, by attacking the exposed flank of the king and his bodyguard at the critical moment when, separated from his main force, Richard attempted to bring about a personal encounter with Henry and his immediate entourage. The first, passively, by standing by with idle arms, awaiting the issue of the battle. In later years the court historian to Henry VII, Polydore Vergil, could not withhold his admiration for the chivalric heroism of Richard's end: 'King Richard alone was killed fighting manfully in the thickest press of his enemies . . . his courage was high and fierce and failed him not even at the death which, when his men forsook him, he preferred to take by the sword rather than, by foul flight, to prolong life.' His death was felt more poignantly by those men who knew him better. From the battlefield the courier John Spooner galloped north with the news to York. There, among the hurriedly assembled mayor and council it brought genuine grief: 'It was showed by . . . John Spooner . . . that King Richard, late mercifully reigning upon us, was piteously slain and murdered, to the great heaviness of the City.'

Today in the Swine Market in Middleham within sight of the entrance to the castle, by the stump of the ancient cross is an amorphous block of stone, eroded by time. Some think this to be the weathered emblem of the last of the Plantagenets, the White Boar of Richard III.

CHAPTER 7

The Dissolution of the Pilgrims

THE GROWING WEALTH of the monasteries did not escape the cove-
tous eyes of kings. As early as 1193 an entire year's wool clip from
the Cistercian, Premonstratensian and Gilbertian houses in England
was commandeered to pay the ransom needed to redeem the crusad-
ing Richard Coeur de Lion from captivity. The mediaeval notion that
the king should live 'of his own', if this ideal survived the disastrous Wars of the Roses, was seen to be wholly inadequate to
meet the financial requirements of strong Tudor government, exposed as it was to the general inflation consequent on the influx of
silver from the Americas. This was clearly grasped by Henry VIII and
his astute minister Thomas Cromwell, the latter the embodiment of
the belief that the Englishman Italianate was the devil incarnate. In
fulfilment of one of Cromwell's principal aims—'to make Henry the
richest king there ever was in England'—a means lay ready to hand
in the diversion of the income of the Church and the spoliation of its
accumulated wealth. A series of Acts of Parliament and royal decrees
began the severance of the links with Rome that marked the Protestant Reformation which was to culminate in the establishment of the
Church of England. Early in 1534 the payment of annates, or first
fruits, to the Pope was prohibited, the money being diverted to the
king's use; and in December of that year the Supremacy Act proclaimed Henry 'the only supreme head on earth of the Church of
England'. Then in March 1536 an Act was passed suppressing the
smaller monasteries: those, that is, with an income of less than £200
a year.

From Yorkshire in the winter of 1535–6 Cromwell's commissioners, Drs Layton and Legh, after the most cursory examination of the

monasteries, wrote to their master: 'There can be no better way to beat the King's authority into the heads of the rude people of the North than to show them that the King intends reformation and correction of religion.' With the intentions of the king and Cromwell in mind, it was not difficult for the commissioners to discover in the lesser monasteries 'manifest sin, vicious, carnal and abominable living'. Why these abuses were restricted to the smaller houses was left unsaid. But as a result of their report—or in accordance with the royal requirements—in the Yorkshire Dales Easby and Coverham Abbeys and the priories of St Martin's, Richmond, and Ellerton-on-Swale were suppressed by May 1536. In January of that year Dr Legh had written to Cromwell: 'Layton is now at Fountains to do your wishes.' Cromwell's wishes are clear from the sequel. The abbot, William Thirsk, whom the commissioners alleged to have made away with the abbey's jewels and plate, was persuaded by them 'to resign privately into their hands'. They had little difficulty in appointing his successor, a canon of Ripon named Marmaduke Bradley. Cromwell was informed that he 'will give you six hundred marks to make him abbot there, and pay you immediately after the election, without delay or respite, at one payment. The first fruits to the King is a thousand pounds, which he with his policy will pay within three years, and owe no man therefore one groat.' Some three years later Abbot Bradley acquiesced without demur to the suppression of Fountains Abbey in return for a sizeable pension. With servants like the practical Cromwell the king's business was in safe hands.

If in the Dales the inflation that was pinching the king had had disturbing effects on landlords and tenants alike, their remedies were not so felicitously available. The landlords responded by increasing the enclosures for sheep-farming (evicting thereby the peasant smallholders) and raising rents and the customary dues—payments such as the ingressum or fine on entry into holdings. These measures, which were almost universal, were bitterly resented by the commons on whom they pressed so grievously. In June 1535 in Craven the enclosures ordered by Henry Clifford, first Earl of Cumberland, and the heavy-handed actions of his unruly retainers, brought about a revolt of the commons. The earl's father, also named Henry, was the 'Shepherd Lord', who had fought valiantly under the Earl of Surrey at Flodden Field:

> From Penighent to Pendlehill
> From Linton to Long Addingham
> And all that Craven coasts did till
> They with the lusty Clifford came.

Unlike the Shepherd Lord, Cumberland was well hated in the county, where for years he carried on a destructive feud with the Nortons of Rylstone in Wharfedale. In 1534 he had brought Lord Dacre to trial for high treason after forcibly seizing his goods. Dacre was acquitted but Cumberland continued to enjoy the favour of Henry VIII. If the Cliffords were well in with the king, the other two great families of the North, the Percies (Earls of Northumberland) and the Nevilles (Earls of Westmorland and Lords Latimer) felt their traditional leadership threatened by the Tudor policy of centralisation. These discontents—chiefly social and agrarian—were now added to by the financial demand for a royal subsidy, the question of the succession to the throne, the religious innovations and finally by the suppression of the monasteries. Rumours began to be rife as to the future intentions of the king and the reviled plebeian Cromwell. Words soon gave way to deeds. Unrest was widespread throughout the country, not only in the North. In August 1536 riots broke out in Cumberland and in September it was reported in London that oaths were being taken in the Yorkshire Dales and that the people were on the verge of rebellion. On Monday, 2 October 1536 a rising of the commons at Louth in Lincolnshire signalled the beginning of that armed protest known as the Pilgrimage of Grace.

In the Lincolnshire revolt the differences between the commons and the gentlemen, whom the former had coerced into joining them, were exploited by the king and Cromwell and, on Henry's promise of a general pardon, the rebels dispersed, although the commons, feeling betrayed by their betters, did so reluctantly. The king showed his contempt for the insurgents in writing to them: 'How presumptuous then are ye, the rude commons of one shire, and that one of the most brute and beastly in the whole realm . . . to find fault with your Prince?' The revolt that spread north over the Humber, however, was a more serious affair, one that, differently led, might have cost Henry his throne. On 6 October Lord Darcy, before taking up his post as the king's steward at Pontefract Castle, had sent his son to the king with the news of risings in Northumberland, Dent, Sedbergh and Wensleydale, adding the warning that 'greater rebellions were to be feared'. The lawyer Robert Aske, the pilgrims' acknowledged leader, came from a junior branch of an ancient Dales' family, the Askes of Aske Hall, at Gilling near Richmond. (This property, which the Askes had possessed for nearly 500 years from the time of the Conquest, is today owned by the Marquess of Zetland.) Far from being the socially insignificant person that the king made him out to be ('a common pedlar in the law' and a man with a 'filed tongue'), Robert Aske was 'cousin to half the gentlemen of Yorkshire'—in fact, by his mother Elizabeth, the daughter of the Shepherd Lord Clifford, he was first cousin to the king's chief supporter in the Dales, the Earl of Cumberland. A religious idealist, he rightly saw that in the North only the religious issues could hold the classes together: on the departure from Yorkshire of early emissaries from Lincolnshire, he had 'bade them God be with them, saying that they were pilgrims and had a pilgrimage gait to go'. On 16 October York surrendered to his forces, and there and then he devised the oath that thenceforth came to be sworn by all the pilgrims:

THE OATH OF THE HONOURABLE MEN

Ye shall not enter into this our Pilgrimage of Grace for the Common-wealth, but only for the love that ye do bear unto God his faith and to Holy Church militant and the maintenance thereof, to the preservation of the King's person and his issue, to the purifying of the nobility, and to expulse all villein blood and evil councillors against the Common-wealth from his Grace and his Privy Council. . . . [Ye shall] take afore you the Cross of Christ, and in your hearts His Faith, the Restitution of the Church, the suppression of those Heretics and their opinions, by all the holy contents of this book.

A copy of this pledge was posted up in Wensleydale and Swaledale on the day following its issue at York.

The Dales, however, had already risen. On 12 October Lord Scrope wrote to the Earl of Cumberland, his father-in-law, informing him that the commons of Mashamshire (many of them Nevilles' tenants) and Nidderdale had risen the day before and had occupied Coverham Abbey and Middleham and were approaching Bolton Castle, where his wife and son were. At Kirkby Ravensworth, the vicar John Dakyn (he was also the vicar-general of the extensive archdeaconry of Richmond) heard of the rising of Richmondshire on the 13th and learnt that the commons, his own parishioners among them, were advancing on Barnard Castle to compel Robert Bowes

and other leading gentlemen to join them as their captains. Both
Dakyn and Bowes, like so many of the gentry, afterwards declared
that they were forced by the commons to ally with them for fear of
their lives and property. Likewise at Jervaulx Abbey the abbot,
Adam Sedbergh, after first escaping and spending some days on
Witton Fell, was coerced into returning to his monastery, where he
was roughly manhandled and threatened with decapitation unless he
joined the insurgents (see pp. 239–40). Unlike the gentlemen of
Lincolnshire, however, in general those of the North needed little
persuasion to join with the commons as their natural leaders, their
grievances, in their own eyes, being real enough.

Later, as a prisoner in the Tower, Robert Aske was interrogated as
to his feelings on the suppressed monasteries:

> First, to the statute of suppression, he did grudge against the same, and
> so did all the whole country, because the abbeys in the north parts gave
> great alms to poor men and laudably served God. In which parts of late
> days they had but small comfort by ghostly teaching . . . the divine
> service of Almighty God is much diminished, great number of masses
> unsaid . . . to the distress of the faith and spiritual comfort to man's
> soul. . . . No hospitality is now in those places kept, but the farmers for
> the most part let and tavern [sublet] the farms of the same houses to
> other farmers for lucre and advantage to themselves. And the profits of
> these abbeys yearly go out of the country to the King's highness, so that
> in short space little money, by occasion of the said yearly rents, tenths
> and first fruits, should be left in the country. . . . Also divers and many of
> the said abbeys were in the mountains and desert places, where the
> people are rude of condition and not well taught the law of God.

After detailing further the good works done by the monasteries to
men of all classes and to the utility of the county—for example, 'as
maintainers of bridges and highways'—Aske adds a remark strange
for that rough and untutored age: 'Also the abbeys were one of the
beauties of this realm to all men and strangers passing through the
same.'

On 16 October Robert Aske with his formidable force of pilgrims
had entered York; four days later Hull fell. On the 21st Pontefract
Castle, where among others Archbishop Lee of York had taken
refuge, was surrendered to Aske by Lord Darcy, whereupon 'the

lords spiritual and temporal, knights and esquires' gathered there solemnly and took the pilgrims' oath. Through the city of York on 20 October rode Lord Latimer (a Neville, the Archbishop of York's steward), Lord Neville (the thirteen-year-old son of the Earl of Westmorland) and Lord Lumley at the head of 10,000 men, bearing with them from Durham the revered scarlet and silk banner of St Cuthbert and the pilgrims' own distinctive banner of the Five Wounds of Christ. They were shortly followed by the Percy contingent, led by Sir Thomas Percy, the popular brother ('Thousands for a Percy!') of the ineffectual Earl of Northumberland, Sir Thomas on the occasion imitating his father the 'Magnificent Earl' in the splendour of his turnout and riding 'a great trotting bay gelding'. Robert Aske and Sir Robert Constable were meanwhile holding musters at Pontefract, where they awaited the host from Mashamshire and the Dales. Here indeed in its military strength was gathering 'all the flower of the North'. The Richmondshire pilgrims were split into two contingents, one joining the insurgents of Mashamshire to march to Pontefract for the general mustering; the others from Swaledale marched, with the men of Durham, to join those from Ripon, Wensleydale and Craven in besieging the Earl of Cumberland, who had retired to defend Skipton Castle.

The Yorkshire Dales resounded to the strains of the pilgrims' marching song, which probably had been composed by a monk of Sawley Abbey, and which in its stirring simplicity and sincerity admirably reflects the religious aspect of the rising:

> Christ crucified
> For Thy wounds wide
> Us commons guide
> That pilgrims be.
>
> God that rights all
> Redress now shall
> And what is thrall
> Again make free
>
> By this voyage
> And Pilgrimage
> Of Young and sage
> In this countree

The leader of the siege against Skipton Castle was a gentleman of Wharfedale, John Norton of Rylstone, with his two sons Richard and Thomas—the last two to be captains in the Rising of the North thirty-three years later. John Norton was motivated not only by his religious beliefs but also by his desire to avenge the private wrongs that his family had suffered at the hands of the Cliffords and particularly of the Earl of Cumberland. Such was the commons' hatred of the earl that, finding the castle impregnable without artillery, they set off to capture Cumberland's daughter-in-law, Eleanor Lady Clifford (an important person as the daughter of the Duke of Suffolk and the king's own sister Mary), together with Lady Clifford's young son and the earl's two daughters, who were at Bolton Priory. It was the intention of the commons to place them in front of their forces in the assault on the castle the following day, and if this failed, 'to violate and enforce them with knaves unto my Lord's great discomfort'. This brutal proposal, however, was foiled by the action of Robert Aske's elder brother Christopher, who was an intimate member of the Earl of Cumberland's household. With the aid of the vicar of Skipton, a groom and a boy, he led Lady Clifford's party at night through the rebels' lines to the safety of Skipton Castle. An order from Robert Aske to join the mustering at Pontefract and Doncaster withdrew the insurgents' forces, leaving the Cliffords' principal castle intact.

When the contingents from the Dales reached Pontefract under their leaders—'Lord Scrope, Sir Christopher Danby, Sir William Mallory, the Nortons, the Markenfields and other knights and gentlemen'—Robert Aske, the pilgrims' commander-in-chief, had an army of more than 30,000 men, facing at Doncaster the very much smaller royal force under the Earl of Shrewsbury and the Duke of Norfolk. If the pilgrims had struck then, as the commons were urging, the result could scarcely have been in doubt. Instead, Aske, who had an absolute faith in Henry's sincerity and saw all the present evils as Cromwell's doing, submitted a list of the pilgrims' grievances to Norfolk for transmission to the king. Meanwhile, on 28 October a truce was agreed, with the condition that both armies be dispersed to allow messengers to be despatched to Henry and for time to be given for his gracious response to be known. Reluctantly the dalesmen were persuaded by their leaders to retire, Aske eloquent in his plea that now their humble requests had been brought to the king's notice, the pilgrimage had achieved its purpose and that royal redress was assured. Norfolk, who was the king's willing tool, wrote to Henry: 'Sir most humble I beseech you to take in good part what-soever promise I shall make unto the rebels . . . for surely I shall observe no part thereof . . . thinking and reputing that none oath nor promise made for policy to serve you mine only master and sovereign can destayne [*sic*] me. . . .' On Henry's behalf Norfolk promised a general pardon and the calling of a parliament. Aske's unquestioning trust in the king's good faith was to prove fatal to the Pilgrimage of Grace—and to himself.

Yet the mistrust in the inclusive pardon, which was proclaimed by the Lancaster herald in Ripon, Middleham, Richmond and other towns in December, was widespread and, when it was heard that Norfolk had been commissioned by the king to take himself to the North to settle all differences, many thought his coming was not to fulfil the pilgrims' requests but to exact Henry's vengeance. In this belief Sir Francis Bigod, lord of the manor of Healaugh, rose in January 1537 and attempted to seize and hold Beverley. Others followed his lead, but with little success, the commons no longer confident in their leaders, since the gentry as a whole, in view of the general pardon, held aloof. As for the king, he continued to dis-semble and to hold his hand. Norfolk was at Fountains Abbey on 14 February when he heard of the rising in Cumberland; by the time he was in Carlisle on the 19th the revolt had been put down by Sir Christopher Dacre. Henry now struck, ordering: 'such dreadful execution to be done upon a good number of the habitants of every town and village that hath offended in this rebellion as well by the hanging of them upon trees as by the quartering of them and the setting up their heads and quarters in every town great and small without pity or respect'. His orders were carried out. Even three months later Cromwell acted against a poor woman who had cut down the rotting corpse of her husband to give it a Christian burial. The king was particularly wroth against the monks of Easby Abbey, who had with popular support (as elsewhere) returned to their suppressed monastery; he gave orders that the monks should be 'tied up [i.e. hanged] without further delay or ceremony, to be the terrible example of others; wherein we think you shall do us great service'. Henry now felt himself free to move against the pilgrims' leaders. The outcome of their trials could be foreseen.

After being indicted at York and committed to the Tower, Lord Darcy was brought to trial in Westminster Hall on 17 April 1537 and found guilty; he was beheaded on Tower Hill on 30 June. Lord Hussey followed him to the scaffold at Lincoln; the choice of venue was intended to be a lesson to the rebels of Lincolnshire; instead it provoked a riot. Already Sir John Bulmer, Sir Stephen Hamerton and William Thirsk, the 'quondam' abbot of Fountains Abbey, had been executed on 25 May at Tyburn. On the same day at Smithfield Sir John's wife, Lady Bulmer, 'a rosy fair creature and a beautiful', was as a woman spared the hanging and quartering; she was burnt at the stake. On 2 June Sir Thomas Percy, Sir Francis Bigod, George Lumley, Adam Sedbergh the Abbot of Jervaulx and William Wood the Prior of Bridlington were executed at Tyburn. Percy and Bigod were beheaded: the others were hanged, drawn and quartered and the heads exposed on London Bridge. For the two principals, Robert Aske and Sir Robert Constable, the king reserved places of execution that would achieve the greatest public effect. In the presence of the Duke of Norfolk Constable was hanged at the Beverley Gate in Hull, his body (as Norfolk reported) 'so trimmed in chains . . . that I think his bones will hang there this hundred year'.

Robert Aske was brought north to await the day appointed for his public execution, 12 July 1537, a Thursday and market day in York. Again, his execution was to be presided over by the Duke of Norfolk and the gentlemen of the Dales, with others prominent in the county including his elder brother John, were summoned to York to be present. None dared disobey. On the last morning Robert Aske was confessed in his prison by the government chaplain, Richard Coren, who sought in vain to extract further names from him. However, Aske did admit that two things 'somewhat aggrieved him': firstly, that Cromwell, 'who spoke a sore word and affirmed it with his stomach', had asserted that all northern men were but traitors; the second, that although both the king and Cromwell had promised him a pardon, nevertheless he was now to die. Brought forth from his cell, in public he confessed that he had sinned against God, the king and the world. Laid upon a hurdle he was then drawn through the streets of York, 'desiring the people ever, as he passed, to pray for him'. On arrival at the Clifford Tower Aske was made to repeat his confession and, as Norfolk had not yet put in an appearance, he was taken within the Tower to await him. When the duke arrived, he proceeded to deliver an address to the crowd gathered to watch the spectacle —an exhortation *more Anglorum*, as a modern Catholic historian has caustically remarked. Aske, who had been led out on to a scaffold on top of the Tower, then once more repeated his confession, before 'asking divers times the King's Highness' forgiveness' and the forgiveness, too, by name, of other high officers of state, including that of the lord privy seal (Cromwell!) 'and thus, after certain orisons, commending his soul to God', he submitted to the justice of Henry Tudor. So died the truest heart of the Pilgrimage of Grace, Robert Aske, begging forgiveness of the very men who, faithless to their given word, had done him to death.

An afterword. John Aske had been forced by Norfolk to sit on the grand jury in York that had brought in a true bill against his brother for treason and conspiracy against the king, and now, with an exquisite refinement of cruelty, he was compelled to witness his brother's execution. It is not surprising that the strain was too much and that he afterwards suffered a severe illness. Robert Aske had petitioned the king, 'to let me be full dead ere I be dismembered'. On this occasion Henry was graciously pleased to be merciful.

If opposition to the suppression of the monasteries had been one of the chief causes of the Pilgrimage of Grace, yet in the Dales resentment against arbitrary proceedings by landlords and the prevailing economic distress had also played a large part—in Richmondshire leaders of the commons frequently adopted the name of 'Captain Poverty'. Rather than saving the monasteries, the pilgrimage hastened the suppression of those which the earlier Act had spared. The rebellion had cost the king much and where else but from the Church was payment to be found? By the time of the final Act of Dissolution in 1539 little was left of monasticism in the Dales. With voluntary or pressurised surrender, or in the case of Jervaulx by the attainder of its abbot, the greater and lesser abbeys and priories had ceased to be. 'Bare ruin'd choirs', ruins majestic still in their dilapidated splendour, alone remained for the romantics of future ages.

The religious oscillations that disturbed the reigns of Edward VI and Mary steadied into the *via media* of Elizabeth, when, with her as 'supreme governor' (a delightful expression of Anglo-Saxon compromise), the Church in England became for most of the inhabitants of the island the Church of England. In the North, however, Catholicism was still strong, but their faith did not prevent Catholics from joining Protestants in the mercenary scramble to purchase the properties of the dissolved monasteries. With their Tudor redistribution of wealth there arose those families of landed gentry, who for almost four centuries thereafter were to perform so important a role in the administration of justice and local government in the countryside, and in the country at large were to constitute the Tory interest within the House of Commons. In Elizabeth's reign England remained a semi-feudal and largely rural nation. In the North the three great families of Percy, Neville and Clifford were still powers in the land and with the Percies and Nevilles and their adherents the old religion had a hold and a charm that were unfelt in centres of bustling urban Protestantism. The Rising of the North may perhaps best be looked on as a historical accident or an irrelevant anachronism, even a reactionary aberration; what is certain is that its aftermath brought much misery to those who least deserved it in the Yorkshire Dales.

In May 1568 Mary Queen of Scots fled the troubles in her own kingdom and sought the protection of Elizabeth; from 15 July she was lodged in Lord Scrope's castle at Bolton in Wensleydale, where she was in fact Elizabeth's prisoner. In the following year a group of peers—Leicester, Arundel, Norfolk and Pembroke—jealous of the 'upstart' Cecil's influence (as they thought) on Elizabeth, secretly pledged themselves to securing the recognition of the Catholic Mary as successor to the English throne, failing an heir born to Elizabeth, and further to bringing about the marriage of Mary with the young Duke of Norfolk, the Protestant son of the Norfolk who had taken part in the Pilgrimage of Grace. Elizabeth, learning of their intentions through Leicester, peremptorily forbade Norfolk think of such a marriage. On 15 September Norfolk left the court in great wrath. Six days later, on the queen's command to return, he retired to his estates. Was this the signal for revolt? After three days of high tension Norfolk submitted. On 11 October he was arrested and lodged in the Tower.

These moves were known in the North, where it was rumoured that the Earls of Northumberland and Westmorland, as Catholics and supporters of Mary to the succession (though not at one on the Norfolk marriage) were under suspicion. Charles Neville sixth Earl of Westmorland had married Norfolk's sister. On 7 November Sir George Bowes, writing to the Earl of Sussex, the lord president of the Council of the North, informed him that Westmorland was assembling his retainers and tenants at Brancepeth, and that with him were the Earl of Northumberland and the Sheriff of Yorkshire, Richard Norton. Some days earlier the two earls had been summoned to court; when they made their excuses the summons was repeated. In refusing to comply, they argued that to come armed would be treason, while to come unarmed would be to place themselves in the power of their enemies at court. Faced with this dilemma, the young and inexperienced Westmorland listened to the advice of hotheads among the gentry—Nortons, Tempests, Markenfields and others —and took up arms; Northumberland seems to have followed only reluctantly. The Rising of the North (or the Earls' Rising), which may be said to have begun on 9 November 1569, not having the popular support of the Pilgrimage of Grace, was doomed from the start.

The military plans of the rebel leaders—if they can be said to have had considered plans—were either to march south to engage the Earl of Sussex, the lord president, at York or to move westwards into Lancashire to recruit their forces. But support everywhere was either lukewarm or not forthcoming and at Bramham Moor near Tadcaster they hesitated before turning back on 24 November. Realising that their strength lay only in the North, they retreated through the Dales and marched to attack Sir George Bowes, who was holding Barnard Castle. On 14 December Bowes was forced to surrender, when 226 of his men, jumping the walls and opening the gates, deserted to the rebels. This was the only military action of the rebellion. A few days later the forces of the earls were in full retreat, with Sussex and the Earl of Warwick in pursuit. The leaders sought safety in Scotland and their troops dispersed, going into hiding or, where they could with safety, returning to their homes. Westmorland later took ship for Flanders, where he was pensioned by the King of Spain. North-umberland was handed over by the Scottish Douglases to the English for the payment of £2,000; he was executed at York and his severed head displayed on Micklegate Bar. He died confessing himself a Catholic, 'I am a Percy, in life and death.' With him to the scaffold he took a gold cross, inset with a thorn, said to be from Christ's Crown of Thorns, given to him by Mary, Queen of Scots. Today this relic is at Ampleforth College.

The full weight of the queen's reasserted authority fell now on the common people, in the Yorkshire Dales the reprisals that followed greatly exceeding those that had taken place after the Pilgrimage of Grace. Martial law was proclaimed, Sussex appointing Sir George Bowes provost-martial to carry out the scarcely condign punishment of the rebels. The queen demanded 700 executions as a salutary lesson and a warning, but these were to be 'wholly of the meanest sort of people'. The well-to-do were attainted—it is said that only nine were executed (others, of course, were fugitives abroad)—and their property was confiscated on behalf of the Crown. Many had to purchase their pardon in the form of fines. Bowes was in Richmond on 8 January 1570 with instructions that allowed him discretion in executing up to 200 rebels in the five wapentakes of Richmondshire. It was reported that 200 rebels had come from Wensleydale, Bishopdale and Coverdale, these dales being in the lordship of Middleham whose steward was the Earl of Northumberland and consequently many of them would have been Percy dependants. On orders from above, care was to be exercised that at least one victim was to be taken from every town or village which had supplied even a single rebel, so that scarcely a Dales' village was spared the reminder of royal supremacy by the grisly sight of a corpse swinging from tree or gibbet. Bowes wrote to his brother that he had put paid to 'six hundred and odd; so that now the authors of this rebellion is (*sic*) cursed on every side; and sure the people are in marvellous fear, so that I trust there shall never such thing happen in these parts again'.

The misery of the dalesmen was completed by the depredation and destruction caused by the Earl of Warwick's troops, who marauded at will. Both the Pilgrimage of Grace and the Rising of the North had made it evident to northerners, and among them the dalesmen, that the time-honoured rule of the feudal nobility and the anarchy that so often went with it, had thenceforth to take account of the newly established strength and authority of the centralised government.

CHAPTER 8

Heiress of the Knight of Pendragon

LATE IN THE year 1663 Lady Anne Clifford set out from her castle of Skipton-in-Craven, built high on a cliff 200 feet (60 metres) above Eller Beck as it flows into the River Aire, departing on one of her semi-royal progresses through her vast northern estates. The old lady herself (she was seventy-three) travelled in a litter slung between two sturdy sure-footed horses; her officials and menservants were on horseback, the women servants rode in a coach; and behind them, in wagons, trundled all the miscellaneous paraphernalia that accompanied a great personage in those days when he or she changed their place of residence. For not only the bedding, carpets, curtains, tapestries and much of the furniture, but also the plate, cutlery and glassware—the main household effects—were removed from one house to be set up afresh in another. Lady Anne's frequent journeys were conducted with all the elements of great state; as hereditary high sheriff and lady of many manors, she had sent on orders ahead summoning the local magistrates, gentry and tenants to meet her at points in her progress, so that at times the number of those in attendance swelled to more than 300—like some colourful oriental caravan *en route*.

Passing through her Craven estates, she made her way up Wharfedale to spend her first night at Kilnsey, at the house of Mr Cuthbert Wade. She delighted in visiting the most remote and inaccessible parts of her immense properties, in taking her lumbering coaches where no coach had previously gone, and relating in her diaries everything that aroused her interest in 'These high wild hills and rough uneven ways.' Next day she went on, noting that it was the first time that she had been to Kettlewell Dale or passed over

Buckden Rakes or the Stake on the rude track that brought her down by way of Bishopdale into Wensleydale to visit her distant relative Mr Thomas Metcalfe at Nappa Hall. The Metcalfes were prominent among the gentry of Wensleydale, a tradition being that Sir Christopher Metcalfe had once in 1556 attended York assizes at the head of 300 of his followers, 'men of his own name or kin', all mounted on grey chargers. It was said that Mary Queen of Scots had been entertained at Nappa by Sir Christopher when she was a prisoner at nearby Bolton Castle. Lady Anne spent two nights at the hall, before taking the road that runs up the dale to the north of the Ure and into Cotterdale, 'where I think never did coach went before'; and, crossing Hell Gill entered Mallerstang where stood Pendragon Castle, recently restored by her. (Today Pendragon remains much as the Elizabethan William Camden described it in his *Britannia*, when it had 'nothing left unto it unconsumed by time, besides the bare name, and an heape of stones'.) Even this indomitable old lady must have realised the difficulties of her passage through 'those dangerous places. . . . Wherein yet God was pleased to preserve me in that journey.' The heiress of the Cliffords was safely at home in the centre of her extensive domains at one of her five castles and she made this complacent entry in her diary: 'So I now kept Christmas here in this Pendragon Castle this year and this was the first time I ever kept Christmas in it, or any ancestors before me, for three hundred years or more, and I now lay in it until the 27th day of January.'

'. . . glad Pendragon—though the sleep of years be on her!' Lady Anne had good reason for her complacency; at last her pertinacity had found its reward. Moreover, and she must have relished it, she was becoming a legend in her lifetime.

Lady Anne Clifford was born in the family castle of Skipton-in-Craven in the year 1590, the only daughter of George third Earl of Cumberland and his wife Margaret Russell. Henry VII, on his accession to the throne after the defeat and death of Richard III at Bosworth Field, had reversed the attainder against John ninth Lord Clifford and restored the title and the estates of the Honour of Skipton to his son Henry, the 'Shepherd Lord', who had come out of enforced retirement, his untutored youthful seclusion in Cumberland. The latter's son, another Henry, had been a boyhood personal friend of Henry VIII and, becoming eleventh Lord Clifford, was created Earl of Cumberland in 1522. It was he who in 1536 had fortified Skipton Castle against Robert Aske and the rebels of the Pilgrimage of Grace. His grandson George, the third Earl, was outstanding in an age remarkable for its men of spirit and one of the brightest ornaments of the brilliant court of Queen Elizabeth.

George Clifford succeeded to the earldom at the age of eleven and was brought up at Woburn and Chenies as ward of Francis second Earl of Bedford, whose daughter Margaret he married in 1577, the wedding being graced with the presence of Queen Elizabeth herself. The groom and his bride were nineteen and seventeen respectively. After the marriage the young couple travelled north on a visit to the Clifford estates and castles—Appleby, Brougham, Brough, Pendragon, Barden and Skipton—which were being administered by Lord Cumberland's mother Anne Dacre. The earl, however, was not cut out to play the part of a country landowner. After some nine years of seemingly happily married life, he fitted out at his own expense the first piratical expedition to the River Plate, exchanging, as his wife put it, 'his country pleasures for new thoughts of greater worlds'. Magnificent in every respect, in appearance, style and manners, he was welcomed at court, as a man after the queen's own virile heart. But he was no mere courtier popinjay. Eleven voyages he made in all, plundering the Spanish Main, suffering wounds, risking shipwreck, nearly dying of thirst; but returning to an English haven, his ships laden with booty, mostly the property of the King of Spain. The treasure piled up on the quays of West Country ports; we hear of 'mother-of-pearl, porcelain dishes, raw silk, cloves, calicoes, pearls, rubies ... elephants' tusks, Turkey carpets, quilts, sarcenet ... ambergris'—and spices, '8,500 quintals of pepper, 900 of cloves, 700 of cinnamon, 500 of cochineal, 540 of other merchandise, with much musk, diamonds and other precious stones'. Of all this the queen had her handsome share; the noble buccaneer, who had risked both purse and life, but small change. 'I shall probably draw little to fill those purses it hath emptied,' wrote Lord Cumberland, 'having as your ladyship well knows been only a fire-maker for others to warm themselves at.'

His greatest reward was perhaps his discerning sovereign's affection; a letter of 1591 is addressed to 'Right trusty and well-beloved Cousin' and is signed 'Your very loving Sovereign, Elizabeth R.' On the death of Sir Henry Lee the queen appointed Lord Cumberland her champion, and the 'Knight of Pendragon' appeared in the tilt-yard to do battle against all comers on behalf of his lady. The beautiful miniature by Nicholas Hilliard portrays him in this role, habited in fine Greenwich armour decorated with golden stars, partly covered by a light blue surcoat bordered with gold; and on his broad-brimmed hat is pinned a lady's glove, the queen's personal favour bestowed on her champion. All these activities and long absences brought about an estrangement from his wife; in addition, we are told by his daughter, he 'fell to love a lady of quality', whose name she leaves anonymous. Two sons born of his marriage had not survived and Lady Cumberland lived a sad separated life, 'looking', as she said, 'as a ghost that wanted the soul of comfort', all her love and attention centred on her daughter Anne. Shortly before his death in 1605, however, Lord Cumberland sought in a touching letter to make amends to his neglected wife, addressing her as 'Sweet and dear Meg', and adding a subscription in his own hand: 'To my dear wife, Countess of Cumberland, give this, of whom, from the bottom of my heart, in the presence of God, I ask forgiveness for all the wrongs that I have done her.' Nevertheless, a greater wrong was yet to be committed.

Lady Anne Clifford was fifteen when her father died, leaving behind him a will that was to be the cause of protracted litigation, royal intervention and almost intolerable pressure on her to bend her will, until, after thirty-eight years, she finally came into possession of estates that were legally hers from the start. The title went to the dead man's brother, Sir Francis Clifford, who became the fourth Earl of Cumberland; but he inherited more than the title. By the will he was left the great Yorkshire estates (the Westmorland property was Lady Cumberland's jointure), with the reversion only to Lady Anne in default of heirs male. In thus providing the means for his brother to support and enjoy the title the late earl was ignoring the fact that in accordance with a deed going back to the reign of Edward II the estates were entailed explicitly upon his child (whether male or female); and since Lady Anne was his only surviving child, the properties and his other titles were rightfully hers. Although the earldom of Cumberland was restricted in descent to the male line, the baronies of Clifford, Westmorland and Vescy and the sheriffwick of Westmorland were not; in law they were now possessed by Lady Anne. Her widowed mother knew this and she devoted the rest of her life in a seemingly fruitless attempt at seeing that justice was done. A petition was made at once and the dowager Lady Cumberland was duly appointed her daughter's legal guardian. In Lady Anne's words, her mother 'showed herself so wise and industrious that she caused diligent search to be made among the records of this kingdom touching these ancient lands, and caused copies to be taken out of them of such records as concerned her said daughter's inheritance'. Lady Anne thenceforth felt that she was in duty bound to her mother as much as to herself and her posterity never to forego her inherited rights. In the summer of 1607 mother and daughter travelled north to inspect the disputed estates. When in Craven, although Lady Anne was not permitted by the new earl to visit Skipton Castle, she was shown the neighbouring Beamsley Hospital, the charitable foundation that Lady Cumberland was building.

With the passing of the years the old queen, who had shown her such affectionate attention, had died and the new king, James I, was on the throne; in 1609, at the age of nineteen, Lady Anne married. Her husband, only a little older than herself, was Richard Sackville Lord Buckhurst, who two days after the marriage became Earl of Dorset on the death of his father and the possessor of the great house of Knole in Kent. The young Dorsets were popular at court. At seventeen Anne had danced in Ben Jonson's *Masque of Beauty*, in attendance on her namesake Queen Anne of Denmark, with whom she was a favourite; two years later she danced again in Jonson's *Masque of Queens*, when her dress was designed by Inigo Jones. In the year following her marriage she took part in yet another court masque, written by her former tutor Samuel Daniel, in which the ladies represented those great rivers of England that were associated with their birth or title, her role being that of the Aire, which flows close by the castle of Skipton.

It is clear from her diaries that the young couple loved each other—she would never utter a word in his dispraise; only one thing came increasingly between them: her obstinate refusal to relinquish her claims on the northern estates. Dorset, so much in the good graces of King James and in the company of Henry Prince of Wales, was extravagant, splendidly spendthrift. Like George Clifford he immersed himself in 'tilting, shooting, bowling-matches and all such expensive sports'. In cock-fighting he saw to it that his birds respectfully lost to the king's, and with their defeat went large sums of money. He needed cash and the present Earl of Cumberland let it be known that a 'composition' might be arranged, whereby for a largish sum of money the Countess of Dorset's claims on the Yorkshire

Above. Looking towards Muker in Swaledale from Crackpot Hall near Keld.
Derek G. Widdicombe
Below. Grinton parish church. *Christine Whitehead*

Above Left. Swaledale. *Christine Whitehead*
Right. Bolton Castle. *Derek G. Widdicombe*
Below. Surrender Mill, Swaledale, with Calva Fell in background. *Christine Whitehead*

Above. Grinton Moor showing Manor Boundary Stone. *Christine Whitehead*
Below. Easby Abbey. *The British Tourist Authority*

Above Left. Barn above Muker, Swaledale. *Christine Whitehead*
Right. The Watch Tower from the Gateway, Skipton Castle. *Derek G. Widdicombe*
Below. The Castle and the River Swale, Richmond. *Derek G. Widdicombe*

Above. Whernside from Bruntscar near Ingleton. *Derek G. Widdicombe*
Below. Fountains Abbey. *The British Tourist Authority*

Above Left. Limestone pinnacle on Pen-y-Ghent. *Derek G. Widdicombe*
Right. The church by the Cowside Beck at Arncliffe in Littondale. *Derek G. Widdicombe*
Below. Pen-y-Ghent, North Ribblesdale. *Derek G. Widdicombe*

Above. Smelt Mill chimney, lead mines, Grassington. *Derek G. Widdicombe*
Below. Kettlewell in Wharfedale from Middlesmoor Pasture. *Derek G. Widdicombe*

Above Left. Old Gang Smelt Mill. *Christine Whitehead*
Right. Bolton Castle. *The British Tourist Authority*
Below. The Strid, Wharfedale. *Christine Whitehead*

estates he held might be discreetly settled. Backed by her mother, she would hear nothing of it. Surely, argued Dorset, the pleasures of the court and Knole, the amiable distractions of London and the South, were infinitely preferable to the wild moors, the waste fells and the ruined castles of the barbarous North? Exasperated by her firm refusal, he once exclaimed, 'Your land transports you beyond yourself, and makes you devoid of all reason.' The countess confessed to her mother: 'In everything I will commend him, saving only in this business of my land, wherein I think some evil spirit works, for in this he is as violent as possible.'

With the death of her mother Margaret dowager Countess of Cumberland in 1616 Anne lost her staunchest ally in her long struggle to preserve what was legally hers. When her husband failed to break or bend her will, at one time by going to the length of separating her from her daughter Lady Margaret, such dignitaries as were brought in—even the Archbishop of Canterbury—were equally unsuccessful in dissuading her from her purpose; so that finally recourse was made to King James I. Here she found a strange ally in the frivolous Queen Anne, who warned her against trusting the matter to the king's decision. In her *Diary*, written at Knole, she recorded how on 16 January 1617 she was summoned to London by her husband:

> Upon the 17th when I came up, my Lord told me that I must resolve to go to the King the next day. Upon the 18th being Saturday I went presently after dinner to the Queen ... [who] promised me she would do all the good in it she could. When I had stayed but a little there I was sent for out, My Lord and I going through my Lord Buckingham's chamber who brought us into the King. ... He put out all that were there and my Lord and I kneeled by his chair sides when he persuaded us both to peace and to put the whole matter wholly into his hands, which my Lord consented to, but I beseech'd His Majesty to pardon me for that I would never part with Westmoreland while I lived upon any condition whatsoever. Sometimes he used fair means and persuasions and sometimes foul means but I was resolved before so as nothing would move me.

Her mother's recent death only seems to have steeled her resolution not to yield.

Three days later Lord Dorset and she were again called into the king's presence, when she found also in the 'Drawing Chamber' her uncle Lord Cumberland, her 'Coz.' Lord Clifford, some important members of the council, the Lord Chief Justice Montague and various legal advisers.

> The King asked us all if we would submit to his judgement in this case. My Uncle Cumberland, my Coz. Clifford and my Lord answered they would, but I would never agree to it without Westmoreland at which the King grew in a great chaff . . . at last when they saw there was no remedy, my Lord fearing the King would to me some public disgrace, desired Sir John Digby would open the door, who went out with me and persuaded me much to yield to the King. . . . Presently after my Lord came from the King when it was resolved that if I would not come to an agreement there should be an agreement made without me.

And so it happened; the Earl of Cumberland was awarded the estates, as left him by his brother's will—the properties in the Yorkshire Dales and the late countess's jointure in Westmorland; to Lady Anne remained the reversion alone in default of heirs male. Lady Dorset was only too happy to receive by way of composition the large sum of £20,000. As Lord Clifford, if not his father the earl, had every reason to expect male issue, the possibility that the northern estates would ever come into the possession of Lady Anne seemed remote indeed.

So while Lord Dorset amused himself as was his wont, going 'much abroad to Cocking, Bowling-Alleys, to Plays and Horse Races', his wife stayed with 'the Child', often sad and solitary at Knole, reading her Bible and improving books, walking in the garden to say her prayers, and at times feeling, as she said, 'like an owl in the desert'. Then, in 1624, at the early age of thirty-five, Lord Dorset died. Of the five children she bore him, the three boys had died early, so now the young dowager countess left Knole, taking with her the two surviving girls, Margaret and Isabella, to live partly in a Sackville dower-house in Sussex and partly in London. At the time of Dorset's death the children had smallpox, which she caught from them. One morning, seeing her 'martyred' face in the looking-glass, she vowed not to marry again. Six years later, to the astonishment of everyone, she broke her resolution by marrying Philip Herbert fourth Earl of Pembroke and Montgomery, a middle-aged widower with children by his first wife, whose nature seems to have been anything but attractive, since he was quarrelsome and violent and as John Aubrey assures us, 'immoderately given to women'. G. C. Williamson in his biography of Lady Anne suggests the reasons for Pembroke's own choice: 'the very remoteness of the quarry, the difficulty of the quest, the unusual character of the triumph, may have stimulated the jaded fancy of the most dissolute wastrel of the Court'. Although they remained husband and wife for twenty years, Lady Anne lived with Lord Pembroke something fewer than five, he spending much time at his quarters at the Cockpit in Whitehall, she living mostly at Wilton in Wiltshire, the great house undergoing during this period extensive alterations under the supervision of Inigo Jones. But her heart resided irretrievably in the North. In 1632 and 1637 Lord and Lady Pembroke put in formal claims for the Clifford property and undoubtedly would have done so again in 1642, had it not been for the outbreak of the Civil War. Her life must have been a lonely one, spent in the company of her daughter Lady Isabella after the marriage of Lady Margaret to the Earl of Thanet. In her diary she wrote, 'the marble pillars of Knole in Kent and Wilton in Wiltshire were to me oftentimes but the gay arbours of anguish'. Apart from their temperaments and personal differences, the couple were separated by their political allegiances: she was a fervent Royalist; he, after much vacillation, came down on the side of Parliament. On Lord Pembroke's death in 1650 a cavalier versifier scathingly wrote of the renegade:

> Here lies the mirror of our age for treason . . .
>
> A traitor to his master, Lord and King,
> A man whose virtues were to lie and swear,
> God damn him! was his constant daily prayer.

In these troubled times policy dictated that Lady Anne live quietly in Baynard's Castle in London, guarding her husband's valuable property stored there. On 21 January 1641 her uncle Francis fourth Earl of Cumberland died at the advanced age of eighty-two. His son Henry, the fifth earl, survived him by just under three years, leaving only a daughter, Lady Cork. Thus, after waiting for thirty-eight years Lady Anne came naturally and tranquilly into her Clifford inheritance. Nevertheless, she had to wait another six years before she could travel north to take possession of what was now indisputably hers. It might have seemed too late; she was nearly sixty. Yet she had more than a quarter of a century of vigorous life before her.

She had come into her own at last. Pious, well-read in the Bible, she thought

> that saying in the sixteenth psalm may be fitly applied: The lot is fallen unto me in a pleasant place. I have a fair heritage. And I may truly say that verse:
>
> > From many noble progenitors I hold
> > Transmitted lands, castles and honours which they
> > swayed of old.

The verses are by her old tutor Samuel Daniel.

Leaving London on 11 July 1649, just six months after the execution of Charles I, on the 18th she reached Skipton, where she had been born, and she entered the castle which she had left as a baby of ten weeks old and where she had never set foot since. The castle, which had been defended by the late Lord Cumberland in the cause of King Charles, had, after undergoing a three-year siege, been dismantled by Parliamentary troops. From an account written in 1682, only six years after Lady Anne's death, by her secretary and agent George Sedgwick of Kendal we read how on her arrival she found

> Skipton Castle, that had been a stately building, scarce affording lodging for herself and her family; so that she was resolv'd to build some lodging rooms in it, notwithstanding the malignancy of the times. Some gentlemen of the neighbourhood, her friends and well-wishers, dissuaded her from it; alleging (and probably enough) that as fast as she built up, Oliver Cromwell would order it to be pulled down. She replied, If they do not take my estate from me, as long as I have money or credit, I will repair my houses, though I were to have them thrown down the next day. This being reported to Oliver,—Nay, says he, let her build what she will, she shall have no hindrance from me.
>
> Thereupon she began with Skipton Castle, and in a year's time made it a very convenient house, though not so stately and large as it was before it was demolished.

'Retain your loyalty; preserve your rights'—Lady Anne lived up to her motto. Quite apart from the troubles arising from the warfare that was being waged in their midst, her tenants had had within a few years to pay two re-entry fines on their lands (fines payable by tenants on the succession of the landlord), and they were resentful and recalcitrant. She soon realised it, candidly admitting that things had begun 'to grow hott betwixt my tenants and mee'. Nevertheless, she was determined to be mistress in her own house and started a course of litigation against individual tenants that was to last for years. Despite her own experience of the inadequacies of the law, she had faith in it; she was naturally, even pugnaciously litigious. On Cromwell's offering personally to intervene on her behalf in matters of her tenantry, she was indignant: what, she who had refused to submit to King James would seek help from the Protector? She would never submit to him, 'whatever hazard or danger she incurred thereby'. Colonel Charles Fairfax, the uncle of the Parliamentary general, describes well her attitude towards her tenants in a letter to his nephew: she would prove a generous and equitable landlord, he declared, 'with such persons whose estates depend upon her award, if they have the good manners to acknowledge it her bounty'. 'Preserve your rights'; it was her rights that she insisted on, nothing more but nothing less either.

From her faithful Sedgwick comes the famous story of the litigated hen. By a feudal custom that had existed for 400 years the tenants of the Honour of Skipton had to pay each year to the lord, in addition to their rents, 800 'boon hens'—it was likewise at Appleby. A rich clothier of Halifax, by the name of Murgatroyd, having bought a tenement near Skipton, found that he was to contribute a single hen. This he flatly refused to do. 'Her ladyship was resolved not to lose that hen, being her ancient right, and the loss of all the rest depending upon that.' She brought an action against Murgatroyd at the York assizes, and won. She gained her hen but it cost her £200 to do so. It cost the loser £200 too—and the hen. This is as the story goes according to reliable authority; but since Lady Anne had become a legend, it was necessary to embroider the tale. It is said that, after her victory, her ladyship invited Mr Murgatroyd to dinner and there, when the two litigants sat down, she had the contested hen served up between them.

Another accretion to the legend is the celebrated letter about a proposed candidate for the parliamentary seat of Appleby, quoted by Horace Walpole as an example of the laconic epistolary style:

I have been bullied by a ursurper, I have been neglected by a Court, but I will not be dictated to by a subject. Your man shan't stand.—
Anne Dorset, Pembroke and Montgomery.

It is certainly 'laconic, stern, decisive'—and discourteous; but it is just as certainly apocryphal.

Within ten days of her arrival at Skipton Lady Anne paid a visit to Barden Tower in nearby Wharfedale, a favourite residence of the 'Shepherd Lord', where he carried out his astrological and mathematical studies in consultation with the monks of Bolton Priory. Her visit was not paid out of familial reverence or idle curiosity. The last earl had left the property to his daughter the Countess of Cork; this alienation Lady Anne would by no means allow. Possession was nine points of the law, but, as G. C. Williamson remarked, Lady Anne 'intended it to include the tenth also'. Taking possession of Barden (which she retained until her death, when it was restored to the Corks), she ordered it also to be put in a state of repair so that she could live in it. Thereupon she made a grand tour of her castles —Appleby, Brougham, Brough and Pendragon—and from there went for a short stay with her cousin Lord Wharton at Wharton Hall, near Nateby, before returning to Skipton. There, she wrote in her journal, 'I employed myself in causing the Bounders to be ridden, and my Courts kept in my several Manors in Craven, and in those kind of Country Affairs about my estate which I found in extreame disorder'. It was while on this tour of her estates that she heard of the death of her husband Philip Herbert Lord Pembroke in January 1650. Now twice widowed she had just turned sixty. It was as if in consciousness of these facts and possibly in remembrance of her loved mother's foundation of Beamsley Hospital, that in the last days of 1650 she bought land near Boroughgate in Skipton and in the following year began building the Hospital of St Anne. This was an almshouse to accommodate twelve sisters, presided over by a mother superior, for women of the neighbourhood too old or infirm to work, an institution where they might live free of rent and rates and with the grant of a small allowance.

Preoccupied as she was with her own concerns of restoring her rights, building and rebuilding and the rehabilitation of her estates, she seems to have turned her back on the political state of England —except when military affairs forced themselves upon her. The notoriously fanatical Roundhead General Harrison quartered himself at her charge in Appleby and, suspecting that she was offering assistance to Charles II but 'not being able to make proof of that, he would needs know her opinion, and dispute her out of her Loyalty, at a time when she slept and lived but at his mercy, giving her Alarms day and night when he listed'. Where she might well have temporised, she was defiant. As Bishop Rainbow of Carlisle reminded his listeners at her funeral sermon, she

> would not easily yield, but . . . having Truth and Loyalty on her side, she would not betray them at the peril of her life and fortune; but boldly asserted, that she did love the King, and that she would live and die in her loyal thoughts to the King, and so with her courage dulled the edge of so sharp an Adversary, that by God's merciful restraint he did her no harm at this time.

However, following the Royalist defeat at Worcester in 1651 and the establishment of Cromwell's protectorate, the tension eased in the North, and Lady Anne went on happily and thoroughly with her work of restoration. With Skipton and Barden now habitable, she turned her attention to the castles of Appleby, Brougham, Brough and finally Pendragon in Mallerstang; and again, after the rebuilding first of Skipton church, she restored or rebuilt the churches or chapels at Barden, Brougham, Mallerstang and elsewhere. On Pendragon Castle she placed a plaque, giving her name and titles, and the date of its reconstruction, and the moving text from Isaiah 58:12: 'And they that shall be of thee shall build the old waste places: thou shalt raise up the foundations of many generations; and thou shalt be called, The repairer of the breach, The restorer of paths to dwell in.' On the little restored chapel at Mallerstang she placed the following inscription, which still may be read there:

> This chapple of Mallerstang after itt had layne ruineous and decayed for some 50 or 60 years was newe repayred by the Lady Anne Clifford Countess Dowager of Pembroke, Dorsett and Montgomery in the year 1663, who also endowed the same with lands which she purchased in Cantley near Sedburgh to the yearly value of eleaven pounds for ever. Isaiah, chap. 54, Ve. 12 Gods name be praised.

Deeply devotional as she was, the scriptural allusion is characteristic; the text from Isaiah reads: 'And I will make thy windows of agates, and thy gates of carbuncles, and all thy borders of precious stones.'

It has been truly said of Lady Anne Clifford that she was born a grandmother; that her natural role was to preside over a numerous progeny. From her two surviving children, Margaret, who married John Tufton second Earl of Thanet in 1629, and Isabella, who in 1647 married James Compton third Earl of Northampton, she was blessed with grandchildren and great-grandchildren, in whose welfare she took great interest. John Tufton, the Thanets' second son, was perhaps her favourite, and he often visited her at each of her castles in turn. Her day-book is full of her entries of their arrivals and departures; she delighted in recalling their first visit and the exact lapse of time since the previous one. When in 1663 Lady Thanet, 'the Child' of Knole, came to Skipton with four of her children, her mother noted in her diary that they had arrived

> about eight o'clock at night into the chamber where I then lay, and wherein I was born into the world, and then I kissed them all with much joy and comfort, it being the first time I saw my Daughter of Thanet, or these four younger Sonnes of hers in Skipton Castle, or in Craven, for it was the first time that they had ever come into Craven.

When her descendants visited her, Lady Anne would despatch them on sightseeing tours of her great estates. In 1670 Thomas Tufton, for whom she had procured the Appleby seat in the House of Commons, paid a visit to his constituents and to his grandmother at Pendragon Castle, coming by way of Greta Bridge and over Stainmore. She sent him off to see the 'remarkable places' in the vicinity: 'Wilborfell; Hugh's Seat, Morvill, and Helgill or Hell Gill Bridge' —Wild Boar Fell, where local tradition has it that the last wild boar in England was killed; Hugh's Seat (High Seat?), Morvill, said to be so named after Sir Hugh de Morvill, one of the four knights who murdered St Thomas à Becket; and the 'Devil's Bridge', which used to span Hell Gill Beck at the southern (Moor Cock Inn) end of Mallerstang Common.

Lady Anne had retained her loyalty, which was to her native North and she had preserved her rights; but she had done more than just preserve them. She had become an institution, and the people of the Dales knew her not as an oppressive landlord but as a benefactress, one whom they saw in the remotest and wildest places of her little kingdom, 'where never did coach went before', the stern-faced old lady carried in her horse-litter, attended by her court of officials, tenants and the neighbouring nobility and gentry. By her own forceful will and attentive care where the lot had fallen to her she had done much to turn the old waste places into pleasant places—a fair heritage. It was more than half a century since she had been made much of by the imperious old queen, since she had danced at the court masques and had been praised by Dean John Donne for her ability to talk intelligently 'on any subject from predestination to sleave-silk'. Now that she was her own mistress she did not have to care whether people criticised her 'for wearing such ill clothes', nor try to remedy it by ordering from Lady St John's tailor a dress of 'sea-water green satin or green damask embroidered with gold'. Her clothes were all made locally; we hear of a black cloth gown which cost her 39s.6d. and Sedgwick informs us that 'a petticoat and waistcoat of black searge was her constant wear, nor could any persuade her to wear others'. It is little surprising to learn that, with her white wimple, her 'Dress [was] not disliked by any, yet imitated by none'. She was unrepentantly herself in the kingdom she had been born to but had taken so long to acquire. This was a great northern lady: homely and at home. Like her clothes, she bought all her provisions, lengths of materials and the little gifts she loved to bestow—the buckskin gloves, ruffles, devotional tracts and the wooden stock-locks—from local dealers, and she paid in cash. She spent her money where it came from: in her rebuilding, in the management of her estates, in many works of piety and charity. Despite her unquestionable authority, she was not censorious of others and was hardest on herself. Having lived with Lords Dorset and Pembroke, she was only too well aware of the ways of the world. The story of her saying that, if she had to visit the restored court of Charles II she would only do so wearing blinkers, does not suggest that the manners there would shock her (how could they after life with Lord Pembroke?), but rather that she preferred her own northern life, that she felt too set in her ways, too antiquated—it was a case of *autres temps, autres mœurs*.

In all her houses life was run with an almost monastic regularity. As she grew older she stayed much in her own room, members of her family and important visitors dining, like her staff and servants, in collegiate fashion at allotted tables, those who were privileged coming after dinner to her chamber, where she talked to them, kissed the more intimate and bestowed on them her carefully chosen presents or small gifts of money. Bishop Rainbow explained how

> She was absolute Mistris of her Selfe, her Resolutions, Actions, and Time: and yet allowed a time for every purpose, for all Addresses, for any Persons; None had access but by leave, when she call'd, but none were rejected; none must stay longer than she would; yet none departed unsatisfied. Like him at the Stern, she seem'd to do little or nothing, but indeed turn'd and steer'd the whole course of her Affairs.

Late in her life she continued her journeys over the high fells, impervious to the difficulties of the wild, unfrequented ways or the boisterousness of Pennine weather. On one day of frost and mist she fainted and when her attendants remonstrated with her for risking her life in proceeding further she replied that, 'she knew she must die, and it was the same thing to her to die in the way as in her house, and in her litter as in her bed'. Increasingly she kept to her room and her day-book, which she continued to write up to the last, records more frequently, 'I went not out all this day.' Towards the end, on being asked how she was, she answered, 'She was very well.' When her sight and hearing failed her, she was heard repeating the eighth chapter of St Paul's Epistle to the Romans, which she knew by heart. She died on 22 March 1676 at the age of eighty-six. If her buildings have mouldered, her memory has endured; in the Conduit Court in Skipton Castle her presence seems to linger still.

Lady Anne had made her will at Pendragon Castle in 1674, leaving the Westmorland property to her elder daughter, now the dowager Lady Thanet, and Skipton Castle and the Craven estates to Lady Alathea Compton, the child of her younger deceased daughter, Lady Northampton. Grandchildren and great-grandchildren, friends and old servants, all were remembered—to her rent-receiver in Craven she left 'fower of my best oxen'. But her wishes were not to be carried out. Using the same argument against the will as she had used against her father's, her eldest grandson, Nicholas Earl of Thanet, stepped in, claiming successfully that the estates should not have been left out of the direct line. Already a rich man, he had little use for castles in the North; Appleby alone was kept in a state of repair, the others were neglected and fell into decay. The wheel had come full circle.

Lady Anne Clifford was buried in Appleby church in the tomb she herself had erected. The address on the occasion by Bishop Rainbow of Carlisle, was characteristic of the age; it is in the language she knew and used so well, the language of Francis Bacon, John Donne, Sir Thomas Browne and John Milton, rich in metaphor, balanced, rhythmic, fresh and vigorous. The life of 'this great wise Woman', he said, was 'fitter for a History than a Sermon'. She had built her tomb 'against this day, on which we are all now here met to give her Reliques Livery and Seizin, quiet possession'.

And while her Dust lies silent in that Chamber of Death, the Monuments which she had built in the Hearts of all who knew her, shall speak loud in the ears of a profligate Generation; and tell, that in this general Corruption, lapsed times decay, and downfall of Vertue, the thrice Illustrious Anne Countess of Pembroke, Dorset and Montgomery stood immovable in her integrity of Manners, Vertue and Religion.

CHAPTER 9

The Solace of Recusancy

RELIGION HAS MEANT much to the dwellers in the Yorkshire Dales. This is historically true, whatever causes the fact is attributed to: whether it is that an awareness of the elemental forces of nature has awakened in dalesmen a Wordsworthian intimation of the presence of an all-pervading, moving, presiding spirit; or whether, at the other extreme, the very harshness of their existence has required some form of relieving narcotic and that they found it, as Marx considered in this 'opium of the people'. It is equally true that the *via media* of the Church of England established by law has not always provided the most suitable medium for their religious aspirations. Some have remained steadfast in their older Catholic beliefs, others have been illumined by the inner light as revealed by George Fox, and others still have found themselves justified by their faith through sanctifying grace and have sought the Christian perfection as preached by John Wesley. Since Henry VIII's break with the Church of Rome many men and women in the Dales have refused the State's legislated prescription for their souls' welfare and, outside the national Church, have found solace in their own conscientiously chosen form of recusancy.

After the passing of the Settlement Acts of 1559 in the first years of Queen Elizabeth's reign the authorities speeded up the process of removing the 'popish monuments of superstition and idolatory' which remained in parish churches in the Dales: the rood-screens, stone altars, images of saints, pyxes, candlesticks, vestments, censers and Latin service books. Despite their renewed activity they were not everywhere successful. The court cases reveal that incumbents and church wardens, with an eye to an uncertain future, frequently hid the offending 'Massing-stuff'. It was the office of the Archbishop of York, the Council of the North and the York High Commission to root out the prohibited articles and punish the offenders. Yet in 1566 the Richmondshire Commissionary discovered the rood images, a pyx, chrismatory, holy oils and a Latin hymnal concealed within Aysgarth parish church. The church wardens reported back that they had now destroyed them. In the following year, however, it was discovered that they had simply hidden them elsewhere; they were then destroyed and the church wardens suffered the humiliation of a public penance. The inhabitants of Masham and its neighbourhood had been in trouble in the Earls' Rising, and in the following year, 1570, not only was the parish church found deficient in Protestant service books but it was learnt that the parish clerk was guilty of sheltering Papist priests, and further that the irons for making communion wafers were still in existence. The public destruction of these last led to riots in Masham and armed attacks on the officials.

In the little church of Hubberholme in Upper Wharfedale may be seen today one of the few survivals of this iconoclastic form of anti-popery in the wooden rood-loft, which is dated as late as 1588, the last year of Catholic Queen Mary's reign. Again, the iron hearse (for the fixing of candles) over the alabaster effigies on the tomb of Sir John Marmion in West Tanfield parish church has, for some unknown reason, escaped demolition. But the destruction of these 'popish monuments' was thorough in the Dales.

Among those who took part in the Pilgrimage of Grace the religious motive, the belief in traditional Catholicism, was powerful; in the Rising of the North this motive was less evident, despite the overturning of communion tables by the rebels, the destruction of Protestant liturgical books and the celebration of Mass according to the ancient rites. However wavering had been the conduct of Percy Earl of Northumberland, he none the less met his execution resolutely confessing himself a Catholic. Fervent Catholics, both priests and laymen, who refused to knuckle under to Elizabethan Anglicanism, took refuge abroad, among them one with Yorkshire connections, William Allen, later to become a cardinal, who in 1568 founded the English College at Douai in France. Priests, educated and ordained on the Continent, slipped back into England to serve remaining Catholics or to undertake the dangerous task of conducting missions. If the penal restrictions had been somewhat haphazard earlier, by this date they had been tightened into a body of extremely harsh law. A priest coming into England after being ordained abroad was liable to the penalty for treason: hanging, then to be cut down while still alive and butchered into quarters. A lay person found guilty of aiding or sheltering a priest was liable to the same capital penalty and the confiscation by the Crown of all his property. Attendance at the Anglican Sunday service was compulsory; local Justices of the Peace were ordered by the Privy Council to seek from the parish authorities the names of those who wilfully absented themselves for four Sundays running, and such offenders were summoned to court and, convicted of Catholic recusancy, were liable to a fine of £260 a year. As an aftermath of the rising, from 1572, when the Earl of Huntingdon became President of the Council of the North, a whole series of harassing laws was enforced against recusants or suspected Catholic sympathisers. If a recusant defaulted in the payment of his fine, two-thirds of his property could be forfeited to the Crown. The authorities had the power to demand that any recusant or suspect take the anti-Catholic Oath of Allegiance. Refusal could mean life imprisonment and confiscation of all property. It is extraordinary that Catholicism in the Yorkshire Dales should have survived.

Yet survive it did, around a hard core of resolute Catholic gentry, the chief of whom were in Richmondshire, the Liberty of Ripon, the wapentake of Claro and in Craven. In 1571 Archbishop Grindal admitted that 'the greater part of our gentry are not well affected to godly religion'. One reason for the survival of the old religion was the steady flow from the 1570s of seminary-trained priests, Jesuits and others, from abroad. Entering the Dales secretly they either served as chaplains in the houses of the gentry or, more frequently, manned the missions, moving in the disguise of gentlemen or chapmen from 'station' to 'station', hearing confessions and performing Masses, often among the faithful in lonely moorland farms and scattered villages or in the privacy of the manor houses of the gentry. A contributory reason for the persistence of Catholic worship was the inability or the reluctance of the authorities to impose the full rigour of the laws. The gentry showed a strong class cohesion, exhibiting on occasions a quite surprising tenderness towards upper-class offenders. Lady Anne Ingilby of the well-known Ripley family is a case in point. Cited as a recusant by the High Commission in 1571, she did not appear when summoned but took a bond to appear later. In the course of the next ten years she signed, by proxy, no fewer than twenty-seven times a succession of such bonds, but she never did appear, sending either a feeble excuse or none at all. Each time the commissioners, who included on more than one occasion Lord Huntingdon himself, felt obliged 'for certain causes moving them' to renew her bond. In May 1581 she was called on to present herself on eight days' warning, but ignoring this she was summoned once again in June 1585. Even then she did not put in an appearance, nor was she ever punished.

During the 1590s and early in the succeeding century the numbers among the Dales' gentry who were openly recusant, suffering fines and penalties in consequence, steadily increased; many others (some maybe as heirs to estates, who were obliged on succession to take the Oath of Allegiance), although conforming, were Catholic-minded, 'mislikers' of the established religion, 'Church-Papists', 'Lady Matins' people'. This success in 'reconciling' dalesmen to the old religion was greatly on account of the missionary activity of the clandestine priests, itinerant seculars who made their dangerous ways around the widespread 'circuits' over the moors, or Jesuits, like Father Richard Holtby, who worked from their 'citadels' in the houses of the gentry. The casualties among the priesthood were heavy; by the end of 1604 forty-seven secular priests or Jesuits in Yorkshire had been executed for treason. Among the laity of the Dales who suffered hanging, drawing and quartering were two of the gentry whose houses had served as 'citadels' for Father Holtby's Jesuits: Thomas Warcopp and Ralph Grimston of Nidd. Warcopp's house at Thornton Woods (the place is thought to have been a remote farmhouse in the Bedale area of Richmondshire or possibly not far distant, in the Liberty of Ripon) was a rest-centre for priests. A married man with a family of small children, Warcopp did not court danger lightly; rather, he was drawn to the religious, contemplative life, far from the hurly-burly of the missions. In 1594 or 1595 he was caught harbouring a priest, Alexander Markland and was gaoled but managed to escape. The following year he was apprehended in the company of Alexander Rawlins, a priest who had been educated at Winchester, Oxford and Rome. Both men were lodged in York gaol, from which Warcopp again succeeded in escaping. From his condemned cell at York Father Rawlins, who was Warcopp's confessor, wrote moving letters to him, sympathising with his desire to follow a contemplative life and assuring him that, if he observed his advice, he need have no fear in failing in his vocation. It was not to be; in 1597 Warcopp was caught for the third time, sheltering another priest, William Anlaby; and the two died as martyrs for their faith. Warcopp's widow was imprisoned in York, where she was still incarcerated in 1600.

In some parts of the Dales the proportion of families among the gentry who were Catholic recusant or Catholic-minded was particularly high. In Craven, in Staincliffe wapentake, of some forty to forty-five gentry families over half were touched with Catholicism. In Claro wapentake two-thirds of the forty-five odd arms-bearing families were Catholic orientated, and these included two of major importance, the Yorkes of Kirkby Malzeard and the Ingilbys of Ripley Castle. The head of the latter family, Sir William Ingilby, who died in 1579, and his son, another William, although strongly suspected of Catholic sympathies by the Earl of Huntingdon, were outwardly loyal officials and conformist but other members were actively Papist. It was likewise in the Liberty of Ripon. A relative of Cardinal Allen, Sir William Mallory, who succeeded the attainted Earl of Northumberland as bailiff of the Liberty in 1570 and who as a member of the Council of the North held high offices until his death in 1602, was accounted by many as sympathetic, although he was active in removing 'superstitious monuments' from Ripon Minster and expressed in a letter to Lord Burghley his regret that one of his sons should have 'abandoned the trew profession of the gospell'. Others of the leading families in the Liberty—Ingilbys of Dacre, Arthingtons of Pateley Bridge, Grimstons of Nidd, Yorkes and Nortons—were all tainted with popery, even if Catholics were more often on the female side. The prevalence of recusancy around Ripon and in Claro owed much to its proximity to Richmondshire, where Catholicism was strongest in all Yorkshire after Cleveland.

In Richmondshire in the wapentake of Gilling West, a great part of which was Crown land in the Honour of Richmond, of the twelve or so local squires some ten were affected with Catholicism, prominent among them being the Lawsons of Brough Hall. Much of Hang West wapentake, with its great upland parishes of Wensleydale, was demesne land of the Lords Scrope of Bolton, who were stewards of the royal Honours of Richmond and Middleham. Emmanuel eleventh Lord Scrope (later Earl of Sunderland) was president of the Council of the North and, however suspect by the more rabid Protestants, was a pillar of the establishment and upholder of governmental policy, being a protégé of the Duke of Buckingham. On his death in 1628 the Richmondshire estate was parcelled out between four illegitimate children, a son John and three daughters, one of whom, Mary, married as her second husband Charles Pow-lett, sixth Marquis of Winchester and first Duke of Bolton, who was brought up a Catholic but apostatised. Other leading families in Wensleydale were divided in their religious loyalties: the Tophams of Agglethorpe, Wyvills of Constable Burton and the cadet branch of the Scropes at Danby and Spennithorne. What is clear from the court records is that by the early seventeenth century Catholic recusancy was widely established among the gentry families and their retainers and servants in the Yorkshire Dales.

In spite of the heavy legal disabilities that Catholics suffered, they had managed to survive, even to prosper, and it was no uncommon thing for them to send their children to be educated on the Continent —the boys to the Benedictine school at Douai or the Jesuit school at Saint-Omer, where a number found their vocation and returned to the Yorkshire mission field. The girls, too, were sometimes sent to convents in France and the Low Countries, some to take the veil, others, like the redoubtable Mary Ward, from near Ripon, to return and carry on their active work of Catholic piety. But the price that Catholic recusants paid was heavy—in presentments, fines, legal fees, bribes and in the support of the priesthood at home and their children's education abroad. One of their means of communicating with fellow-Catholics, of attending confession and Mass and of contributing to the raising of funds, was at the periodic race meet-ings, which were extremely popular among the Jacobean gentry. The Catholic Thomas Meynell recorded one such meeting in his com-monplace book: 'Anno domini 1623. Mense Aprilis there was seaven horses which did rune at Richemond for a Bowle worth 12 li . . . and a Salte worth six, the first horse to have the best, the second the next, Sir William Gascoigne did win the first, I myself did win the second with a Nagge called Frontino of coler white'. In the Dales the Catholic religion had a strong pull on the country folk, since it was associated with traditional festivities and rustic revelry, soon to be submerged in Puritan severity. 'Dost think because thou art virtuous that there will be no more cakes and ale?' Mystery and 'rush-bearing' plays, mimes in the church and dancing in the churchyard were not stilled at a stroke. The Papists of Ripley in about 1608 used to pipe and dance in the churchyard during Evensong. From 1595 we hear of the Egton interlude players, a troupe of Catholic actors, led by two recusants, Robert and Christopher Simpson, who were much in demand among widespread rural audiences with what their enemies called their 'popishe playes'. The performance of these plays gave a useful cover for meetings for Mass and the Sacraments and for the collection of funds.

In 1609 the Simpsons were invited to bring their Egton company into Nidderdale to entertain an audience of some hundred persons at Gouthwaite Hall, the property of the Catholic Sir John Yorke. The hall was within an enclave of almost exclusively Catholic gentry, many of them possessors within the preceding century of the lands of former granges of the dispossessed abbeys. Sir John was offered his choice among the players' repertoire—two of Shakespeare's recent plays, *King Lear* or *Pericles*, *The Three Shirleys* or the piece entitled *St Christopher*. Appropriately he chose the last, which seems to have been a version of an old morality play. In it the character Reprobus, a man with no religion, desiring to serve the greatest man on earth, takes service with the emperor. He is soon disappointed in the emperor's greatness, when he observes that the latter is ruled by a great fear, that of the Devil. So he switches his allegiance to the Prince of Fiends, only to find that he too lives in fear, in dread of the Crucifix. Relinquishing therefore the Devil's service, he takes himself to a holy hermit, is instructed by him, does penance, and with a new life opening before him he is christened with the name of Christopher. The Catholic Simpsons then added an epilogue to point the moral for their own day. This was a serio-burlesque dialogue between a Catholic priest armed with a crucifix and a Protestant clergyman holding a Bible. The priest naturally gets the better of the argument and wipes the floor with his opponent, who is carried off-stage by a troop of devils—one of whom was played by young Christopher Yorke, who later entered the Carthusian Order.

Under the Stuarts governmental policy towards Catholic recusancy, although the laws remained strict (a new Oath of Allegiance was introduced in 1609), tended towards a practical *modus vivendi*, whereby recusants served as milch-cows for the profit of the Crown. From 1627 the Commission for Compounding with Recusants exacted a high tax from nonconforming Catholics in return for the assurance that they might lease back those lands that had been seized and secure immunity from further molestation. The period of the Civil War and the Protectorate, however, proved a sore trial for

Catholics. If a recusant had supported the Royalist cause he was regarded either as a traitor (in which case his whole estate was seized) or as a delinquent (when four-fifths of it were confiscated). Figures from the West Riding give some picture of the severity of the blow. Of sixty-one recusants who suffered sequestration (all but seven of them gentry), twenty-nine were penalised simply as Papists, nine as delinquent Papists and twenty-three as traitor Papists. It might have seemed as if Catholicism in the Dales would never recover; but the succeeding events showed the toughness and the pliancy of the recusants. Typical of these adaptable holders of the old religion was the career of Sir Solomon Swale of Swale Hall, Swaledale. Swale, of Grinton and Gray's Inn, had been a recusant in 1641, but he appears to have escaped presentment—in fact, he seems to have been politically a trimmer of the first water, and the services of a priest were required to reconcile him to the Church in 1660. As an MP he moved the resolution of the House for the restoration of Charles II in 1660 and for this he was awarded with a baronetcy. In 1670 he was Sheriff of Yorkshire; from Grinton he had moved to another Swale Hall, which he built at South Stainley. His will, made shortly before his death in 1675, reveals both the man and his times:

> I blesse God by His grace for making me a member of His Roman Catholique Church militant, hoping that I may be of the Church triumphant in heaven. And I blesse God that my self & ancient family have been constantly loyall to the Crowne although I have suffered much therefore in the last rebellious tymes & I charge my children & posterity that they be & continue to be loyall as they expect God's blessing, & I have impaired my health & my estate by waiving my good practice in the law & serving constantly the Crowne & my country in Parliament being the first that moved in the then House of Commons the 7th of Maye 1660 to proclaim his Matie King the next day & for that motion His Sacred Matie was graciously pleased to make me the first baronet in Yorkshire of his creating . . . I charge my son & heir apparent Henry Swale Esq. that he spare not his purse in the good education of my grandsonne, but that he will breed him abroad at school to be a good scholar by God's blessing & about his age of 21 years to admit him to the Inner Temple to study the Common Laws. . . .

A Catholic, always with a cautious eye to the main chance, Sir Solomon bequeathed his best horse to his good Catholic friend the Duke of York, afterwards King James II.

The brief revival of Catholic hopes during the reign of James II was dispelled by the Glorious Revolution of 1688. Those recusants who had Jacobite sympathies (which they might well have shared with Anglican Tories) were now faced with the penalties for refusing a new Oath of Allegiance to William and Mary and all Catholics alike were liable to the land tax (to fight 'King William's war'), which for them was doubled. This double land tax for Catholics continued throughout the eighteenth century and into the nineteenth and it proved a heavy drain on often encumbered estates. The Jacobite scares of 1715 and 1745 naturally caused the authorities to look more closely at possible Catholic sympathisers but they could find little in the Dales to arouse anxiety. The Yorkshire Fairfaxes and Stricklands, who had known Jacobite connections, moved mostly outside the Dales. However, in 1718 Roger Strickland, whose father Robert and uncle Admiral Sir Roger had died at the Court of Saint-Germain-en-Laye—he himself had been a page to the Old Pretender and had served in the French army—returned to Yorkshire to claim successfully an inheritance at Catterick. He married a Scrope of Danby and settled in Richmond. In 1745 he was arrested and interrogated but was soon released as posing no threat. The tradition that the Scropes had in that year stored arms at Danby Hall is not supported by evidence. In 1784 Simon Scrope declined to take the new oath for Catholics, since he had already subscribed to that of 1778, which called on him to defend George III against all conspiracies and attempts against his person, throne and dignity. The reasons that Scrope gave were symptomatic of enlightened Catholic opinion in the Dales: he found 'conspiracies' far too strong a word and 'dignity', 'so strong I can't get over it'. The age of active persecution for recusancy was closing and a climate of toleration approaching which allowed the relieving Acts for Catholics at the end of the eighteenth century and the Emancipation Act of 1829.

By the middle of the seventeenth century the seamless garment of the one Catholic Church was rent into a multitude of antagonistic sects. Royalist and Episcopalian clergymen had been replaced by Puritans but in the unseemly scramble for the richer benefices the poor parishes, of which there were many in the Dales, were often left with no incumbent at all. Among Puritans the sects proliferated: Presbyterianism was making a bid for national acceptance, opposed by

Congregationalists (Independents, Brownists), Baptists, Ranters, Seekers, Familists, Separatists and a hundred others. The ideological turmoil of the country had penetrated the Dales. Typical of these North Country seekers after the truth was the Separatist preacher Thomas Taylor, an Oxford graduate from the West Riding, who held a living at Preston Patrick at the head of Morecambe Bay, but refused the £50 in tithes entitled to him. In the northern Dales of Yorkshire and on the neighbouring borders of Lancashire and Westmorland Seekers were numerous and had organised themselves in a monthly meeting, to which farmers, artisans, small dealers and labourers rode or trudged for miles to attend, drawn by favoured preachers. Taylor had connections with similar-minded people in Swaledale and, when he was in dispute with his own flock over the question of infant baptism, he accepted a post in Richmond in 1651. It was Thomas Taylor or men in sympathy with his views, like John Audland and Francis Howgill, who most probably invited George Fox into the Dales, hearing of his success in the south of Yorkshire.

George Fox was born in 1624 at Fenny Drayton in Leicestershire, the son of a Puritan weaver and church warden. Serious, solitary, virtually self-taught, from boyhood Fox devoted himself to the study of the Bible, in which he believed implicitly—if it were interpreted aright; that is, according to the eternal Light of Christ which shines within each and everyone. Yet this Inner Light was denied by the priests (the clergy, of whatsoever denomination, even dissenting, were always 'priests' to Fox) and they disallowed that any might possess it. At nineteen he left home and his apprenticeship to a shoemaker and country dealer (in which he had shown himself highly capable and uncommonly honest) to visit London and to travel the country, questioning, arguing, preaching in the 'steeple-houses' or the open air and being thrown into prison for his pains—all the time in turmoil and agony of mind. His quest for the truth among the vociferous sects went unanswered, until one day, 'when all hope in man was gone, then, O then, I heard a voice which said, "There is one, even Jesus Christ, that can speak to thy condition," and when I heard it my heart did leap for joy'. Fox's conviction was confirmed: the true religion was to be found in following the precepts of the divine Word as it is illuminated in each man's soul, if only he sought the 'guidance of the Inner Light', the 'Spirit of the Lord', the 'revelation of the Divine Will'. He had found his mission: to overturn the priests who offered their wares for sale in their steeplehouses, to 'win a general convincement' that Christ was the Light within every man and woman. The characteristic Quaker beliefs and usages were present very early: the familiar brotherly address of 'thee' and 'thou', the refusal to pay tithes or to take oaths ('Christ commands me not to swear at all, as does the Apostle James'), or to offer 'hat-honours', the absolute honesty of speech and action and the repudiation of all violence. For Quakers Christ's coming had abolished tithes as well as the Levitical priesthood. Despite the revilings of the mob, frequent beatings-up and imprisonment, George Fox persisted in proclaiming his evangelical message through the English towns and countryside and such were his powers of persuasion, his sincerity—and perhaps his homespun appearance (he wore clothes of leather, his hair down to his shoulders, surmounted by a broad-brimmed white hat)—that he brought 'convincement' to many troubled minds.

Responding to the call from the Dales, in the summer of 1652 Fox came north and it was in crossing from the West Riding into Lancashire that he had his vision on Pendle Hill, as he relates in his *Journal*: 'And so we passed on warning people as we met them of the day of the Lord that was coming upon them & as we went I spied a great high hill called Pendle Hill & I went on the top of it with great ado it was so steep: but I was moved of the Lord to go atop of it: & when I came atop of it I saw Lancashire sea: . . . & the Lord let me see atop of the hill in what places he had a great people. . . .' That night at an inn he had a further vision as to who this great people might be. 'And the Lord opened to me at that place: & let me see a great people in white raiment by a river's side coming to the Lord: & the place was near John Blaykling's where Rich. Robinson lived.' These names suggest that it was not only the Lord who 'opened' to him, but those who had invited him to the Dales, acquainting him with a place where he could lodge and be well received. The *Journal* (written many years later) is unclear as to Fox's route through the Dales, but he states that he came up 'Wensydale' and reached the market town on market day. This could be Hawes. There, he says, 'I went into the steeplehouse & after the priest had done I declared the day of the Lord to the priest and people, and turned them from the darkness to the light & from the power of Satan unto God.' From Wensleydale he proceeded westwards, preaching as he went. His reception was mixed: at one house they tried to lock him up as a madman; at an inn they came at him with clubs and knives, but 'the Lord preserved me by his power'. In Garsdale he arrived at the house of a Major Bousfield, where he was received kindly by those present, and some were 'convinced'. He continued through Grisedale and Dentdale, convincing 'many'. On meeting a man and enquiring the way to Richard Robinson's at Brigflatt's, Fox was asked from whence he came, and he replied, 'From the Lord'. Passing through Sedbergh, he reached Robinson's small farmhouse, which still stands today at the end of Brigflatts Lane. The events of the next ten days have been generally regarded as marking the foundation of Quakerism and the Religious Society of Friends.

The following day was Whitsunday, 6 June 1652. Robinson took George Fox to a meeting of Seekers at Borrat, the house of Justice Gervase Benson, a leading townsman of Sedbergh, whose support gave weight to Fox in the town. Of Borrat he wrote, 'This was the place that I had seen the people coming forth in white raiment: & a mighty meeting there was & is to this day near Sedbergh which I gathered in the name of Jesus.' On the Wednesday the annual Hiring Fair took place and Sedbergh was thronged with young men, maid-servants and prospective employers. Fox addressed a crowd from a bench beneath a yew tree in St Andrew's churchyard. There he again convinced many, among them the Separatist preacher Francis Howgill, who declared, 'This man speaks with authority and not as the Scribes.' On the following Sunday—'the next first day', as Fox called it—Francis Howgill and John Audland were to preach to Seekers in the morning at the little chapel on Firbank Fell and Fox was invited to attend. He did not go into the chapel, but withdrew to the fellside, where he sat down on a rock. Then—the rock is marked today with an inscription—in the afternoon he preached a momentous three-hour sermon that was listened to attentively by more than 1,000 people from the Yorkshire Dales and Westmorland,—'among whom I declared freely and largely of God's everlasting truth and word of life'. Many were convinced and from these beginnings the 'Valiant Sixty', the converted 'Publishers of the Truth', went out to face ill-usage and imprisonment in proclaiming George Fox's message of the Inner Light.

The seeming trivia of some rigid Quaker observances—for example, the refusal to give 'hat-honours'—were considered by them as being symbolic of greater matters. The symbolism was not always easy for the uninitiated to understand. When William Simpson felt called by the Lord to demonstrate the necessity of stripping power from hireling priests and corrupt officials, he took off his clothes and ran stark-naked through the streets of Skipton-in-Craven. The magistrates appeared to accept the validity of the symbolism, since they did nothing; not so the populace who beat, punched, pummelled and kicked him. Some years later William Simpson stripped again and displayed his nudity to the dismay of Skipton residents, who did not understand that this time his symbolic action was to demonstrate that, unless they saw the Light, they too would be stripped as naked as he. The Quakers' flouting of conventions and their preaching in and out of season could, while 'convincing' some, irritate others. A contemporary saw them as:

> These kind of vermin swarm like caterpillars . . .
> Some preach, or prate, in woods, in fields, in stables,
> In hollow trees, on tubs, on tops of tables.

Fox was indefatigable in spreading the Light. Cromwell listened to and respected him, but men might smile when he wrote to the Emperor of China and Prester John and even to Pope Alexander VII, exhorting him to be 'godly'. The letters went unanswered. Of two Quakers who went to Rome to convert the Pope one was hanged and the other clapped in prison as a madman.

Nearer home, however, Quaker preaching convinced many of the dalesmen, particularly in Craven, Dentdale and Richmondshire. Two of Fox's leading disciples, Thomas Taylor and James Nayler, carried his message into Richmondshire; by 1669 there were some forty to sixty Quakers in Richmond, about sixty in Grinton, a 'conventicle' at Downholme and a small group at Marrick. Six years earlier there had been twenty Quakers in Masham as compared with the thirty-five Catholics there. It is understandable that the tolerance of Charles II and James II should have appealed to all Dissenters, both Protestant and Catholic; yet the Anglican Tory squire felt that he had fanatics all about him. To the ordinary upholder of the religious establishment all nonconformists were confusedly lumped together as being hostile to society.

It was not considered right for Quakers to marry outside the Society of Friends; this was to prove a serious stumbling-block and ultimately result in a diminution of their numbers. As early as 1689 the Swaledale meeting was distressed at John Tomlin's 'disorderly-ness in taking a woman of the world to wife before a priest', and at Ian Gallaway for acting likewise, 'contrary to Truth and over the heads of Friends'. By the first decades of the eighteenth century the number of Quakers in the Dales was dwindling through backsliding and marriage to non-Quakers; but the principal cause of their decline was undoubtedly the coming of John Wesley.

Today Fox's followers still attend their meeting houses at Skipton, Settle, Bainbridge, Countersett, Carperby and Richmond, but it is the Brigflatts meeting house, outside Sedbergh, which draws Quak-ers from all over the world. A narrow lane leads down between hedgerows of hazel to the River Rawthey; behind it towers the green-grassed contour of Holme Fell. In 1652 Brigflatts was a hamlet of flax-weavers, whose cottages clustered around the village green and pump. Few houses now remain; one of them, Richard Robin-son's, where George Fox stayed, faces the end of the lane, a short distance beyond the meeting house of 1675, the earliest of its kind in the North of England. Before these, on the right, is the Quaker burial ground, bought from Robinson for ten shillings, an enclosed plot beneath the trees—sycamores, a fine copper beech, and cypresses. On a June morning among the long grass, wet with rain, grow bluebells, bright and fresh against the sombre, low, curved tops of the Quaker tombstones. All are alike, the earliest being that of Thomas Sharpe, who was buried in 1657, the latest dated 1980.

The meeting house, with its whitewashed exterior, set as it is in an old-fashioned English garden, suggests at once the peculiar quality and the quiet charm of the Quaker way of life. Within, uncomprom-ising in the simplicity of its white walls and the plain oak of the benches, panelling and balustraded gallery, the impression is of serenity and stillness, the avoidance of anything extraneous to the indwelling of the Spirit. All is not unrelieved severity, however. On the small, sturdy oaken table in the centre of the room stands a vase of freshly cut flowers.

In 1767, in the middle of his fifty years of tireless proselytising, John Wesley wrote to his brother Charles: 'I find a wonderful difference in myself when I am among those who are athirst for God. . . . On this account, the North of England suits me best, where so many are groaning after full redemption.' In that year it was estimated that the groans had ceased for some 6,000 Methodists in Yorkshire—half, that is, of the sect's national total. In the Dales Wesley found the fields 'white unto harvest'. The quite extraordinary response of dalesmen to the call, when (as Southey put it) 'Wesley blew his trumpet and awakened those that slept', owed something to the man, something to the message he proclaimed and much to the audience whom he addressed.

From the earliest days of the Oxford Holy Club, founded by Charles Wesley at Christ Church in about 1729–30, John Wesley had displayed his evangelical fervour; but it was not until after his disastrous Georgia venture (and the fear experienced on the voyages out to America and back) that meetings with the Moravian Brother Peter Böhler had convinced him that salvation came through faith alone. This revelation came early in 1738 when Wesley was thirty-four; thenceforth, as he said, he was 'translated out of darkness into light'. With his passionate belief in faith, 'the free gift of God', 'sanctifying', 'justifying' faith, and the conviction of 'conversion', of a 'new birth', open to all who accepted Christ, Wesley was off and away. And away it was; the *sine qua non* of Wesley's success was his untiring activity, his perpetual journeying. Unlike the mystics and the Quakers—and in agreement with Dr Johnson, who complained against those who claimed an 'Inner Light'—for Wesley ' "stillness" and inaction brought no spiritual balm'; he refused to be 'swallowed up in a dead sea of stillness'. As a result his missionary activity was ceaseless; in his fifty years of active work he travelled, mostly on horseback, some quarter of a million miles—the distance from the earth to the moon. His appeal was to the hearts of men; unlike other clergymen of the Church of England (the Church he never left), he took his message that salvation was a gift for all to the people in churches, houses, the streets and the fields ('all the world is my parish'), preaching with an eloquence that acted as 'a thunderclap on the consciences' of many. Wesley's message of hope swept over the Yorkshire Dales; today it is still recalled by dalesfolk in remote parts that John Wesley once passed that way.

His first connection with the Dales was while he was in his early twenties and a Fellow of Lincoln College, Oxford, when he considered applying for the mastership of a school in Skipton-in-Craven. What attracted him was its remoteness, 'scarce accessible on any side', which would enable him to continue uninterrupted with the serious business of his own salvation. The post, however, went to another. With Wesley this social exclusiveness was a passing phase; from 1739 on, when he began his missionary work, he became immersed in sinful humanity. In 1742 he first carried his mission north, staying with the stonemason convert John Nelson at Birstall in the West Riding on his way to Northumberland, where he was to be gratified by the huge success of his field-preaching. In the autumn of 1743 Wesley was in Wensleydale, where he preached in Wensley's beautiful parish church of the Holy Trinity, with its silent evidence of departed Scropes. The congregation could not make him out. Was he a Quaker? An Anabaptist? Finally they settled for a 'Presbyterian –Papist'. (Both Quakers and early Wesleyans were frequently taken for Catholics.) The following summer he visited nearby Redmire and Bolton, when roughs pelted him with stones until 'one stalwart fellow . . . seeing how meekly he bore it' defied them to touch a hair of his head. Methodism came to the northern Yorkshire Dales largely by way of neighbouring County Durham, where its call was felt strongest among the miners of Weardale and Allendale. A 'class' was established in Barnard Castle in Teesdale in 1747 under the leadership of the itinerant lay preacher Jacob Rowell, whom Wesley appointed to supervise mission work in the Dales. Conversions were soon abundant in Arkengarthdale and Swaledale, where the leadminers and small farmers and their wives showed a willingness to 'off-load their weight of sin'. The Methodist singing had a powerful appeal to these people: with them brother Charles' hymns struck a resonant chord, even such dire verses as:

> Ah, lovely appearance of death!
> What sight upon earth is so fair?
> Not all the gay pageants that breathe
> Can with a dead body compare.

Wesley did compose, however, such deserved favourites as 'Jesu, lover of my soul'.

When John Wesley came to Swaledale in June 1761 he stayed at Blades with the Spencely family, who had 'fitted up a cottage for preaching adjoining their house'. He found 'an earnest, loving and simple people', whom he 'exhorted not to leave the Church though they had not the best of ministers'. His own ultimate nonconformity was, as he saw it, forced on him; he was never a recusant. Yet in upper Swaledale nonconforming Wesleyans were later to outnumber

Anglicans. In 1768 he preached there to 'a large and attentive' congregation and found 'the society one of the most lively which I have ever met with in England'. Next day, however, in Richmond he could not approve of members of the Yorkshire militia, 'a more rude rabble rout I never saw; without sense, decency or good manners'. His message was unacceptable to them. Later, however, he was to write of the Barnard Castle circuit: 'I have not found so deep and lively a work in any other part of the Kingdom as runs through the whole Circuit, particularly in the dales that wind between these horrid mountains.' (His words, curiously for him, reflect the contemporary cult of the Picturesque.) He was in Swaledale again in the summer of 1774, when in his *Journal* he records: 'Tues. 14 June. We crossed over the enormous mountains into lovely Wensleydale, the largest by far of all the Dales, as well as the most beautiful.' However, there he discovered 'bitter dissension' among the preachers, so that 'the poor sheep have all been scattered'. In Redmire 'the people stood staring on every side, as if we had been a company of monsters'. There he preached ('Believe in Lord Jesus, and thou shalt be saved'), reminding the elder listeners that they had heard him thirty years earlier in Wensley church. Afterwards, 'the people were profoundly civil ... bowing and curtseying on every side'. On he rode to Richmond, where in Newbiggin he observed that the militia 'behaved with decency', since their officers were present. Then on to Barnard Castle, where an hour in a cold bath 'refreshed' him. That evening he preached once more. This was a day in the life of a man of over seventy.

Redemption, however, could be difficult; conversion, as Wesley's own *Journals* suggest, was no easy matter. People had to be 'purged before they are fed', at times 'to be torn to pieces', when they 'fell with extreme agony both of body and soul', suffering 'violent sweats and heavings of the breast' or 'such pangs as I never saw', 'strainings as it were to vomit', vehement 'groanings for deliverance'. In Otley in the summer of 1759 the torments of his congregation had caused some unfortunates 'to burst out into loud and ardent cries', lasting for fully two hours; others uttered 'dismal shrieks, one crying "I am in hell, O save me, save me!"' (When the travail of the pangs was over, the new birth might be greeted with ecstatic shouts of 'Glory! Glory!') However, on his coming again to Otley in 1766 he found the town 'run mad. Such noise, hurry, drunkenness, rioting, confusion, I know not when I have met with before. It was their feast day! A feast of Bacchus or Venus or Belial? O shame to a Christian country! However, both the small and the great rabble were so engaged that they had no leisure to molest us.' It is clear that in Otley they 'did not run well'. Yet it was from this town that there came the 'sister' much loved by Wesley, Elizabeth Ritchie, 'one of our Lord's jewels', who, born in 1753, had been, in Methodist terminology, a class leader in her twenties and who attended him on his death-bed in 1791.

In his half century of mission work John Wesley covered most of the Dales, preaching, exhorting, interrogating and receiving latterly the homage of the converted. Although his *Journals* reveal more of the state of souls than of the beauty of the countryside, more the glory of God's grace than of His other works, Wesley did at times have an eye for the landscape through which he passed.

> We reached Grassington about ten. The multitude of people constrained me to preach abroad. At Pateley Bridge the Vicar offered me the use of his church ... it was not large enough to contain the congregation. How vast is the increase in the work of God! Particularly in the most rugged and uncultivated places! How does he 'send the springs of grace' also 'into the valleys that run among the hills!'

After visiting Jervaulx Abbey he remarked on 'what a stately pile it was once', adding that it lay 'in a delightful country, the more so when contrasted with the horrid mountains'. In the summer of 1779 he went out of his way to visit High Force in Teesdale and when he was in his eighties, in May 1786 he thought it worthy of recording that he 'rode through the lovely country to Barnard Castle'.

His language, steeped in that of the Bible, often strikes strangely nowadays on our 'unscriptural' ears. To young Mrs Sarah Ryan, aged thirty, he wrote, 'You have refreshed my bowels in the Lord. . . .' Both John and his brother Charles employed this intestinal metaphor in their hymns—a huge output of some good, much bad but for the most part indifferent verse such as:

> Let the bowels of Thy love
> Echo to a sinner's groan.

and

> Praise God, from whom pure blessings flow,
> Whose bowels yearn on all below.

None the less the Wesleys spoke the language of the people, their voices touched the hearts of thousands of dalesmen, waiting 'to be set at liberty by the Lord'. It may be said of John Wesley that he, a latter-day Paulinus, more than any other single man brought religion into the Dales. If Catholicism lingered among the gentry, there was a latent Puritanism among the labouring classes and this was the source that Wesley tapped. But it would be an over-simplification to look on religion in the Dales as a class matter. Earlier in Richmond-shire in 1662 when the Congregationalist-minded rector of Bedale, the Rev. John Gunter, was dismissed under the Act of Uniformity, the fourth Lord Wharton appointed him steward of his manors of Healaugh and Muker. Lord Wharton, of strong Puritan sympathies, made his shooting-lodge at Smarber Hall in upper Swaledale available about this time for nonconformist meetings; and in 1689 he built and endowed a chapel there for the use (it is variously said) of Presbyterians and Congregationalists. In 1690 he founded a charitable trust to provide Bibles for the children of poor nonconformist families. The Wharton Trust, which is still in existence, was subsequently taken over by the Established Church but since 1896 it has been administered by Anglican together with nonconformist trustees. But from the time of Wesley's coming it was Methodism that reigned in these regions, both in its Wesleyan or (the thing Wesley himself feared) its breakaway forms.

During the nineteenth century Methodism became associated —and in some minds identified—with the temperance movement, a curb on the heavy drinking, particularly among Dales' miners. Entries in an unpublished diary of the Wesleyan Joseph Smithson of upper Swaledale illustrate his social interests and John Wesley's still prevailing influence:

1842. November 6th. Jeremiah Watson of Crackpot was found drowned at the bottom of George Spence's field. He is supposed to have gone in on the 4th of this month, being intoxicated with drink.—This backend a night school has begun at the Wesleyan school room Low Row . . . December 1st. A new public house was opened at Low Row. Pigeon shooting and a great deal of sin and wickedness. It lasted three days. And we of the Low Row sunday school are trying to raise a Wesleyan day school to carry about 20 scholars free.

Interspersed throughout the entries are timely admonishments addressed by the diarist to himself, alluding to the frailty of human nature: 'The wages of sin is death. Rom. 7:23'; 'Curseth is he that continueth not in all things written in the book of the law as spiritual, but I am carnal cold under sin. Rom. 7:14'. It would seem that Joseph Smithson and others in Low Row still fell far short of Wesley's ideal of Christian perfection. The fields might have been 'white unto harvest' but there remained tares among the wheat.

CHAPTER 10

Eyes for the Picturesque

IF IT WAS the Grand Tour that placed the Yorkshire Dales on the map of the Picturesque, it was only after the Treaty of Ryswick in 1697 that this continental finishing school became a necessary completion to the education of the young English gentleman. Earlier travellers in the North of England, like the Tudor antiquarians John Leland and William Camden, had little eye for the landscape; their eyes would be more often on the roads—frequently unsurfaced rocky or muddy tracks, impassable after heavy rain. Few contemporaries wished to emulate the exploits of the intrepid Lady Anne Clifford. Yet it was another adventurous lady, Mistress Celia Fiennes, who not so many years later in the reign of William III traversed the Dales on horse-back and left a breathless account in her *Journeys* (1697–8), a description that likens her experiences to what her father had told her of the Alps.

She had a meticulous eye but, in the taste of her age, her predilection was for cultivated places, 'neate' mansions of the gentry in their parks and gardens, with their 'squaires' of turf, gravelled walks, 'knotts of flowers', topiary work, 'vistos' and terraces, fountains and the warbling 'melody of Nightingerlls' from artificial water-pipes. Steep hills made 'travelling tedious and ye miles long' and allowed her only a view of 'ye clouds'. However, her eye was all-embracing; she noted that

that which adds to the formidableness of Blackstone Edge is that on the one hand you have a vast precipice almost the whole way both as one ascends and descends and in some places the precipice is on either hand; the hill took me up much tyme to gaine the top and also to descend it and put me in mind of the description of the Alps in Italy, where the clouds drive all about and as it were below them . . . ; this was the account my father gave of those Alps when he passed them and I could not but think this carryed some resemblance tho' in little.

Richmond she found 'a sad, shatter'd town and fallen much to decay and like a disregarded place'. A somewhat later traveller, Daniel Defoe, in his *A Tour of the Whole Island of Great Britain* (1724–7), likewise preferred to notice signs of thriving humanity, of cultivation and populous industry to the 'waste and almost uninhabited vales'. Within half a century this way of seeing things was to be completely changed; the Peak district of Derbyshire, the English Lakes and the Yorkshire Dales were to gain a vogue which they have never lost. It was the cult of the Picturesque that proved to be the 'curing of the evil itch of over-valuing fforeign parts', as Celia Fiennes put it; henceforth home-keeping youths might cultivate at home their homely wits.

Typical of young Englishmen making the Grand Tour were Horace Walpole and Thomas Gray, who were abroad in the years 1739–41. In Italy, like so many of their countrymen, they were much taken with—'ravished by' is hardly too strong a word—the landscapes of Claude Lorraine, Gaspar Poussin and Salvator Rosa. Their imagination was powerfully affected by what they saw in the scenery and in paintings, which gradually took shape with them as an aesthetic category—the Picturesque. In 1739 Walpole wrote of the landscape of Savoy: 'Precipices, mountains, torrents, wolves, rumblings, Salvator Rosa. . . .'; and he described a road as 'winding round a prodigious mountain, and surrounded by others, all shagged with hanging woods, obscured with pines, or lost in clouds! Below, a torrent breaking through cliffs, and tumbling through fragments of rocks! Sheets of cascades. . . . This sounds too bombastic to one that has not seen it, too cold for one that has.' In the following year Gray used the word 'picturesque' to describe a Roman scene: 'You cannot pass along a street but you have views of some palace, or church, or square, or fountain, the most picturesque and noble one can imagine.' At the Grande Chartreuse he was 'intoxicated with the sublimities', and exclaimed, 'Not a precipice, not a cliff, but is pregnant with religion and poetry.' Although the term became part of the fashionable jargon of 'connoisseurship', and after the publication in 1756 of Edmund Burke's essay on the Sublime and the

Beautiful somewhat confused with these concepts, yet it long retained something of the meaning of 'painterly' or 'suitable to the
painter's brush', and the painters to whom reference was principally
made were the same Claude, Poussin and Salvator Rosa. It was these
three who formed the canon of taste for the Picturesque landscape.
The purchase of their paintings, genuine or spurious, and their
proliferation through engraved prints served to throw a strong
'Italian light on English walls'. The Grand Tourists returned to their
native land with their eyes and their imaginations coloured by what
they had seen. In order to view the English landscape bathed in the
same warm, golden glow of a painting by Claude Lorraine a tinted
glass was invented (the Claude-glass), with which every Picturesque
tourist was equipped, to transform the duller northern scene into the
dawn or sunset splendour of classical Italy. And what might have
been, without the Claude-glass, lacking to the eye was more than
compensated for by the sublime heights of their imaginative invention.

The ordinary visitor to Keswick today would be astonished at the
description of the place written about 1760 in a famous letter to Lord
Lyttleton by Gray's friend, 'the ingenious Dr Brown':

> At Keswick you will, on one side of the lake, see a rich and beautiful
> landskip of cultivated fields, rising to the eye in fine equalities, with
> noble groves of oak happily disposed; and clinging to the adjacent hills,
> shade above shade, in the most various and picturesque forms. On the
> opposite shore, you will find rocks and cliffs of stupendous height,
> hanging broken over the lake in horrible grandeur, some of them a
> thousand feet high, the woods climbing up their steep and shaggy sides.
> . . . A variety of waterfalls are seen pouring from their summit, and
> tumbling in vast sheets from rock to rock, in rude and terrible magni-
> ficence, while on all sides of this mimic amphitheatre the lofty moun-
> tains rise around, piercing the clouds. . . . To give you a complete idea
> . . . would require the united powers of Claude, Salvator and Poussin
> . . . beautifully dreadful.

With this letter, when it was published in 1767, the Picturesque was
firmly launched on a credulous world; it sent Thomas Gray, Arthur
Young and many others to the Lakes and to the Yorkshire Dales to
have their eyes opened to their native resources of the Picturesque
and their minds 'horridly and delightfully' roused into recognition.

The poet Dr John Dalton, could find a rewarding solace in the wildness,

> Horrors like these at first alarm,
> But soon with savage grandeur charm
> And raise to noblest thoughts the mind.

Thomas Amory, however, cavilled that his description fell short of Dales' reality. John Cunningham, after visiting Yorkshire, greeted his discovery of the Picturesque there with an appreciative apostrophe, 'Delightful Horrors, hail!'

In 1756 there appeared the first volume of an extraordinary book, whose setting was 'Richmondshire' but a Richmondshire that never was, although its descriptions of scenery do have at times a curiously impressionistic ability to evoke brilliantly parts of the Great Scar Limestone country of Craven's caverns and the wilder, more remote hills and valleys of Teesdale, Nidderdale, upper Swaledale and Wensleydale. This is Thomas Amory's *The Life and Opinions of John Buncle, Esquire*, a rumbustious picaresque extravaganza in the Picturesque; in fact, so extravagant is it that it has been seriously stated that the author was a madman and that anyone who enjoys it must be suffering a similar mental disorder. It is, however, a most entertaining work and one's own appreciation and admiration are buttressed by the knowledge that they were shared by so discriminating a critic as Charles Lamb.

The hero, a convinced Unitarian, after going down from Trinity College, Dublin, quarrels with his father over the Athanasian Creed, is promptly cut off from paternal support and leaves Ireland for England in search of material assistance from a university friend, who lives on his estate vaguely near 'Brugh under Stainmore'. Buncle, as Miss Harriet Noel, the first of his many loves, says of him, is 'an odd compound of a man', and his oddity is given ample play in his wanderings in unknown Richmondshire; indeed, it seems that Amory set him down there for the very reason that it was then little known and therefore offered the fullest scope for the Romantic and the Picturesque. It is clear, however, that Amory was well acquainted with the Yorkshire Dales. As Buncle makes his loquacious way through 'a country that is wilder that the campagna of Rome', he meets in the most unexpected places the most unexpected persons —or rather, after a certain time the reader will not find it at all unexpected that Buncle should come upon a delightful 'mansion' in an isolated romantic spot and discover within all the refinements of luxurious living: a dinner ready, 'a fine dish of trouts, roasted chickens, tarts and sparragrass', bottle after bottle of excellent wine, and the company of 'glorious' young women. These paragons of beauty, lovingly described, will deliver or listen attentively to disquisitions on Providence, the Athanasian Creed, Christian-Deism, Hebraic circumcision, the 'Abrahamic succession', algebra, Newtonian 'fluxions' and anything else under the sun. They are, 'most glorious girls . . . capable of adding greatly to the delights of philosophy' since, 'thinking blooms and good humour itself in a human figure'; in short, they are 'fine northern girls'. He marries some five or six of them, who die, after usually not more than two years of connubial bliss, and he accepts their loss as providential:

> It was not fit for me to sit snivelling for months, because my wife died before me, which was, at least, as probable as that she should be my survivor; but instead of solemn affliction, and the inconsolable part, for an event I foresaw, it was incumbent on me, after a little decent mourning to consecrate myself to virtue and good fortune united in the form of a woman.

With the garrulous and mercenary Buncle as guide we are taken on a Picturesque tour of romantic Richmondshire.

The author did know the Dales; but it would seem that he stored the impressions that the wildness, grandeur and the contrasting charm of certain secluded spots made upon him and, recollecting them in tranquillity, dipped into this store to compose the descriptive scenes that are so much a part of this incredible book.

> With the rising sun then I set out, and was charmed for several hours with the air and views. The mountains, the rocky precipices, the woods and the waters appeared in various striking situations every mile I travelled on, and formed the most astonishing points of view. Sometimes I was above the clouds, and then crept to enchanting valleys below. Here glens were seen that looked as if the mountains had been rent asunder to form the amazing scenes, and there, forests and falling streams covered the sides of the hills. Rivers in many places, in the most beautiful cascades, were tumbling along; and cataracts from the tops of the mountains came roaring down. The whole was grand, wonderful, and fine.

If suffering some change in the process of his imagination, the potholes and caves of the Great Scar Limestone countryside of Craven are recalled:

> The lake I have mentioned was the largest I had seen in this wild part, being above a mile in length, and more than half a mile broad; and the water that filled it burst with the greatest impetuosity from the inside of a rocky mountain, that is very wonderful to behold. It is a vast craggy precipice, that ascends till it is almost out of sight, and by its gloomy and tremendous air, strikes the mind with a horror that has something pleasing in it. This amazing cliff stands perpendicular at one end of the lake . . . and has an opening at the bottom, that is wide enough for two coaches to enter at once. . . . How far it goes, I know not, being afraid to ascend more than forty yards; not only on account of the terrors common to the place, from the fall of so much water with a strange kind of roar, and the height of the arch which covers the torrent all the way: but because as I went up, there was a sudden, an increase of noise so very terrible, that my heart failed me, and a trembling almost disabled me . . . the frightful sounds encreased, and as quick as it was possible for me, I came into the day again.

From 'the Stanemore part of Richmondshire', the 'Stanemore Alps', a 'vast tract of mountains, glens, and valleys, forest, rock and water, the most wonderful land in the world', brought Buncle to Richmond, which from his account seems socially, at least, to have improved, since Celia Fiennes visited it.

> The delightful romantic situation of Richmond, and the fine curiosities about the town, will afford you an agreeable entertainment for a couple of days; and if you like going at night to a club of very worthy, sensible men of this town, who are very civil to strangers, you may pass the evening in a very pleasing way: or if you have a taste for dancing, and prefer the conversation of a fine girl to a pipe and more serious discourse, there is a small polite assembly of as pretty women as ever gladdened the heart of man. My method, while there, was to smoke one night with the club; and the next I devoted to the ladies. . . . Life and truth and charm were in perfectiom in those Richmond girls.

And in their company we may leave him.

In character John Buncle (or rather the author Thomas Amory) could hardly be more dissimilar from the shy, retiring, exquisite Thomas Gray, who, in returning from the Lakes, visited the Dales in the autumn of 1769. He carried with him, as was customary with the Picturesque travellers of his time, his Claude-glass, until he broke it in a fall. Gray's travelling companion, Dr Wharton, being overcome by asthma and unable to continue, was kept posted by Gray with details of his journey:

> Ingleborough ... was now completely wrapped in clouds all but its summit, which might have been easily mistaken for a long black cloud too, fraught with an approaching storm. Now our road begun gradually to mount towards the *Apennine*, the trees growing less, & thinner of leaves, till we came to Ingleton ... it is a pretty village situated very high & yet in a valley at the foot of that huge creature of God *Ingleborough*. ...
>
> The nipping air (tho' the afternoon was growing very bright) now taught us we were in Craven. The road was up & down (tho' nowhere very steep). To the left were mountain-tops (Weryside) [Whernside], to the right a wide valley (all inclosed ground) & beyond it high hills again. In approaching Settle the crags on the left drew nearer to our way, till we ascended *Brunton-brow*, into a cheerful valley (tho' thin of trees) to *Giggleswick* a village with a small piece of water by its side covered with coots. Near it a Church, which belongs also to Settle & half a mile further on having passed the Ribble over a bridge arrived at Settle.

The following day, 13 October, Gray set out to visit Gordale Scar, of which he gave the celebrated description that as recently as the 1970s brought Margaret Drabble to Yorkshire, to see for herself what he had described. The wind was blowing from the north-east:

> day gloomy and cold ... came to *Malham* (pronounced *Maum*) a village in the bosom of the mountains seated in a wild & dreary valley. From thence I was to walk a mile over very rough ground, a torrent rattling along on the left hand. On the cliffs above hung a few goats: one of them danced & scratched an ear with its hind-foot in a place where I would not have stood stock-still
>
> For all beneath'the moon.
>
> As I advanced the crags seemed to close in, but discovered a narrow entrance turning to the left between them. I followed my guide a few paces, & lo, the hills opened again into no large space, & then all farther away is barred by a stream, that at the height of almost 50 feet gushes from a hole in the rock & spreading in large sheets over its broken front dashes from steep to steep, & then rattles away in a torrent down the

valley. The rock on the left rises perpendicular with stubbed yew-trees & shrubs, starting from its sides to the height of at least 300 feet. [Today, against a blue sky it is reminiscent of the steep hillside, with cypresses, at Ravello on the Sorrentine peninsula.] But these are not the thing! It is that to the right, under which you stand to see the fall, that forms the principal horror of the place. From its very base it begins to slope forwards over you in one black & solid mass without any crevice in its surface, and overshadows half the area below with its dreadful canopy. When I stood at (I believe) full 4 yards distance from its foot, the drops which perpetually distill from its brow, fell on my head, & in one part of the top more exposed to the weather there are loose stones that hang in the air, & threaten visibly some idle Spectator with instant destruction. . . . The gloomy uncomfortable day well suited the savage aspect of the place, & made it still more formidable. I stayed there (not without shuddering) a quarter of an hour, & thought my trouble richly paid, for the impression will last for life.

And this was from the pen of one who had been 'intoxicated with the sublimities' of the Grande Chartreuse. The Picturesque had become more than a way of seeing; it was to become a way of life in that efflorescence of feeling that marked the Romantic Movement.

Leaving these 'horrors', Gray travelled to Skipton, where he saw 'the good Countesse's' castle, but did not visit it; then on to Otley.

First up *Shodebank*, the steepest hill I ever saw a road carried over in England, for it mounts in a straight line (without any other repose for the horses, than by placing stones every now & then behind the wheels) for a full mile. Then the road goes on the level on the brow of this high hill over Rumbald-moor, till it gently descends into *Wharldale*: so they call the Vale of the Wharfe, & a beautiful vale it is, well-wooded, well-cultivated, well-inhabited, but with high crags at a distance, that border the green country on either hand. Through the midst of it deep, clear, full to the brim, & of no inconsiderable breadth runs in long windings the river . . . [a] fine & copious stream.

John Buncle's ecstatic descriptions of the Dales stimulated the curiosity of travellers to visit them, among others Arthur Young, who in the late 1760s made his *Northern Tour*, collecting information on the state of English agriculture. Young had frequent complaints to make on the state of the roads; and occasional praise for the new turnpikes that were beginning to make the Pennines more easily accessible. Having a few days to spare, he tells us, he was 'induced to employ it in a little excursion into Stainmore, of which I had read such wonders in the life of John Buncle'. He was not disappointed; for the eyes of this prosaic observer of soils, crops, manures and prices had been opened to the Picturesque. At Greta Bridge he paused to inspect the fine art collection at Rokeby, the seat (at that time) of Sir Thomas Robinson; then on he rode up the beautiful dale of the Tees, by way of 'Bows' and 'Bernard castle':

> Leaving Bernard castle, towards Eggleston, the road runs along a steep woody precipice, the border of a long winding valley, with a river meandering through it. You look down on the tops of tall groves, in a manner most exquisitely picturesque. You next come to a romantic valley, nobly lined with steeps of wood, and a rapid stream winding through it. . . . Pursuing the beautiful line of country we next come to Eggleston; romantically situated among rocks, steeps of wood, raging torrents, beautiful cascades, a fine assemblage of the noble touches of nature. . . . Advancing towards Middleton, from the hill before you descend to the village, the most glorious prospect opens to the view, that imagination can picture; you look down upon the left over a noble extensive valley intersected with hedges and a few walls into sweet inclosures, which being below the point of view are seen distinct, though almost numberless; the scattered trees, the houses, villages &c. &c. ornament the scene, in a manner too elegant to admit of description. Beneath your feet at the bottom of a vast precipice, rolls the Tees, which breaks into noble sheets of water, and throws a magnificence over the scene, that is greatly striking . . . the trembling reflections of the sunbeams from so many spots in such a range of beauty, has an effect astonishingly fine: Elegant beyond all imagination.

From 'this paradise, the sport of nature in her gayest mood', where all is 'elegantly romantic', the 'terrible sublime' is near at hand, to act as an aesthetic foil:

> Pursuing your track through this delicious region, you cross some wild moors, which contrast the pictures you have beheld, and render those that follow more particularly beautiful. After passing Newbigil [New-biggin], you come to a spot called Dirt Pit [an example of the English felicity in topographical nomenclature], one of the most exquisite bird's-eye landscapes in the world: it is a small, deep, sequestered vale, containing a few inclosures of a charming verdure, finely contrasted with the blackness of the surrounding mountains.

The cult of the Picturesque did open English eyes to the natural beauties of their countryside, but we may feel it was too public, too standardised a view, too conventional a taste, and the descriptions too stylised and overwritten to be acceptable—even when they are not necessarily untrue. Perhaps the *reductio ad absurdum* of this cultivation of the Picturesque is to be found in the work of the Rev. William Gilpin, whose *Observations Relative Chiefly to Picturesque Beauty* were published in 1786. Gilpin actually sets out to formulate the 'rules' for the 'correctly picturesque'. Nature herself is a crude worker, often lacking the good taste and refinement of the connoisseur; but these blemishes may be removed, rectified by 'a little practice in the rules of picturesque composition'. There is a confusion here as to what the artist, the descriptive writer or simply the spectator has come to see—and what, in fact, he does see. (We are on the road to Sir George Sitwell and his imagined advice to one of his sons: 'Well, my boy, it needs improving. Remove that hill; throw out some water there, a sheet of water; trees, avenues of trees; statues, yes, statues and urns, perhaps an obelisk; and in the far distance a grove enclosing a Temple of the Winds.') The Picturesque had become an aesthetic strait-jacket and damaged the Dales by directing the visitor's eye to what it was supposed to see—a stereotyped, idealised vision—rather than allowing it the untrammelled freedom of seeing for itself.

Gilpin, although he prescribed rules for improving on nature, fiercely denounced those who deformed her works. For him ancient ruins, in which the Dales abounds, were natural objects—in fact it has been suggested that he looked favourably on Henry VIII and Cromwell for having provided us with so many splendid shattered fabrics of abbeys and castles. He is scathing in his criticisms of the 'improvements' made to Studley Royal and Fountains Abbey by the owner, the dismissed chancellor of the exchequer at the time of the South Sea Bubble, John Aislabie, and his gardener William Fisher. Today the visitor to these beautiful grounds would think differently. Yet Gilpin's strictures are not without their point.

> The area, which such a scene naturally suggests, is that of retirement —the habitation of cheerful solitude. . . . Instead . . . the whole is a vain ostentation of expence; a mere Timon's villa, decorated in a taste debauched in its conception, and puerile in its execution. Not only the reigning idea of the place is forgotten; but all the great master-strokes, in every shape are defaced.

He goes on to describe the valley and ruins of Fountains Abbey:

> Such was the general idea of this beautiful valley, and of the ruins which
> adorned it, before they fell into the hands of the present proprietor. . . .
> He found [them] indeed somewhat ruder than even picturesque beauty
> required; and a little might have been well done. But *his improvements*
> have no bounds. He has pared away all bold roughness, and freedom of
> the scene, and given every part a trim polish. A few fragments lying
> scattered around the body of the view are *proper*, and *picturesque*. They
> are *proper*, because they account for what is defaced; and they are
> *picturesque*, because they unite the principal pile with the ground; on
> which union the beauty of composition, in good measure, depends. [A
> note here refers the same idea to mountains, to building—and to cattle.]
> In the room of these detached fragments, which were the proper, and
> picturesque embellishments to the scene, a gaudy temple is erected, and
> other trumpery wholly foreign to it.—It is a difficult matter, at the sight
> of such monstrous absurdities, to keep resentment within decent
> bounds. I hope I have not exceeded.

The widespread cult of the Picturesque was mocked at more than
once in the novels of Jane Austen. In *Sense and Sensibility* Marianne
explains to Edward that much of the talk was 'mere jargon', everyone pretending to feel and describe landscape 'with the taste and
elegance of him who first defined what picturesque beauty was':

> 'I like a fine prospect,' said Edward, 'but not on picturesque principles. I
> do not like crooked, twisted, blasted trees, I admire them much more if
> they are tall, straight and flourishing. I am not fond of nettles or thistles
> or heath blossoms.'
> Marianne looked with amazement at Edward.

Although Samuel Taylor Coleridge was not unmoved by scenery
which he found 'most wild and romantic', a corrective to the almost
universal disposition to see nature through Picturesque eyes was
provided by William Wordsworth:

> for this
> Although a strong infection of the age
> Was never much my habit.

Still less it was for 'Wordsworth's exquisite sister', Dorothy; it was something far removed from the Picturesque that inspired her to write, 'A fine moonlight night—The moon shone like herrings in the water.' A film had dissolved from before her eyes and it was through her eyes that the poet so largely saw. On Christmas Eve 1799 Wordsworth wrote a long letter to Coleridge, in which he described how he and Dorothy walked through Wensleydale to take up their residence in Dove Cottage, Grasmere. Having spent the night at Askrigg, early next morning they visited the waterfall in Whitfield Gill, of which Wordsworth gave him a highly appreciative, detailed and accurate account. They left the 'spot with reluctance but highly exhilarated'. Hitching a lift on a farm cart, they arrived at Hardrow and, after warming themselves before a cottage fire, made for the Force.

> After cautiously sounding our way over stones of all colours and sizes encased in the clearest ice formed by the spray of the waterfall, we found the rock which before had seemed a perpendicular wall extending over us like the ceiling of a huge cave, from the summit of which the water shot directly over our heads into a basin and among fragments of rock wrinkled over with masses of ice, white as snow, or rather as D. says like congealed froth. The water fell at least ten yards from us and we stood directly behind it, the excavation not so deep in the rock as to impress any feeling of darkness, but lofty and magnificent ... a scene so exquisitely beautiful. The spot where we stood was as dry as the chamber in which I am now sitting, and the incumbent rock of which the groundwork was limestone veined and dappled with colours which melted into each other in every possible variety. On the summit of the cave were three festoons or rather wrinkles in the rock which ran parallel to each other like the folds of a curtain when it is drawn up; each of them was hung with icicles of various length, and nearly in the middle of the festoons in the deepest valley made by their waving line the stream shot from between the rows of icicles in irregular fits of strength and with a volume of water that momently varied. . . . In such a situation you have at every moment a feeling of the presence of the sky. Above the highest point of the waterfall large fleecy clouds drove over our heads and the sky appeared of a blue more than usually brilliant.

Here is direct observation, factually reported; it has not been seen through a Claude-glass and coloured by classical associations and landscape painting.

In the summer of 1807 William and Dorothy Wordsworth made

an 'excursion' on horseback and by carriage into Wharfedale, to visit Bolton Priory. Afterwards they went on foot over the moors to Gordale and Malham, which Dorothy had not previously visited. William was much taken with the beauty and the historical associations of the environs of Bolton Priory; the fortunes of the Cliffords (particularly the vicissitudes of the 'Shepherd Lord') and the Nortons interested him deeply; and about the time of this visit were written the poems 'Song at the Feast of Brougham Castle', 'The White Doe of Rylstone' and 'The Force of Prayer', all of which deal with characters and incidents connected with this spot. In his notes to 'The White Doe' he quotes with appreciation a description of the place by Dr Whitaker in his well-known *History of the Deanery of Craven*. This description is Picturesque but without the defects of the style; much of what Whitaker describes can be seen today: a wooded landscape of idyllic beauty—when not encumbered with visitors that is.

> Bolton Priory stands upon a beautiful curvature of the Wharfe, on a level sufficiently elevated to protect it from inundations, and low enough for every purpose of picturesque effect. Opposite to the East window of the Priory Church, the river washes the foot of a rock nearly perpendicular, and of the richest purple, where several of the mineral beds . . . are twisted by some inconceivable process into undulating and spiral lines. To the South all is soft and delicious; the eye reposes upon a few rich pastures, a moderate reach of the river, sufficiently tranquil to form a mirror to the sun, and the bounding hills beyond. . . . But all the glories of Bolton are on the North. Whatever the most fastidious taste could require to constitute a perfect landscape, is not only found here, but in its proper place. In front, and immediately under the eyes, is a smooth expanse of park-like enclosure, spotted with native elm, ash, etc. of the finest growth: on the right a skirting oak wood, with jutting points of grey rock; on the left a rising copse. Still forward are seen the aged groves of Bolton Park, the growth of centuries; and farther yet, the barren and rocky distances of Simon-seat and Barden Fell contrasted with the warmth, fertility and luxuriant foliage of the valley below.
>
> About half a mile above Bolton the valley closes, and either side of the Wharfe is overhung by solemn woods, from which huge perpendicular masses of grey rock jut out at intervals . . . the Wharfe itself is nearly lost in a deep cleft in the rock [the dangerous Strid], and next comes a horned flood enclosing a woody island—sometimes it reposes for a moment, and then resumes its native character, lively, irregular and impetuous.

Wordsworth, in a preface to 'The White Doe of Rylstone', draws attention to the differences between his treatment of the mediaeval incidents in the poem (the eclipse of the Nortons in the Earls' Rising) and the methods of Sir Walter Scott. Scott first came to stay with his friend, J. B. S. Morritt, at Rokeby Hall on the River Tees near Greta Bridge in 1809. It was to Morritt that Scott dedicated his long poem, *Rokeby*, 'the scene of which is laid in his beautiful demesne'. Scott's work is central to the Romantic Revival and this particular poem brought the lovely countryside in which it is set to the notice of a wide public. He chose the setting, he said, because 'the place itself united the romantic beauties of the wilds of Scotland with the rich and smiling aspect of the southern portion of the island'. This part of Teesdale Scott made peculiarly his own: Barnard Castle, Greta Bridge, Ravensworth, the Rivers Tees and Greta, Caldron Snout and High Force, Rokeby Hall and Mortham Tower, Brignal Woods and the Roman camp of Lavatrae (behind the George Inn—now the Morritt Arms)—all are there; Brignal giving rise to one of Scott's most popular lyrics:

> And you may gather garlands there
> Would grace a summer Queen.

This appeal of the Dales to the Romantics is perhaps best exemplified by the painters, especially in Thomas Girtin and, above all, J. M. W. Turner, who was *par excellence* the painter of the Yorkshire Dales. It was in Yorkshire that as a young man he made the acquaintance of Squire Fawkes of Farnley Hall, near Otley in Wharfedale, a meeting which grew into a firm friendship. After contemplating the Wharfedale scene Turner painted the extraordinary *Hannibal Crossing the Alps* in 1812; it is now in the Tate Gallery. He supplied only some twenty of the 120 water-colour drawings that had been commissioned for T. D. Whitaker's *History of Richmondshire* (1819–21). This is to be regretted, since the pictures are of a rare beauty, delicate harmonies of amber, browns, blues and greens, of which Ruskin wrote glowingly, 'The foliage is rich and marvellous in composition, the rock and hill drawing insuperable, the skies exquisite in complex form.' No one better than Turner depicted the natural features of the Dales: the hills, clouds, rock formations, woods, rivers, waterfalls, the atmosphere and the extraordinary contrasts of light—of sunshine, mist and the louring majesty of threatening storm. This dramatic quality, so essentially Romantic, is seen in his view of Semer Water. From the shore, behind the Carlow Stone, the middle distance is deep in shadow; behind, the folds of the hills merge in a swirl of clouds, through which rays of the sun break, to bathe in a brilliant light the background of clouds and the fellside.

The grandeur of the Dales' scenery has at times proved too much for some painter's Romantic inspiration and for his brush. One such failure was James Ward (who has been called 'the Michelangelo of the Picturesque') in his colossal painting of Gordale Scar—it measures 140 × 131 inches (355 × 332 centimetres). At the time of writing, it is exhibited in Gallery 14 at the Tate. Wordworth's friend, Sir George Beaumont (himself a Picturesque painter, who carried about with him an original Claude, which he placed beside his easel as he painted) considered that Ward, in selecting Gordale Scar, had chosen a scene 'beyond the range of art'. And in this—although not in his condemnation of Turner—Sir George was doubtless right.

Like the Wordsworths others from the Lakes' literary community made forays into the Dales of Yorkshire, among them Robert Southey. In *The Doctor*, a charming book in which his erudition is worn with a disarming ease, Southey has the birthplace of his hero in the limestone country of Craven.

Daniel, the son of Daniel Dove and of Dinah his wife, was born near Ingleton in the West Riding of Yorkshire, on Monday 22 April, old style, 1723, nine minutes and three seconds after three in the afternoon. . . . Daniel, the father, was one of a race of men who unhappily are now almost extinct. He lived upon an estate of six and twenty acres which his father had possessed before him, all Doves and Daniels, in uninterrupted succession from time immemorial, farther than registers or title deeds could ascend. The little church, called Chapel le Dale, stands about a bow shot from the family house. There they had all been carried to the font; there they had each led his bride to the altar; and thither they had, each in his turn been borne upon the shoulders of their friends and neighbours. Earth to earth had been consigned there for so many generations, that half of the soil in the churchyard consisted of their remains. . . . On three sides there was an irregular low stone wall, rather to mark the limits of the sacred ground, than to inclose it; on the fourth it was bounded by the brook whose waters proceed by a subterraneous channel from Wethercote cave . . . on the other side of the brook, the common with its limestone peering everywhere above ground, extended to the foot of Ingleborough. . . .

The house of the Doves was to the east of the church, under the same hill, and with the same brook in front. . . . It was a low house, having before it a little garden. . . . You entered between two yew trees clipt to the fashion of two pawns. There were hollyhocks and sunflowers displaying themselves above the wall; roses and sweet peas under the windows, and the everlasting pea climbing the porch. Over the door was a stone with these letters:

$$D$$
$$D + M$$
$$\text{AD}$$
$$1608$$

It was, that is, an early seventeenth-century Dales' farmhouse, built in the natural local limestone, of the type, perhaps, originating in the old Viking longhouse.

The houses in neighbouring Dentdale are of a gayer appearance, frequently being whitewashed over and the windowsills and doorways picked out in bright pure colours, like houses in the Lake District. It is in *The Doctor* that Southey gives the account of 'the terrible knitters e' Dent', told to him by the pipe-smoking old Betty Yewdale and written down in dialect. In the eighteenth and nineteenth centuries knitting was a cottage industry in the Dales, carried out not only by the women but by the menfolk and children also as a necessary addition to the family income. During the Seven Years War (1756–63) the government placed large orders for supplying the army with the soldiers' worsted stockings:

'It was about six an' fifty year sin, in June, when a woman cam fra' Dent at see a Nebbor of ours e' Langdon. They er terrible knitters e' Dent—see my Fadder an' Mudder sent me an' my lile Sister, Sally, back we' her at larn at knit. I was between sebben an' eight year auld, an' Sally twea year younger. . . .

'Weel, we dud'nt like Dent at a'—nut that they wer bad tull us—but ther way o' leeving—it was round Meal—an' they *stoult* it int' frying pan, e' keaeks as thick as my fing-er. Then we wer *stawed* we' sae mickle knitting.

So the two little things planned to escape and one day between 'Kursmas an' Cannalmas' they managed to do so, walking in their wooden clogs in terrible wintry conditions from Dent back to their home in the Lakes.

Southey, in advance of his time, was sensitively aware of social conditions and of the changes that were coming over English society —changes that were to continue in the aftermath of the Napoleonic Wars and with the acceleration of the Industrial Revolution. In 1807 he published *Letters from England*, ostensibly translated from the Spanish of the young Don Manuel Espriella, who sends home accounts of life in contemporary England. He is travelling by stage-coach 'over the sierra of Stainmoor, a cold and desolate tract', where at Bowes some schoolboys are picked up.

> At Bowes begins the great grazing country for children. It is the cheapest part of England, and schools for boys have long been established here, to which tradesmen, and even some parents of higher order who think money better than learning, send their children from all the great towns, even from the western provinces,—but London supplies the greater number. . . . These schools are upon the most economic plan, a pension of sixteen pounds sterling pays for every thing, clothing included. For certain they are kept on Spartan fare; but the boys, who were from different schools, spake well of their masters, and had evidently been happy there.

Some thirty years later Charles Dickens was to paint a grimmer picture; but Regency England had given way to the Victorian era—the Picturesque to the scene depicted by Friedrich Engels—and the transition was to bring much hardship to the Yorkshire Dales.

CHAPTER 11

Leaden Echoes

IN THE LAST quarter of the eighteenth century the pattern of radical
social change which is summed up in the term the Industrial Revolution was beginning to have its effects on the age-old economy of the
Yorkshire Dales. Thenceforth changes comparable with those that
had earlier taken centuries were encompassed in decades. From the
late sixteenth century and throughout the seventeenth century the
common-field system had been transformed; walled enclosures
('crofts') had been built around the villages and parcels of the
commons and waste had become consolidated, by exchange and
intake, within dry-stone walls. The results were beneficial to both
crops and stock, so that by the eighteenth century the practice of
enclosure had been intensified; and in 1801 the earlier private Acts of
Parliament which had allowed this were confirmed by a further Act
that systematised and facilitated the procedure. It was from this time
that the familiar walls of the Dales, that look as if they are a natural,
primaeval part of the landscape, came into existence: first, the
common fields and meadows, then the higher hillsides and finally the
great expanses of the moors themselves. To a practised eye this
walling can be dated, from the earliest seemingly haphazard croft-
walling around the nucleated villages to that of the intakes (again
often irregularly shaped) and lastly to the long, straighter walls of the
high fells. In the Dales 'to fence' signified 'to wall', and the skilled
craft of dry-stone walling came into being, giving employment to
specialists in the work, who in the early part of the nineteenth
century, when the enclosures were at their height, might be expected
to complete a rood of 7 yards' (6.4 metres') stretch of 'weel thruffed
wall' in the course of a day. It is difficult to imagine today the Dales'

scene, before the common fields and meadowland, the woods and moors were partitioned out in this way.

For the dalesfolk farming, which was predominantly pastoral (particularly in the upper dales), had been traditionally supplemented by cottage industries and in certain localities by mining, chiefly of lead but with some extraction of coal and iron. Arkwright's invention of the water-frame in 1769 and the adaptation of his machines to water-power may be seen as symbolic of the Industrial Revolution. In 1794 the Birbeck family had a wool warehouse in Skipton, where the wool was brought, and after 'sorting and combing it is spun at the Company's mills at Linton and Addingham . . . and made into stuffs, viz. shalloons, calimancoes, and all sorts of double-goods'. Near Settle the Claytons were spinning cotton in their mill at Langcliffe and shortly after flax was being spun in Nidderdale. By the end of the eighteenth century there were water-powered mills in Airedale and Wharfedale for the spinning first of cotton. In Wensleydale as early as 1784 the mill at Aysgarth Falls was producing spun cotton; later it was converted to the production of woollen yarns. About the same time in Swaledale and in the north-west around Sedbergh mills driven by the plentiful supply of water were also turning out woollen yarns for use in the widespread home-knitting industry. Mechanical power and an adequate labour-force were among the first essentials for the development of the textile industry—and for that of mining, as well as for the production of iron and steel. The application of James Watt's inventions in the harnessing of steam provided an accelerating increase of power; enclosures and a change from arable to pastoral farming in the lower dales, demanding fewer hands, helped to supply the required labour. The great textile industries, that of woollens in West Yorkshire and of cotton goods in Lancashire, now took root and blossomed—if such expressions are appropriate to the human misery they brought with them. At the same time came the rapid extension of the iron and steel industries—and, to provide power for all, the extraction of coal. The growth of these industries profoundly affected life in the Dales.

In 1794 inspectors from the Board of Agriculture reported on the farming conditions they found there. The increasing population in the new industrial areas was already demanding an ever-increasing supply of farm produce. Drovers from Scotland still brought their great herds of cattle to the markets at Settle, Skipton and to the periodic fairs, like that held on Malham Moor, and for fattening in the richer southern pastures. Improvements arising from the enclosures of the meadowland and in the breeding of cattle led to an increased amount of dairy-farming in the lower dales, while in the uplands farmers kept a few milking animals alongside their flocks of sheep. (The black-faced Scotch sheep were now gaining a hold, especially on the rougher moorland grazing.) The inspectors found that in Dentdale there was 'a considerable quantity of butter salted in this tract, and disposed of at Skipton. . . . Few cattle are fed but great numbers of milk cows are kept, and large quantities of butter and cheese produced.' In Nidderdale the butchers' stalls in the market at Pateley Bridge 'declared that the inhabitants were in no danger of starving for want of butcher meat'. The men were also impressed by the number of pigs that were reared in the district on oatmeal (oats was one of the few arable crops to survive), the hams being sent to the London market and to the manufacturing districts of Lancashire. In Wharfedale, Wensleydale, Swaledale and Teesdale butter, cheese and meat (mutton, beef and cured hams) were being produced for the growing markets at Ripon, Skipton, Richmond, Barnard Castle (in County Durham) and, over the Westmorland border, Kendal. However, market fluctuations resulting from the Napoleonic Wars and their aftermath, the repeal of the Corn Laws and the periodic depressions that were to continue throughout the nineteenth century and after, taken together with the enclosures and the shift from arable to pastoral farming, meant that fewer people were able to find a livelihood from Dales' farming alone. Another reason for the inability of the farms to support their inhabitants was that the division among the descendants on the death of the holder of land held by copyright led to uneconomically-sized holdings. The drift away from the land to the coal-mines of County Durham, the woollen factories of the West Riding or the cotton mills of Lancashire had begun, an exodus that was to end, with the failure of the supplementary industries, in a depopulation of the Dales, particularly in the upper regions, and the desolation of previously flourishing upland farmsteads.

In the first decades of the nineteenth century the living conditions in the North Riding of Yorkshire—the cost of foodstuffs, rents and labour—were among the cheapest in the country and it was this fact perhaps above all that had prompted the proliferation there of cheap boarding schools for boys. Southey had already written about these cheese-paring educational establishments before they came to the notice of Charles Dickens; but it was the latter who, in his novel *Nicholas Nickleby*, brought the full horror of the facts home to the British public. Dickens travelled by stage coach to Yorkshire with his friend Hablot K. Browne just before Christmas 1837 and they put up and were warmed and cheered after a shivering winter's journey by the genial hospitality of the George Inn, near Greta Bridge in Teesdale. (The present Morritt Arms is a pleasant hostelry, with wall paintings and mementoes that recall Dickens.) In a preface to his novel Dickens expressed his disgust at the whole race of ignorant, bullying schoolmasters, like the infamous Mr Wackford Squeers of 'the Academy called Dotheboys Hall at the delightful village of Dotheboys near Greta Bridge in Yorkshire':

> Of the monstrous neglect of education in England, and the disregard of it by the State as a means of forming good or bad citizens, and miserable or happy men, private schools long afforded a notable example. Although any man who had proved his unfitness for any other occupation in life, was free, without examination or qualification, to open a school anywhere; although preparation for the functions he undertook, was required in the surgeon who assisted to bring a boy into the world, or might one day assist, perhaps, to send him out of it; in the chemist, the attorny, the butcher, the baker, the candlestick maker; the whole round of crafts and trades, the schoolmaster excepted; and although schoolmasters, as a race, were the blockheads and imposters who might naturally be expected to spring from such a state of things, and to flourish in it; these Yorkshire schoolmasters were the lowest and the most rotten round in the whole ladder.

It is the tradition that Dickens visited neighbouring Bowes and, with a fabricated letter of introduction, sought a meeting and showing over the school of one William Shaw. But Shaw was suspicious of his visitor and Dickens did not gain an entry; instead, he strolled into the wintry churchyard nearby. There, it is said, seeing north of the chancel the tombstone of a boy, George Ashton Taylor, who at the age of nineteen had died at Mr Shaw's Academy in 1822, he had the germ of an idea that developed into the distressing life of Smike in his novel. On another Yorkshire trip Dickens again stayed in Teesdale, this time at Barnard Castle at the King's Head Hotel, and it was there that the watchmaker's shop, which was across the road from the hotel, gave him the idea for *Master Humphrey's Clock*. The King's Head had fallen on bad times, but recently it has happily been refurbished and refurnished in a manner more befitting its role of ancient coaching inn.

The traditional source of wealth and employment in Yorkshire, the wool trade, had survived the Dissolution of the Monasteries, the monastic labourers having been superseded by others, who carried on the production, collection and processing of the fleeces, if no longer primarily for the export trade in raw wool. Licensed dealers, pedlars like the 'broggers' of Halifax, bought and collected the wool from the outlying farms and distributed it to be scoured, carded, combed and spun. Much of the work had been traditionally done in the homes of dalesmen, the cottage crafts performed by women and children to eke out the often meagre living from their farms. Before the advent of the factories, the spun yarn, the product of the hand spinning-wheel, was woven into cloth on individual looms (or those owned and worked jointly by a group of cottagers) or was used in knitting. Knitting had been carried on in the Dales for the market from Tudor times. In 1724 Daniel Defoe was struck by the knitters of Richmond—'here you see all the people, great and small, a knitting; and at Richmond you have a market for woollen and yarn stockings, which they make very coarse and ordinary, and they are sold accordingly; for the smallest siz'd stockings for children are here sold for eighteen pence per dozen, or three halfpence a pair, sometimes less.' Throughout the century the Richmondshire knitters were suppliers of long yarn stockings and seamen's woollen caps for the substantial trade with the Low Countries. At the beginning of the nineteenth century the hosiers collected weekly from the cottage knitters of Sedbergh and Dent as many as 840 pairs of stockings of a finer wool. It was not only the women and children who knitted; men took up the pursuit in their spare time—the dalesfolk were 'terrible knitters'. In Wensleydale and Swaledale the lead-miners would take out their knitting sheaves during rest periods, so that these breaks were described as 'having six needles'. Even the navvies who were employed in the construction of the railway over Blea Moor on the Carlisle line knitted in their leisure hours. Until early in the present century, in the long winter evenings, the women would gather round a neighbour's fire to chat, tell tales or sing to the accompaniment of the click-click of knitting needles. Adam Sedgwick, who was born in Dent vicarage in 1785 and later became Woodwardian Professor of Geology at Cambridge, describes in his *A Memorial to Cowgill Chapel* such a 'ganging-a-Sitting' of his childhood:

> They took their seats; and then began the work of the evening; and with a speed that cheated the eye they went on with their respective tasks. Beautiful gloves were thrown off complete; and worsted stockings made good progress. There was no dreary deafening noise of machinery; but there was the merry heart-cheering sound of the human tongue. No one could foretell the current of the evening's talk. They had their ghost tales; and their love tales; and their battles of jests and riddles; and their ancient songs of enormous length, yet heard by ears that were never weary. Each in turn was to play its part, according to the humour of the *Sitting*. Or by way of change, some lassie who was bright and *renable* was asked to read. . . . She would sit down; and, apparently without interrupting her work by more than a single stitch, would begin to read—for example, a chapter of *Robinson Crusoe*. In a moment the confusion of sounds ceased; and no sound was heard but the reader's voice, and the click of the knitting needles, while she herself went on knitting: and she would turn over the leaves before her (as a lady does those of her music-book from the stool of her piano), hardly losing a second at each successive leaf, till the chapter was done. . . . Such were the happy family 'Sittings', in which labour and sorrow were divorced, and labour and joy were for a while united.

Southey gives one of those knitting songs in *The Doctor*, simple and direct as a nursery rhyme:

> Sally an' I, Sally an' I,
> For a good pudding pye,
> Taa hoaf wheat, an' tudder hoaf rye,
> Sally an' I, for a good pudding pye.

This they sang for every needle and when they came to the end they would cry 'Off', and then begin all over again, changing 'Sally' for another name. The income derived from the sale of these knitted goods, if small, was steady, until it dwindled and died in competition with the output from the mechanised factories. It is said that the value of woollen articles produced in Wensleydale and Swaledale amounted about the year 1823 to some £40,000 annually.

Another source of supplementary income for the small Dales' farmer was from mining, principally of lead. Lead had been mined in the Dales since the time of the Brigantes and the Romans. Many of the technical terms used by the miners reflected an Anglo-Viking origin —'wrowt' (wrought), 'grooves' or 'greaaves' (groves), 'toema' (bouse teme), 'meare' (meer)—and the name of the most famous of all the mines, Old Gang in Swaledale, suggests that the Anglian-speaking inhabitants recognised it as an ancient working. Bede in his *Ecclesiastical History* describes how Eadberth in the second half of the seventh century had sheeted the roof of a wooden church on Lindisfarne with lead; and after the Norman Conquest lead was much in demand for the roofing of castles and churches. In 1145 Count Alan of Brittany, Lord of the Honour of Richmondshire, granted to the Cistercian monks of Jervaulx Abbey the right to excavate ores of iron and lead within the Forest of Wensleydale. Some thirty years later Roger de Mowbray made a similar concession in upper Nidderdale to the same order, to the monasteries of Fountains and Byland—this was the district around Greenhow Hill, already mined centuries previously by the Brigantes and Romans. The main areas of Dales' mining were roughly two: Swaledale and Arkengarthdale with the north side of Wensleydale; and south of this the tract from Nidderdale west to Grassington with an extension to Malham. After the Dissolution of the Monasteries the Clifford Earl of Cumberland came into possession of the Grassington mines and those of Nidderdale passed into the ownership of the Yorke family; in Swaledale and Arkengarthdale the purchase from the Crown by Thomas Lord Wharton of the manor of Muker in 1544 (to which was added in 1556 half of the manor of Healaugh) brought the early controlling interest in the mines there to the Wharton family.

Until the seventeenth century prospecting for lead had been undertaken by independent working miners, who most often combined mining with the running of a farm or smallholding. In 1603 the Earl of Cumberland brought miners from Derbyshire to open up the mines on Grassington Moor. Throughout the seventeenth century mining in Wharfedale centred chiefly around Grassington Low Moor and Appletreewick. Early in the century the Greenhow mining village had begun to grow but many of the miners still lived on the farms in the neighbouring valleys. Others came to occupy cottages spread out along the Grassington—Pateley Bridge road. As early as 1546 Leland had been at Bolton Castle in Wensleydale and went from 'there to a place in a great Rock a 2 miles of where my Lord Scrope seeketh for lead'. This would possibly be the Keld Head group of mines between Preston-under-Scar and Wensley; other mines were in Apedale nearer Castle Bolton. Gradually in the seventeenth and eighteenth centuries companies were formed to work areas of consolidated leases, the best known being that promoted by Quakers, the London Lead Company, which was incorporated in 1692 under William and Mary. In about 1676 Lord Wharton's steward, Philip Swale, formed a partnership with Robert Barker of a Derbyshire mining family to work on lease Old Gang in Swaledale. In nearby Arkengarthdale the manor had been bought in 1656 by Dr John Bathurst of Blackfriars, London, who had been Oliver Cromwell's physician. The doctor had at first leased the mines (before buying the manorial rights) from the citizens of London, who had been given them by Charles I in payment of debts. His five groves (a unit of seam measurement) were worked by partnerships—four of four persons, one of three—who were paid according to the loads of ore extracted. Some twenty miners (one a widow) were thus employed. The Bathurst mines prospered and on the doctor's death the manor, and with it the mines, passed to his son Charles, whose initials (or possibly those of his own son, another Charles) formed the title of the famous C. B. Company, which operated the lead-mining in the dale. East of Arkengarthdale at Hurst mines that had been worked since Roman times were leased in 1718 by Lord William Powlett, the lord of the manor of Marrick, as a large-scale capital venture, with a stipulation that 147 men were to be employed.

All these undertakings gave employment to numbers of dalesmen, who might work a shift in the mines or be engaged in the ancillary occupation of providing turf for the smelting mills, timber and haulage, and other tasks, while maintaining their farms in the meantime. Both their womenfolk and children found remunerative work in such activities as dressing, crushing and washing the ore. An early method of discovering the workable presence of lead was known as 'hushing' and walkers on the high fells today may come upon the remains of these old hushes. On the hillside above where ore was thought to exist a dam was constructed. When a sufficient quantity of water had accumulated the dam was breached and the rush of water, tearing away rocks and subsoil, revealed (if they existed) the precious veins of ore. Work was then carried on with pick and shovel. Shafts might be sunk to tap the vein and these were either joined by cross-cuts or levels were driven straight into the hillside to meet the vein. Prospectors were permitted to try for lead anywhere except on enclosed land and, should they be lucky enough to find it, they were recognised as the owners of the vein and had the right to work it for the distance of a 'meer' (27–32 yards, 24–29 metres), the 'founder's meer'; the ownership remaining theirs for as long as they continued excavating on a regular basis. Men either worked in partnership in this way or as direct employees of the mining companies. One such independent partnership at Arngill in Swaledale discovered a vein that brought them £400 in eight weeks. A partnership of, say, four men would usually work in pairs in two shifts of six hours a day. On Grassington Moor in good times work would be carried on 'round the clock', in three shifts of eight hours. The extracted ore had to be dressed and smelted, then the pigs of lead would be loaded on to pack-horses and long trains of as many as thirty animals wended their way over the ancient green-tracks or rough stony paths—the jagger lanes—to the lead merchants at Stockton, Boroughbridge or Gargrave, thence to be shipped or otherwise transported to London and abroad.

At the beginning of the nineteenth century Great Britain was the world's largest lead exporter until production from the Spanish mines, where the presence of silver in the ore cheapened the price, and the output of Germany and the United States put paid to the industry in the closing decades of the century. A hundred years earlier, at the end of the eighteenth century, more rational management and an increased use of water- and steam-power, with improved machinery—such as that undertaken by the Duke of Devonshire at Grassington Moor—had led to a great increase in Dales' production. The Pomfret–Denys royalty in Swaledale (which included the A. D. Company), the result of intelligent direction and increased capital expenditure in Old Gang and Surrender mines, advanced from an annual average of some 583 tons in 1786–9 to 958 tons in 1790–3, and reached an average of over 2,000 tons in the years 1800–9. In 1801 Old Gang alone produced 3,252 tons; in 1858, when the output was at its height, the production of the Swaledale mines was 6,576 tons. The average price of lead was £27.5s. a ton in 1825; by 1894 imports from abroad had reduced it to a mere £9.11.9d. In 1801 the population of Swaledale was 5,699 and it touched its highest point of 7,433 twenty years later; then, with the decline and cessation of most mining in the dale, it fell to 2,483 in 1901. The palmy days of Dales' mining were a thing of the past.

Mining had not only rewarded the large capitalists but had also supplemented the earnings of many small farmers in the Dales; and its failure meant poverty and enforced emigration—Yorkshire miners taking their knowledge and skill to the lead mines of the United States and Canada. However, for the fortunate few the developments of the Industrial Revolution had brought wealth and an enhanced social position. One such family was the Knowles of Swaledale, who from humble origins rose in the course of the nineteenth century into the ranks of the county families. First mention of Edmund Alderson Knowles was made in 1796 as a small farmer, who joined in partnership with another to try for lead on Whitaside Moor. Their articles of agreement are dated 3 December of that year. Five years later he is cited as one of the ten shareholders, mostly working miners, in the important Lane End Mine. In addition to his farming and mining activities he was putting out wool for the hand-knitters of the dale; he had turned hosier and was soon the lessee of a neighbouring fulling mill. When Edmund died in 1835 his sons carried on the wide interests that he had built up: they had invested in the lead mines in Arkengarthdale, Old Gang and Beldi Hill and in the coal mine at Tan Hill; they were established as worsted spinners and built a steam-powered mill at Haverdale for the spinning of yarn and the manufacture of carpets. Other Dales' families, like the Garths of Crackpot, moved with the times and shared largely in the extended industrial interests of the dalesmen; enterprise was not solely confined to comparative 'incomers', who were primarily investors in lead-mining, rich men such as Dr George Robinson of Reeth or Sir George Denys of Draycott Hall, Fremington.

It was the impetus of the Industrial Revolution that broke down the barrier that had hitherto preserved the remoteness of the Yorkshire Dales—their inaccessibility. Earlier the roads were, 'in a very ruinous condition and, in some Places, not only narrow and incommodious, but also impossible for Wheel-carriages, and sometimes very dangerous for Travellers'. Private enterprise led the way, a series of Turnpike Acts providing for the construction and repair of roads and the charging of their users at toll-bars. In the 1750s the Keighley to Kendal and Richmond to Lancaster turnpikes were constructed; on the former the charge for a horse and trap travelling the whole distance was as much as 9s.6d. By 1770 Arthur Young could report progress, although he deplored the state of some of the roads over which he passed. The Turnpike Act of 1761 improved the roads around Sedbergh, through which the Lancaster to Newcastle connection ran; and along this, speeded the new public stage coaches such as the 'Lord Exmouth'. Another reconstituted road joined Sedbergh with Wensleydale, through Garsdale. Naturally the Dales did not lend themselves to the construction of canals, although the Leeds and Liverpool Canal was extended to Skipton-in-Craven in 1774. Most remarkable among the early road contractors was John Metcalfe, who, having been blinded by smallpox at the age of six, was known as Blind Jack of Knaresborough; along with Mother Shipton he became one of the most celebrated worthies of that town. Sightless as he was, he was able to swim, fish, play the fiddle and act as local guide through Knaresborough Forest; to become entangled with two women simultaneously and elope with one; to serve in the 1745 Rebellion; to deal in fish, and in 1754 to begin his innovations in road-building that were to revolutionise their construction. He died, aged ninety-two in 1810, after building some 180 miles (288 kilometres) of roads—one of which, through formerly an impassable bog, needed no repair whatsoever for twelve years after completion.

Improved roads and canal links were not in themselves, however, enough to open up the Dales. It was not long before pack-horses, wagons, barges and coaches became overtaken as the principal means of transport and communication by the auspicious advent of the railways which outstripped them in both speed and cheapness. On 27 September 1825 George Stephenson himself drove his 'locomotive' steam engine from Darlington to Stockton in neighbouring County Durham; nine years later the first goods' and passenger service in Yorkshire was opened between Leeds and Selby. In the forties Leeds was joined with Rotherham, and south by the Rother Valley with Derby and London; to the north the line was pushed forward to Skipton and on to Hellifield and Ingleton. In this same decade Darlington was linked with Richmond and the pigs of lead from Swaledale piled up on Richmond station. About the same time the Nidd was crossed at Knaresborough by a viaduct 90 feet (27 metres) above the river and a branch line from York reached Pateley

Bridge. From Northallerton a line was laid through Wensleydale to Bedale and Leyburn in 1856 and twenty years later it was continued on to the dale's head at Hawes. The extension of the line from Richmond to Reeth in Swaledale, although often mooted, was never accomplished. The triumph of railway engineering in the Dales was achieved with the construction of the Settle to Carlisle line between 1870 and 1875. This stretch passes through some of the most magnificent countryside in England, but the problems confronting its builders were formidable, demanding the highest technical ingenuity and a prodigious expense of human labour. And of life, as a visit to the little church of Chapel-le-Dale in Ribblesdale will reveal. There in the graveyard, within sight of the summits of both Whernside and Ingleborough, lie buried the remains of some hundred navvies and others who died in the course of the line's construction.

In summer the shanty towns of felt-lined huts which arose must have resembled those of the Australian goldfields; in winter, when roaring blizzards whipped up the blinding snow, they would have been more reminiscent of the Klondike. After rainfall they were a sea of mud in which wagon-horses sank up to their bellies. The names of these camps recall the Victorian era in its many aspects: Garlic Huts, Jericho, Battlebarrow Bank, Sebastapol, Salt Lake City, Batty Wife Hole and Batty Green. The last, near Ribble Head, at one time housed some 2,000 inhabitants and possessed a post office, school, library, a mission house run by the Manchester City Mission and a hospital built to meet the smallpox epidemic of the late spring of 1871 which resulted in the deaths of many. Life was rough, at times grim; beef cattle were driven up and sold on the hoof almost at the doors; drink was cheap and bare-knuckle fights were frequent; the Methodist missioners had their hands only too full. The difficulties presented by the terrain were taxing on human ingenuity and resources: at Intake Bank twelve months' tipping produced no visible effect; at Arten Gill it was necessary to dig down over 50 feet (15 metres) into the moor to strike a rock basis for the arches of a viaduct; the Blea Moor tunnel, 2,629 yards (2,403 metres) in length and in places 500 feet (152 metres) below the surface, required the simultaneous work of sixteen gangs for five years, excavating from either end and sinking seven ventilating shafts. Today in the summer the Yorkshire Dales railway runs excursion trains over this most beautiful section of the line. Leaving the Eden Valley the traveller passes down lovely Mallerstang, within sight of the ruins of Pendragon Castle; from the claustrophobic tunnels he emerges suddenly to find himself on a lofty viaduct, overlooking from on high the variegated greens of meadows and trees in Garsdale and Dentdale; and then he comes out into Ribblesdale and the sweeping grasslands of the Limestone country of Craven, with the pale greys of its screes and dry-stone walls and the towering masses of Ingleborough and Pen-y-Ghent; a jouney so unimagined in its diversity, so revealing of the beauty of the Pennine landscape.

If the coming of the railways facilitated and cheapened the movement of goods into and out of the Dales, it also did much to redress the exodus of the indigenous population, which accompanied the falling off in demand for hand-knitted articles and the closing of the lead-mines towards the end of the century. The railways brought the tourists. It was not only the rich who arrived in the first-class carriages, to greet the grouse on the moors with a fusillade of shot on the morning of the Glorious Twelfth, but increasingly from mid-century on the middle-classes found the Dales a pleasant place in which to spend their summer holidays and from the newly industrialised cities came the poorer classes to pass a day in the welcome freshness of the countryside. From the fifties enterprising carriers advertised their wagonettes at Skipton railway station, which met the trains from and to London and the Midlands and ran in Wharfedale, conveying the visitors between Skipton and Grassington or Bolton Abbey. With the better-off, educated Victorians science was much in vogue; amateur geologists, botanists, naturalists, speleologists and other earnest and well-informed enquirers abounded; and where better than the Yorkshire Dales to engage in their scientific pursuits among the wonders of Limestone, Millstone Grit and Yoredale Series or register their enthusiastic discoveries of flora and fauna? The cult of the Picturesque had given way before the study of nature, the Claude-glass before the collector's specimen box.

The Victorian shift from aesthetic to intellectual interest is well exemplified in the visitors to Malham Tarn House. Malham Tarn is high on the moors, some 1,300 feet (396 metres) above sea-level, between the valleys of the Ribble and the Wharfe. It is a lake of glacial origin, about half a mile (0.8 kilometres) square, lying in a hollow formed in the boulder clay on a bed of impervious Silurian slate, its water withheld by a moraine. The house stands in the woods on its northern shore beneath the Limestone crag of Highfolds Scar.

There has been a dwelling on this spot for at least 400 years but much of the present building was erected in the eighteenth century for James Lister of Gisburn, later the first Lord Ribblesdale, who occupied the house as a shooting lodge. In 1852 the Malham Moor, Malham and Kirkby Malham estates were sold to James Morrison, who left the properties to his son Walter on his death in 1857. Walter Morrison spent much of the year there until his own death in 1921. The eastern Victorian wing of the house and a 'Romanesque' campanile (recently demolished) were added by the latter and the mixture of architectural styles was gently mocked by his friend Charles Kingsley. Walter Morrison, who was educated at Eton and Balliol and was for a time a Liberal MP, was unmarried and immensely rich, his wide and generous benefactions being so discreetly carried out that he was regarded by many as an eccentric, self-absorbed miser. His one and only piece of self-advertisement was perhaps the little stained-glass figure in the Founder's Window in the chapel of Giggleswick School, 'the mosque with a copper dome', that he built at a cost of more than £50,000 and bestowed on the school, of which he was a governor, in the year of Queen Victoria's Jubilee. Although Morrison played the host to his house-guests on the occasions of the grouse-shooting, his own liberal and scientific interests are revealed by the celebrated visitors who stayed at Malham Tarn; among them such eminent Victorians as Henry Fawcett, the blind economist; Charles Darwin, Thomas Hughes, the author of *Tom Brown's Schooldays*; Lord Avebury, John Stuart Mill, John Ruskin, Sir William Harcourt and Charles Kingsley.

In his *Proserpina*, which was published in 1879, Ruskin underlined to his devotees the moral that could be learned from the contrast between 'distressed and happy wildness' among plants in a state of nature—illustrating the distress by the brushwood and undergrowth of an uncultivated part of his own garden and the happiness from a memory of his stay at Malham—'the thorniness and cruelty of the one, and the softness of the other'. The passage shows Ruskin at his best and his worst; the pathetic fallacy was never more evident.

The other piece of wild growth was among the fallen blocks of limestone under Malham Cove. Sheltered by the cliff above from stress of wind, the ash and hazel wood spring there in a free and perfect freedom, without a diseased bough, or an unwholesome shade. I do not know why mine is all encumbered with undergrowth, and this so lovely that scarce a branch could be gathered without injury;—while underneath, the oxalis, and the two smallest geraniums (*Lucidum* and Herb-Robert) and the mossy saxifrage, and the cross-leafed bedstraw, and the white pansy, wrought themselves in wreathes among the fallen crags, in which every leaf rejoiced, and was at rest. . . . In Malham Cove, the stones of the brook were softer with moss than any silken pillow —the crowded oxalis leaves yielded to the pressure of the hand, and were not felt—the cloven leaves of the Herb-Robert and the orbed clusters of its companion overflowed every rent in the rude crags with living balm; there was scarcely a place left by the tenderness of the happy things, where one might not lay down one's forehead on the warm softness, and sleep.

In 1858 Charles Kingsley was in Yorkshire gathering materials for a proposed book on the Pilgrimage of Grace, a work that was never completed. On 5 July he wrote to his wife from Malham Tarn House:

Here I am at a most charming place, built by old Lord Ribblesdale —now belonging to Mr Morrison, an Oxford First Class man. . . . The house looks out of fir-woods and limestone scars over a lake a mile square, and simply the best trout fishing I have ever seen. It belonged to the old monks of Fountains, and will come into the book with the old Percys and Cliffords connected with it. My largest fish today was 1½ lb (a cold north-wester); but with a real day I could kill 50 lbs. . . . I have got such flowers! *Actea spicata*, for instance. Tomorrow I may get some fresh species.

Four years later, when Kingsley came to write *The Water Babies*, Walter Morrison's house, the walks on the moors and especially the sight of Malham Cove were fresh in his mind. Like Dickens, Kingsley had a tender social conscience and in this book he did intend to try to ameliorate the condition of chimney sweeps' boys; and, like Dickens, he succeeded—the Chimney Sweepers Act, which forbade the exploitation of boys was passed in 1864. It is usually held that Sir John Harthover and Harthover Hall are modelled on Walter Morrison and Malham Tarn House. The story goes that Kingsley, asked to explain the presence of black markings on the face of Malham Cove, had replied jokingly that they had been left there by the sooty fingers of a little sweep's boy. Any such resemblances to Malham are confined to the first part of the story; the second part, which describes Tom's adventures with the living creatures of the river, reflects the Victorians' accurate scientific knowledge of such things; in the third part Kingsley mounts the pulpit, and ruins the tale. In Tom's escape across the moors Kingsley vividly depicts the limestone Craven landscape. Tired, hot and thirsty, Tom reaches the top of the moor, and looks over 'Vendale':

Below him lay, spread out like a map, great plains, and farms, and villages, amid dark knotts of trees. They all seemed at his very feet; but he had the sense to see that they were long miles away. And to his right rose moor after moor, hill after hill, until they faded away, blue into the blue sky. But between him and those moors, and really at his very feet, lay something, to which, as soon as Tom saw it, he determined to go. . . .

A deep, deep green and rocky valley, very narrow, and filled with wood; but through the wood, hundreds of feet below him, he could see the clear stream glance. Oh, if he could but get down to that stream! Then, by the stream, he saw the roof of a little cottage, and a little garden set out in squares and beds. And there was a tiny little red thing moving in the garden, no bigger than a fly. As Tom looked down, he saw that it was a woman in a red petticoat. . . .

So Tom went down; and first he went down three hundred feet of steep heather, mixed up with loose brown gritstone, as rough as a file. . . . Then he went down three hundred feet of limestone terraces, one below the other, as straight as if a carpenter had ruled them with his ruler. . . . First, a little grass slope, covered with the prettiest flowers, rockrose and saxifrage, and thyme and basil, and all sorts of sweet herbs. . . . At last he came to a bank of beautiful shrubs; whitebeam with its great silver-backed leaves, and mountain-ash, and oak; and below them cliff and crag, with great beds of crown-ferns and wood-sedge; while through the shrubs he could see the stream sparkling, and hear it murmur on the white pebbles. He did not know that it was three hundred feet below.

If the picture Kingsley paints is not that of Malham Cove, it is wonderfully evocative of the countryside, informed with the scientist's as well as the artist's eye for detail. Today Malham Tarn is National Trust property; the old house has been converted into a Field Study Centre, under the direction of Dr R. H. L. Disney. Walter Morrison is buried in the charming nearby village of Kirkby Malham, in the fifteenth-century church of St Michael the Archangel, his coat of arms appearing with others closely associated with the spot—Percies, Cliffords, Metcalfes and that of the former abbots of Fountains Abbey.

With the demise of the hand-knitting industry and the failure of the lead-mining, the Dales reverted at the turn of the century to their traditional economy—that, for the most part, of small independent pastoral hill-farmers. Butter- and cheese-making were still important among the cottage industries—the celebrated Wensleydale cheese, Swaledale, Cotherstone and others were the work and the pride of the farmers' wives. As the sources of work dried up, the dalesfolk departed in search of employment elsewhere, the men to the industrialised areas of the West Riding and Lancashire or the Durham coal-mines, the girls often going into domestic service. For those who remained life centred very much on the family and the local community; it was inescapably parochial, even people from neighbouring dales were looked on as foreigners. Marriages were most frequently made within the dale. In their leisure time, such breaks as their hard laborious lives allowed them, the dalesfolk had to create their own amusements: they had the weekly markets, the annual shows, the silver band festivals, the church or chapel choirs, the fairs, sports and dances. The widespread Methodism in the Dales frowned on the public houses. The men—those for whom self-culture was an incentive—might go to the literary institutes, where on the winter evenings they would find a glowing coal fire, newspapers, books and companionship. If this kind of life bred a self-reliance, it was not always conducive to a wide and varied culture; and if there were brilliant exceptions to this, and much good-neighbourliness, there were also boorishness, sometimes mutual mistrust and suspicion of strangers. The harsh way of life made too many purely physical demands on many dalesfolk and the chapel offered only an inadequate source of spiritual replenishment.

Mechanisation, which from the Industrial Revolution on had transformed the textile, iron, steel and mining industries, has only comparatively recently been applied extensively to agriculture and, more particularly, to that sub-division of it—hill-farming. In the Dales the farms are mostly small in acreage, consisting of meadowland, rough grazing and rights on the moors (sheepgaits, heughs or heafs). The raising of sheep and cattle is judiciously combined; there is very little arable; of crops hay is all-important, the mainstay of the pastoral economy. Traditionally when cattle were stocked they were not kept close to the farmhouse and a central milking place but scattered over the holding, the cows milked among the meadows and the stock wintered in the fine stone byres, which are such a feature of the landscape. The sheep spent most of the year on the moors, only being brought down at certain times, for example, at lambing and dipping. Up until the last war the depopulation of the Dales, which resulted in the loss of that occasional labour which was required to help out the farmer and members of his family at haymaking ('hay-timing'), had been made good by Irish farm-workers, who came over for the season, many often going each year to the same farm. Since then tractors and machines have replaced the handsome horses and the need for such intensive labour. The hay, which was cut from the grass-rich meadows, had not far to be carted, being stored in the upper floor of the byres, where in the winter it was conveniently fed to the animals below. This convenience, however, was offset by the necessity of the farmer making his way from the farmhouse to the outlying byres, often in atrocious blizzards, in order to feed, water and muck out his stock. The coming of the Milk Marketing Board lorries—and with the sale of the milk the arrival of a regular cheque—has brought about an almost complete cessation of traditional butter- and cheese-making, only few farmers' wives now practising this age-old art. More recently many of the less accessible farms have given up dairy-farming for the market entirely, concentrating on their sheep and on rearing and fattening their cattle; with this change has come the appearance of the great cream-coloured Charollais bulls in the fields and the replacement of the former pure Friesians or Shorthorns by cross-bred herds.

EEC membership and the existence within its common agricultural policy of subsidies for hill-farming, have made possible the erection of large byres ('stock sheds'), centrally placed, in which greater numbers of animals can be wintered. These have become conspicuous in the Dales' countryside, frequently to its disadvantage. Recent experiments in silage, mechanically carried out, have increased the nutritive value of the hay, besides facilitating the work and lessening the risks attendant on bad weather, of the hay-timing. Everywhere one goes on the moors one sees the sheep, most often the black-faced Swaledales, a local variant of the black-faced breeds native to the Pennine areas of the North of England and related to the Scotch Blackface. The Swaledale has gained in popularity in recent years; it 'has proved itself to be a bold, hardy sheep, well fitted to endure the hardships of exposed and high lying situations. It is of an alert nature and a good thriver. The ewes make most excellent lamb rearers'. Part of the flock of Swaledale ewes are frequently crossed with another breed (Wensleydale or blue-faced Leicester) in order to obtain a larger type of lamb for the market. Anyone who has seen the magnificent animals at the traditional gathering of Swaledale breeders in May at Tan Hill, on the border with County Durham, will not be surprised to learn that Swaledale pure-bred rams ('tups') can fetch upwards of £14,000.

Prosperity, to whatever degree, has come perhaps too recently to the Dales to alter radically the character of dalesfolk or the appearance of the landscape. In the last respect the powers of the Dales National Park authority to control unsuitable building, if at times used with consideration and tact, have not always been so happy —for example, in its refusal to allow the restoration of some derelict farmhouses, usually beautiful stone buildings of the seventeenth and eighteenth centuries. Dalesfolk have often resented the purchase of houses by 'incomers' for holiday purposes. Nevertheless the tourists and holiday-makers have brought a very helpful supplement both to the farming communities and to tradesmen; many housewives are glad of the additional income derived from the provision of bed and breakfast. Yet if times are more prosperous, memories are long. There are living dalesmen who can remember the shock of their father's death from an accident in the mines or goring by a bull and their mother's struggle to preserve what little there remained. They remember, too, evenings after school, when they did their stint in breaking stones 'the greets' for the maintenance of the parish roads. They are wary of economic or political panaceas for prosperity. Deep down they are conscious that they are dalesmen, in their being and their end an inextricable part of the Yorkshire Dales. A canny caution is with them the way of life.

Of all those who have written of the Dales it is perhaps William Wordsworth who best expresses that sense that comes over the minds of those who walk the high fells alone, the only human thing amid the solitude of nature and beneath the encompassing sky. I refer here principally to the meditative Wordsworth of *The Prelude*, who identifies that sense, or spirit

With high objects, with enduring things—
With life and nature—purifying thus
The elements of feeling and of thought,
And sanctifying, by such discipline,
Both pain and fear, until we recognise
A grandeur in the beatings of the heart.

For to Wordsworth

Above all
Did Nature bring again that wiser mood
To look with feelings of fraternal love
Upon those unassuming things that hold
A silent station in the beauteous world.

It is to such an observer that much will be revealed that is not immediately visible or explicable in the vagaries of dalesmen or in the unexpected vagaries of the Dales themselves.

CHAPTER 12

The Eastern Dales

THE CATHEDRAL CITY of Ripon stands upon high ground above the River Ure, close to where it is joined by its tributaries, the Laver and the Skell. From perhaps as early as the sixth century Ripon was an important centre (or a stage) in the Anglo-Saxon settlement of the western dales, as their tribal name *in Hrypum* would suggest. Prominent among the somewhat later Saxons was Bishop Wilfrid, a highly contentious figure during his lifetime, the upholder of the rites (and the rights) of the Roman Church, as was demonstrated by his stand at the Synod of Whitby in 664, by his personal appeals to the Pope, and by the council which was held on the River Nidd in 705, when papal letters confirmed him in the disputed possession of his monastery at Ripon. The *confessio* beneath the church that Wilfrid built was retained by the Normans as the crypt of the church they erected on the site of his monastery; the church which was to become a cathedral again more than eleven centuries after Bishop Wilfrid's death, when Bishop Longley was raised to the restored see in 1836.

In Norman times the manor of Ripon was held by the Archbishop of York and the great Archbishop Thurstan entertained a group of monks from St Mary's Abbey, York, there at Christmas 1132 and granted them an uncultivated, inhospitable tract on the archiepiscopal estates in Skelldale. Although Alfred the Great had created Ripon a borough in 886 and presented the wakeman and aldermen with the still-existing horn as token of the charter, prosperity in the Middle Ages rather favoured the monastic community at Fountain's Abbey than the royal borough of Ripon. Both lived from wool. In 1534 John Leland wrote of Ripon, 'Now idleness is sore increased here and cloth making almost decayed.' Only a few years later the great Norman storehouse at Fountains lay empty of wool. In Ripon at nine each evening since time beyond record the wakeman's horn has blown at the market cross: 'Except Ye Lord Keep Ye Cittie, Ye Wakeman Waketh in Vain.' By the side of the Skell, when the last visitor has left the abbey grounds, the silence is unbroken save by the plaintive cries of the water-fowl.

At the dissolution of Fountains in 1539 the abbey lands embraced a vast holding of some 30 miles (48 kilometres) from the boundary of St Wilfrid's of Ripon to the slopes of Pen-y-ghent in the west; and throughout this extensive region the monks have left their indelible mark: in the place-names of Fountains Fell and Fountains Earth Moor, in buildings, in the green roads—one would almost venture to say, in the way of life. For after the disposal of its properties, the economic basis of the monastery, particularly the sheep-rearing, cattle-raising and the lead-mining, was continued, transferred as the properties were into private hands. At its foundation Fountains was most fortunate architecturally in being granted lands by the Skell, in that it had on the spot a most beautiful stone for its buildings. Only a few miles to the west begins Millstone Grit country—a stone which, though having excellent properties for building purposes, tends in weathering to discolour, leaving ugly sooty surfaces that give the houses, however good architecturally, a dismal, dispiriting air—far different from the pale beauty of the limestone of Craven, or the calcareous sandstones. The magnificent edifices that remain at Fountains, considered in conjunction with the abbey's estates in the Dales, allow us to form a very clear mental picture of the life in a great Cistercian abbey in the Middle Ages.

The buildings that we see today were begun after the destruction wrought by the supporters of William, the deposed Archbishop of York, in 1147 by Abbot Richard and continued by his successor Robert, who, as a chronicle relates, 'restored the fabric of the church and constructed sumptious buildings'. Abbot Robert died in 1179. The next stage was undertaken by John of York (1203–11) and finally completed by John of Kent (1220–47). The main work, then, was carried out in the Transitional Norman and the Early English styles. The only major building after 1250 was that done by one of the last abbots, Marmaduke Huby, when shortly before the Dissolution he built the Perpendicular great north tower. The beauty of the architecture is perhaps best seen from the east, where the glorious Chapel of the Nine Altars, with its Early English lancet windows flanking the great Perpendicular east window, is reflected in the still waters of the Skell. Here can be appreciated to the full the crispness, the freshness, the sober delicacy of the Cistercian style of monastic building—something very near perfection. All this is enhanced by the exquisite quality of the stone—the palest of greys, but warm, responsive to the light, intensely living. It is a great pity that in the second, eastern transept (Nine Altars) the contrast between the pale masonry and the slim supporting piers, with their eight detached shafts of dark mottled Nidderdale marble can no longer be seen. (There are pieces of this marble in the abbey museum.) The beauty of this stone when used for domestic purposes can be seen in nearby Fountains Hall, built c. 1611 by Sir Stephen Proctor (the unscrupulous Collector of Fines on Penal Statutes), using material from the abbot's lodgings and monks' infirmary.

NIDDERDALE

From Fountains the *conversi* made their way over Pateley Moor into Nidderdale, to visit there and farther to the west the abbey's widely scattered granges and mines. John Buncle's Picturesque descriptions of Richmondshire, however highly imaginative, have a validity throughout the Yorkshire Dales: everywhere the traveller, after long traverses of often desolate high fells, descends from these lonely stretches of moor to find himself in beautifully wooded valleys, through which sparkling streams water rich meadows, with attractive stone-built villages, farmhouses and the greater houses, dating from Tudor times onwards, standing in their well-kept parklands —the unsuspected contrasts demanded by devotees of the Picturesque. Nothing could be in stronger contrast with the woods, hedges, fields and streams of prosperous Mashamshire and the Liberty of Ripon than the wild fellsides on which rise the becks that form the headwaters of the River Nidd.

The sources of the Nidd are on Great Whernside and the waters of the infant river are almost immediately caught up and held in the reservoirs of Angram and Scar House, which, remote and isolated as they appear, are only some 9 miles (14 kilometres) as the crow flies from East Witton in Wensleydale, little more from Masham and fewer than 5 miles (8 kilometres) from Kettlewell in Wharfedale. But this is another world, enclosed in its mountains; a landscape that betrays the presence of Millstone Grit, tough, dark, unyielding, so that its upper fellsides appear grim and forbidding. The dale quickly changes though and by the time the Nidd has reached the charming hamlet of Ramsgill the wildness has given way to a scene of pastoral serenity, deep-green meadowland and stately trees. Peacocks used to fan their tails beneath the sycamores on the lawns in front of The Yorke Arms. But they have gone, like the ancient family of Yorke, whose estates once extended over much of Nidderdale. Behind the rather meagre nineteenth-century parish church is the gable-end of a chapel raised by an abbot of Byland, whose abbey had property here, along with that of Fountains. From the churchyard in the evening a delectable view is to be had, looking south towards Gouthwaite reservoir, which, having achieved a settled maturity as a lake, has now more than a suggestion of some Scottish loch. On the north-western shores of the reservoir, above the road, the light grey stone of the re-cently renovated rectory and its terrace balustrade shows how out of place this material appears among the predominating gritstone.

Secluded in its pleasant valley lies Pateley Bridge, its houses dark from their millstone grit but relieved by the brilliant greens of its encompassing woods. This was a staging post for the monks of Fountains Abbey, close to their mines on Greenhow Hill, from which the ore was brought to be treated in neighbouring Smelthouses. Across the river at the hamlet of Bewerley abbot Marmaduke Huby built a chapel and lodging for a priest, which still stand; but the great house of the Yorkes that was here, was demolished in 1926, their sole memorial being some ruins known as Yorkes' Folly, which rise on the hilltop to the south. From Bewerley a road climbs steeply up Greenhow Hill, remembered by Rudyard Kipling, whose family lived for a time at Pateley Bridge, in *Soldiers Three*, with his Yorkshireman Learoyd. The road leads over bleak Bewerley Moor, with wide views over an expanse of moorlands, and past Stump Cross Caverns, spectacular for their stalactites and stalagmites, to Hebden and Grassington, the whole region being riddled with worked-out lead-mines. To the east of Pateley Bridge, a short distance to the south of the road from Ripon and Fountains, are the fantastic Brimham Rocks, a curious geological survival from Per-mian times, the product of wind erosion on masses of Millstone Grit, the action of fierce desert winds and sandstorms in a torrid climate, so difficult now to imagine here. From extreme heat to extreme cold: as the Nidd flows south-easterly and then for a while almost due east, it passes through what was once a glacial lake. Here the dale opens out and the landscape takes on the aspect of well-wooded, rich, arable farmland around Ripley.

Ripley Castle has been the home of the Ingilbys for generations —there must be few houses in England that have remained in the hands of one family for so long. In the late fourteenth-century church of All Saints, opposite the castle gatehouse, the Ingilbys were buried; one tomb, which was brought from an earlier church that slid into the river, is of Sir Thomas de Ingilby, who died c. 1369, and his wife. Their children stand by the tomb's side. Below a fulsome tribute to Sir William Ingilby (1618) are the words, 'No pompe nor pride. Let God be honoured', said to have been placed there by order of Oliver Cromwell. Traditions or legends have persisted about the activities of the Ingilby womenfolk at the time of the battle of Marston Moor in 1644. Jane Ingilby is said to have taken part in the fighting and to have returned wounded to Ripley. Thither, after the battle, came the victorious Cromwell, to receive a very cool welcome from Lady Ingilby, whose husband Sir William had sided with the Royalists. The chatelaine is said to have met Cromwell with a brace of loaded pistols on her apron strings, to have allowed him only a sofa on which to repose, and to ensure his good behaviour and that of his men, to have sat up all night watching. Asked later why she had two pistols, she replied that she might have missed with the first. Gunshot marks on the east wall of the church have been thought to mark the execution there of Ripley men of the defeated cause. In the churchyard is a circular pedestal with curious niches for penitents' kneeling, the remnants of a weeping cross of perhaps Saxon origin. In the nineteenth century Sir William Amcotts Ingilby whimsically adapted Ripley to resemble a village in Alsace-Lorraine, with its Gothic *Hôtel de Ville*, his castle looked upon as the *Schloss* and instructions at his lodge to 'Parlez au Suisse'.

At Knaresborough the Nidd has carved a precipitous gorge in the magnesian limestone, where high on the cliff overlooking the river and the magnificent trees on its bank stand the ruins of the castle built by the Norman Serlo de Burgh. It was here that Hugh de Morville and his fellow murderers fled after they had slain Thomas à Becket in Canterbury Cathedral. Following Marston Moor the castle was held by the Royalists, until they were starved into surrender by Fairfax; it was then dismantled by command of Cromwell. Cut in the cliff-face is a house, Fort Montagu, hewn by a weaver in the late eighteenth century, the laborious task of excavating his strange three-storeyed dwelling taking him sixteen years. Its neighbour is the curious little chapel of Our Lady of the Crag, long attributed to St Robert of Knaresborough, the monk from Fountains Abbey, who lived as a hermit in another cave a short way downstream. In fact the shrine was built under license from Henry IV in 1408. A third Knaresborough cave-dweller in the sixteenth century was the celebrated Mother Shipton, the veracity of whose remarkable prophecies regarding the march of science has not been diminished by her slipping up so badly on her last:

> The world to an end shall come
> In eighteen hundred and eighty-one.

From Knaresborough the Nidd flows on, past the field of Marston Moor to join the Ouse at Nun Monkton.

WHARFEDALE

The River Wharfe has its source high in Langstrothdale Chase, where the Oughtershaw Beck joins the Green Field Beck at Beckermonds (Norse, 'the meeting of the streams') and flows down Deepdale, past Hubberholme, where, after the confluence of the Cray and Kirk Gills, it enters Wharfedale, properly so called. As in the nomenclature in the upper reaches of Wensleydale, these Norse names betray the origin of the early settlers. Similarly, with the curious Yockenthwaite; but here there are survivals of still remoter periods in a Bronze Age stone circle and the remains of Iron Age settlement. These so much older inhabitants seem to have found Wharfedale to their liking for they have left their traces in more than one spot and especially lower down the dale at Grassington and Ilkley, the latter with stones marked with the mysterious cup-and-ring and the swastika, this apparently a fertility symbol. After the Conquest Langstrothdale Chase was a royal forest and at Buckden the king's verderers had their lodge to protect the abundant deer and game. The chase was granted by the king to the powerful Percy family and from them by way of marriage it came into the possession of the Cliffords of Skipton Castle. Up Wharfedale late in the seventeenth century trundled the lumbering coaches of Lady Anne Clifford. One can appreciate 'the good Countesse's' achievement today as one climbs the limestone terraces of Kidstones Fell beneath the heights of

Buckden Pike (2,302 feet, 701.5 metres above sea-level). The road up Langstrothdale Chase, which passes Oughtershaw Hall, perched among the trees on the side of the ravine, and the school there designed by John Ruskin, climbs to an altitude of just under 2,000 feet (609 metres)—it is claimed to be the highest piece of asphalted road in Yorkshire—before it descends Wether Fell to Hawes in Wensleydale. Winter is not the time to travel over these gaunt and sparsely populated fells; in summer they have their own austere beauty with the broad sweep of the moors, the bracing air and the lonely cries of birds.

In the churchyard of St Michael's at Hubberholme one can feel very close to these early Vikings, looking out over the hillside with its stumpy trees that is possibly very little different from what they saw. The church, however, is Norman with its squat west tower and low-roofed nave and aisles; and, inside and out, its roughly finished stonework. Here is one of the few rood-lofts in England to escape the destructive zeal of the reformers; its date is 1558, during the reign of Catholic Queen Mary. Perhaps the very remoteness of Hubberholme saved it. The pews are modern, carved by Robert Thompson and marked with his signature of a tiny mouse. On the other side of the bridge stands the George Inn, until recently the property of the Church but now in private hands. An ancient custom is still observed here on the first Monday of the New Year in the ceremony of 'land-letting', the lease of 16 acres (6 hectares) of pasture, the rent of which goes to the poor of the parish. The bids come from the local farmers, who constitute the 'Commons' of the bar; the 'Lords', the vicar and the church wardens, sit in the parlour. It is a social occasion rather than a parliamentary one, and conversation and drink flow freely before the landlord provides his customary obligation of luncheon. When this is finished the bidding begins and competition can be brisk until the vicar accepts the highest bid: the pasture is let for another year and the poor profit.

The road down dale follows the already sizeable Wharfe on its eastern bank to Kettlewell (Norse, 'Chetel's spring'), which lies directly below Great Whernside. A very steep road climbs immediately from the village street in a north-easterly direction. It passes the entrenchments of Venutius and his Brigantes on Cam Head and takes its narrow and gated way through wild, striking scenery between Cover Head Moor and Little Whernside to come down into the gentler pastoral landscape of Coverdale. The main road crosses to the west bank of the river at Kettlewell, but those with time to spare may take the narrow lane (with passing places), which continues to the east of the Wharfe to Grassington. This offers fine views through the trees of river, meadows and the great overhanging limestone cliff of Kilnsey Crag, passing beneath Bastow or Green Wood, a nature reserve, which in spring and summer is bright with a profusion of wildflowers, among them some rare and exquisite varieties. To the west of the Wharfe opens Littondale, with its Viking-sounding river the Skirfare, thought by many to be one of the most unspoilt and beautiful of the Yorkshire dales, set as it is in the Great Scar Limestone country.

From Arncliffe in Littondale, where in the church of St Oswald by the Skirfare are given the names (and the accoutrements) of local dalesmen who fought at Flodden Field, a road ascends by Cowside Beck and, passing Darnbrook House in its steep valley, crosses the flanks of Fountains Fell to Malham Tarn. Another road from Hatton Gill, higher up Littondale, runs below Pen-y-ghent (2,278 feet, 694 metres), to descend into Ribblesdale at Stainforth. The presence of limestone is visible in the frequent scars but it is equally evident in the smooth emerald surface of those beautiful grasslands, the turf springy underfoot, the grass close-cut from centuries' cropping of sheep, impeccable as a lawn. It seems as if Nature has covered over the bare limestone frame with a soft living pelt of greensward. This countryside was the source of the wealth of Fountains Abbey; on these fells grazed the monastic flocks in the charge of their shepherds and across them, following the old green lanes, passed the pack-trains of the *conversi*. Just to the south was the principal grange for their Craven estates at Kilnsey, and from it the ancient green track of Mastiles Lane was the monks' thoroughfare to the grange at Malham. In springtime Littondale is gay with daffodils and prim-roses and hidden away among the limestone clints grow rare species of wildflowers.

If Grassington, enmeshed in its maze of roads, is rather too popular for all tastes today, its popularity is clearly long-standing, since in the vicinity are notable monuments of earlier inhabitants from the Bronze and Iron Ages, from the Roman period and through-out the Middle Ages. Here are to be seen the round and disc barrows of Bronze Age peoples and the camps and settlements of their succes-sors of the Iron Age; the hut circles of the latter have yielded important remains and the field-system employed by the Celtic tribesmen is clearly visible. The discovery of a pig of lead dating from the age of Trajan is proof of the early exploitation of the mines but it was from the late sixteenth century on that Grassington and Hebden Moors became honeycombed with the shafts of the lead-miners. If Grassington was then a miners' metropolis, the exhaustion of the seams by the end of last century was succeeded by the arrival of the visitors, so that it has since flourished as a tourist centre.

The church of St Michael and All Angels serves the parishes of Grassington, Hebden, Linton and Threshfield, but it stands removed from all four villages, not far from the gaunt structure of the disused Linton Mill on the bank of the Wharfe. It is an unusual building, with its squat, square bell-turret above an early fourteenth-century west window, parts of the chancel being Norman. A writer, describing the church in the mid-fifties, praised the authorities for their trust in allowing their treasure, a little Romanesque brass crucifix, possibly dating from the ninth century, to be placed on an aisle pillar for all to see. Alas, their trust was misplaced; it has recently been stolen.

Linton village must be one of the most charming in Yorkshire, its houses clustered among the trees around its green, through which flows a stream, crossed by stepping stones and by a clapper and a pack-horse bridge, as well as the modern motor one. Across the green stands a surprising edifice, very splendid for so small a place. This is the chapel and almshouses of Fountaine's Hospital, which was founded in 1721 by Richard Fountaine, a member of an old Linton family, who made his fortune in London Dick Whittington-wise. The architect of this Vanburgh-like building is not known, Laurence Whistler, the biographer of Vanburgh, being uncertain whether it was by Vanburgh or Hawkesmoor or both. At nearby Threshfield are two seventeenth-century buildings of interest: the manor house, with its impressive three-storey porch and unusual six-spoked wheel-window and, just off the main road, the mullioned grammar school, which was founded in 1674. The village of Thorpe is so well hidden in its fold in the hills that, it is said, the local people in the fourteenth and fifteenth centuries took refuge here from Scottish raiders and were consistently overlooked by the marauders. The beautiful bridge at Burnsall is the successor to one which was repaired in 1612 by Sir William Craven, another Dales' Dick Whittington, who, born in neighbouring Appleetrewick, was Lord Mayor of London in 1610 and was also the benefactor of Burnsall in its grammar school and the restoration of the parish church. In Appletrewick, a village mentioned in *Domesday* and now with its three halls, Sir William is remembered in the pleasant inn of The Craven Arms.

The church of St Wilfrid of Ripon at Burnsall is approached by an unusual weighted lych-gate, possibly of the late seventeenth century. It is assumed that there existed an Anglo-Saxon wooden church when St Wilfrid visited Burnsall about 700. Remnants of some eleven gravestones of the Saxon and Viking periods have been discovered here and placed in the church, including cross-heads and shafts and two hogback tombstones; the font is remarkable for its Norse-Danish markings, although it dates from about the Norman Conquest. On the wall of the north chantry is a sculptured panel in alabaster, depicting the Adoration of the Magi, part probably of a fifteenth-century reredos. In the chancel are the arms of Sir William Craven, who restored what was possibly in the main a fourteenth- and sixteenth-century church in 1612.

Wharfedale, from Barden Bridge and Tower to Bolton Priory, presents a wooded landscape of quite incomparable beauty. There the broad reaches of the Wharfe, which temporarily narrow into the treacherous mill-race of the Strid, are enclosed within the magnificence of the woods, largely of oak and ash, and have as their background the tawny hummocks of the moors. From the height of the road the river, seen through the trees, sparkles over its rapids or gleams in sheets of molten silver. This enchanting scenery that so captivated the painter Turner is coloured deeply by the historical associations of the spot with the families of Clifford and Norton. History relates, and around it legend has embroidered, the events that took place here with strong contrasts of piety and tragedy. Both scenery and history had a profound appeal for William Wordsworth, who recalled them in 'The White Doe of Rylstone', 'The Force of Prayer' and 'Song at the Feast of Brougham Castle'. Turner's feelings —and perhaps his own—were expressed by John Ruskin in 1856 in *Modern Painters*:

> Up the valley the limestone summits rise, and that steeply, to a height of twelve hundred feet above the river, which foams between them in the narrow and dangerous channel of the Strid. Noble moorlands extend above, purple with heath, and broken into scars and glens; and around every soft tuft of wood, and gentle extent of meadow, throughout the

dale, there floats a feeling of this mountain power, and an instinctive apprehension of the strength and greatness of the wild northern land. It is to the association of this power and border sternness with the sweet peace and tender decay of Bolton Priory, that the scene owes its distinctive charm.

Ruskin in this passage echoes the response of Sir Walter Scott to the scenery at Greta Bridge.

The impressive ruins of Barden Tower and its chapel stand amid the trees on a height above the crossing of the Wharfe by the beautiful Barden Bridge. The original buildings, a hunting lodge of the Cliffords of Skipton Castle, were reconstructed by Henry Clifford, the Shepherd tenth Lord, after 1485, when the attainder against his father, Butcher Clifford, had been reversed by Henry VII. It was restored, like so much else, by Lady Anne Clifford in 1658–9 (she may have rebuilt Barden Bridge at the same time, since it is of that date), although her legal title to the property was, to say the least, precarious—but few would care to dispute with that imperious lady. After the death of the Butcher Lord, killed at Ferrybridge in 1461, the young Henry Clifford was romantically hidden away by his mother to escape the vengeance of his father's enemies and brought up unschooled among peasants loyal to his family:

> Love had he found in huts where poor men lie . . .
> The silence that is in the starry sky,
> The sleep that is among the lonely hills.

On his regaining his titles and his estates he spent much time at Barden, studying alchemy and astrology and keeping in close touch with the Augustinian canons at Bolton Priory. As an old man he led the men of Craven to the victory of Flodden Field in 1513.

The Augustinians were transferred in 1151 from Embsay, where the monastery had been endowed by Cicely de Rumilly in 1120, at the desire of her daughter Alice, when she founded Bolton Priory, as legend has it, in memory of the tragic death of her son Egremond, drowned by the faltering of his hound, as they leapt the swollen Strid. Found Bolton Priory she did; but her son was still living in 1154. Wordsworth made use of another legend when he wrote of the white doe that accompanied Emily Norton as she prayed in Bolton Priory for the soul of the last to remain of her martial brothers, the gentle

Francis, assassinated on Standard Hill on the further side of the Wharfe. Tradition also tells of the White Horse of Wharfedale, which rises from the Strid, foretelling a fatal accident there. At the Dissolution of the Monasteries Bolton Priory and its lands were sold in 1542 to Henry Clifford second Earl of Cumberland and from his descendants they came into the possession of the Cavendishes, dukes of Devonshire. Bolton Hall, built round the monastery's gatehouse, is a shooting lodge of the present duke. On the attainder of Richard Norton for the part he and his family played in the Earls' Rising, their ancestral estates in Craven also went to the Clifford Earl of Cumberland. Margaret, daughter of Francis second Earl of Bedford and third Countess of Cumberland, endowed in 1593 nearby Beamsley Hospital as an almshouse for poor women of the parish and this was subsequently 'finished more profusely' by her daughter Lady Anne Clifford. Today it stands in a state of neglect and disrepair, the garden a tangle of weeds and the little circular chapel in it, which seems to have been converted into miserable bed-sitting rooms, remains filthy and forlorn. After nearly four centuries one wonders if the trustees have kept their trust. Lady Anne, in emulation of her mother's charity, founded St Anne's Hospital for the same purpose in Skipton. It has vanished.

How perfect the Early English style of ecclesiastical architecture can be is shown by the lovely lancet southern windows of the nave of Bolton Priory, this part of the church being retained at the Dissolution to serve the parish, while the remainder was allowed to decay. The last prior, Richard Moone, not forseeing the fate that was so soon to befall his monastery, began in the 1520s building the Perpendicular great west tower, with its splendid traceried window which, however, masks the beautiful work of the earlier west end. Prior Richard's tower remained unfinished and unroofed at the apex of the window arch; it is only today, in 1983, in the restoration of the church that is now taking place that the work which Henry VIII's confiscation stopped is to be completed.

From the recently and expensively refurbished Devonshire Arms at Bolton Bridge a road runs east, passing Beamsley Hospital, over the moors to Blubberhouses and thence to Ripley, Harrogate and Knaresborough. Down Wharfedale the road continues, through the village of Addingham to Ilkley, Burley-in-Wharfedale and Otley, running between the tree-lined bank of the Wharfe and the high fells of Rombalds Moor and The Chevin to the south.

Long before the Romans built their fort at Olicana at the time of Agricola (AD 40–93), the fells above Ilkley were inhabited by prehistoric Bronze and Iron Age tribesmen, who have left visible traces of their existence in cairns, rock engravings, barrows, hut-circles, field-systems, enclosures and entrenchments. The famous cup-and-ring motif, consisting of an incised ring around a hollow cup, has been thought perhaps to be a sun symbol, characteristic of the food vessel culture of the Early Bronze Age. Specimens of these and pictorial descriptions of life in Roman Olicana, can be seen in the museum that has been installed in the early seventeenth-century manor house, which stands near the parish church of All Saints, both buildings being within the ancient perimeter of the Roman fort. In the churchyard three ninth-century Anglo-Saxon crosses have been erected. The tallest is of great interest, having on the front the figure of Christ above single twisted beasts and a pair of them in panels, and on the reverse the symbols of the four Evangelists as four draped half-figures. The shortest shaft, with a half-figure, perhaps of an angel, and single beasts in panels, could be as early as *c*. 800. Much of Ilkley dates from the nineteenth and twentieth centuries, when the town had a certain fashion as a spa; but a fine seventeenth-century bridge remains, though used now only by pedestrians; and on the hill to the north, overlooking it, stands the stone, twin-gabled Tudor Myddleton Hall, once the house of the Catholic Middletons and now a retreat of the Passionist Fathers.

Otley, the birthplace in 1718 of the celebrated cabinet-maker Thomas Chippendale, is today a small industrial and market town for the lower dale. Almost to its outskirts extend the grounds of Farnley Hall, standing in its beautiful 200-acre (80-hectare) park. It is owned by the Horton-Fawkes, descendants of an old Yorkshire family, whose undoubtedly most famous (or infamous, depending on how you regard him) member was Guy Fawkes. The family was and is Protestant, Guy being a convert to the older faith. He was described by a no doubt sympathetic observer, Father Greenway, as a man 'of great piety, of exemplary temperance, of mild and cheerful demeanour, an enemy of broils and disputes, and faithful friend . . . whose society was sought by all the most distinguished . . . for nobility and virtue'. A strange character for a would-be murderer but, as he said, 'dangerous diseases require a desperate remedy'. It seems that Charles I, son of James I, against whom his plot was directed, held nothing against the family, since in his difficulties he wrote to Thomas Fawkes, requesting the loan of £13. The Old Hall at Farnley is of Elizbethan origin but the existing façade is Jacobean. The present owner has recently demolished the large Victorian wing which stood on its right and in its place has made a pleasant formal walled garden, which is entered by a columned gateway, dated 1624. To the left of the Old Hall was added in 1786 a Georgian wing, which has been regarded as the masterpiece of the undeservedly too-little-known architect John Carr, 'Carr of York'.

Not long after this wing was built, in 1797 a young, shy painter, J. M. W. Turner, first came to Farnley Hall as the guest of Walter Fawkes, and the two men, very dissimilar in character, became friends, the friendship lasting, with many visits of Turner to Farnley, until Squire Fawkes' death in 1825. Early in his career Turner was very much a water-colourist and he was enchanted by the scenery of the Yorkshire Dales which he painted in all seasons, travelling incessantly in search of those striking contrasts that so delighted the Romantic taste. It has been said that Turner's first Yorkshire visit turned him from a talented student into the painter he became. Quoting from Milton's *Paradise Lost*, he apostrophised this northern landscape, which called out all the reserves of his latent talents:

> Ye mists and exhalations that now rise
> From hill or steaming lake, dusky or grey
> Till the sun paints your fleecy skirts with gold.

Walter Fawkes bought many of Turner's water-colours and formed a valuable collection, of which many remain today at Farnley Hall. It is from Turner's sketches of the rooms in Carr's wing that the present owner has been able to redecorate them in their early form so as to reproduce the interior of a Georgian house in an age when English cultivated taste could hardly be faulted. The result is both magnificent and exquisite, beautiful in conception and carried out to the last detail. In the drawing room, which is hung with the paintings of Turner and such contemporaries as Copley Fielding, the pale harmonies of Turner's colour have been caught up and reflected in the stucco-work of the ceiling and in the furnishing of the room, to provide, with the elegance of the white marble chimneypiece, a setting for the paintings that is quite perfect. The dining room is equally gracious, with its delicately carved chimneypiece and its grisaille panels by Theodore de Bruyn. As in these rooms, so in the lofty main hall, with its Ionic columns and great staircase; indeed, in all the other rooms of Carr's splendid houses the same exquisite standard is maintained. This is the other side of the Picturesque coin; the preoccupation of an age acutely sensible to the aesthetic criteria of taste. In this they were often, as here, admirably successful. And the grounds of Fountains Abbey prove, *pace* the Rev. William Gilpin, no exception.

CHAPTER 13

The Western Dales

TODAY MALLERSTANG IS in Cumbria but both topographically and historically it clings to its past as part of the Yorkshire Dales. Lying beneath High Seat (2,328 feet, 709 metres), between Mallerstang Edge and Wild Boar Fell—only 4 feet (1.2 metres) lower—where the tradition is that the last wild boar in England was killed, the dale is the catchment area for the numerous becks that descend from the fells and form the headwaters of the River Eden, which proves the exception to the rule of the Dales' rivers by flowing northwards to end its course in the Solway Firth. South of the village of Nateby stood the stronghold of the marcher lords Wharton, whose estates once extended into Swaledale. A farmhouse has been built around the remains of the mediaeval castle, of which a handsome gateway still stands, with the arms of the Whartons prominent above the arch. Wharton, Lammerside and Pendragon Castles—their ruins in Mallerstang are a reminder that this was once frontier territory, to be defended against the inroads of the Scots. This whole region is one of watersheds. To the south of Mallerstang, on Abbotside Common, is the source of the River Ure, which as a tiny stream flows south past the little Lunds Church and, turning east at the Moorcock Inn, runs down Mossdale, where it is joined by the becks of the remote enclave of Cotterdale under Great Shunner Fell. To the west of the Moorcock, beyond the railway viaduct on the Settle–Carlisle line, are the headwaters of the River Clough, which descends rapidly to the west through Garsdale to meet the River Rawthey near Sedbergh. Among the woods of sparsely populated Garsdale a number of becks from the north and south, from Baugh Fell and Rise Hill, feed the Clough, adding their waters to its own sparkling cascades. High on the side of

Widdale Fell passengers on the expresses to Scotland, emerging from the tunnels on Blea and Mossdale Moors, may look down over the trees and streams of Dentdale and Garsdale.

DENTDALE

Dentdale, through which the River Dee flows, is quite unlike the other dales in that it has about it a softness, even a gaiety, which derives perhaps from the presence of hedgerows of hazel and thorn and from the cheerful colour-washed houses, as if the inhabitants had deliberately put out of mind the harsh, grey austerity of stone. Even the cobbled streets of Dent Town (to give it its older name) and the huge slab of shap granite in its main street, raised as a memorial to Adam Sedgwick, its most distinguished son, serve to mark the contrast and to point to the surrounding landscape, at once so brilliantly green, prosperous and mellow. Both Dentdale and neighbouring Deepdale have something almost alpine in their appearance and this suggestion of foreignness must have been even stronger in earlier times, when the houses of the narrow streets of Dent retained their first-floor galleries. If it was from thrift, it was surely somewhat unfeeling for the inhabitants to pave the approach to the porch of St Andrew's church with gravestones, some with their inscriptions clearly visible; if the dead may bury the dead it still comes as a bit of a shock as a stranger to tread on their memories. This Norman-founded church, which came under the spiritual care of the monks of Coverham Abbey, has been much rebuilt but is chiefly Perpendicular in style. Remarkable are the Jacobean high box-pews of the sidesmen, with the monograms of former owners either carved or executed in brass-headed nails. These sidesmen (synodsmen, statesmen, questmen) have constituted a form of popular representation in parish affairs since 1429; they were, and are, twenty-four yeomen farmers, who, with the bishop, share the patronage of the living and still administer local charities.

Adam, the son of the Rev. Richard Sedgwick, the vicar of Dent for fifty-four years, was born in the old parsonage here in 1785. He was educated at Sedbergh School, took orders and, after being for many years Professor of Geology at Cambridge, died there in 1873 and was buried in Trinity College Chapel. None the less he remained a Dentdale man all his days. The much-travelled and voluminous writer William Howitt has a pleasant story to tell of his meeting with

Sedgwick. One day he and his wife were walking in one of the dale's narrow lanes, when they met a rough-looking countryman slashing at a hazel hedge. Stopping to have a word with him, they found that he was singularly well-informed on country, particularly Dales', matters. Howitt (who wrote a book entitled *The Rural Life of England*), in thanking him for his useful information, pressed a coin into his hand, telling him to refresh himself with a pint of ale. Some months later in London Howitt was present at a scientific meeting when, among the distinguished persons present, he was exceedingly disconcerted to discover in the Woodwardian Professor of Geology the hedge-cutting dalesman.

It was from a bench beneath a yew in the churchyard of St Andrew's at Sedbergh in June 1652 that George Fox preached to the crowd gathered in the market town for the annual Hiring Fair. On the following 'first day' Fox preached again, the momentous sermon on Firbank Fell. St Andrew's was described by Nikolaus Pevsner as being 'a typical West Riding church', that is, with a solid west tower, a long low nave and aisles, which are not structurally divided from the chancel, and with chancel chapels. Though founded by the Normans and with Norman remains, it is in the main a thirteenth-century church. Among the monuments of interest is one, with a bust by R. W. Sievier, of John Dawson, the shepherd boy from Garsdale, who worked his way to become a surgeon and is remembered as a brilliant mathematician. Before his death in 1820 he had been a most successful master (to judge by the senior wranglers he produced) at Sedbergh School. Another distinguished master at Sedbergh was Hartley Coleridge, son of the poet, although, dogged with failure as the unfortunate Hartley was throughout his life, his tenure there was transitory. The school was founded in connection with a charity in 1528 by a Howgill boy, who became Provost of Eton, one Roger Lupton. Suppressed with the chantry by Henry VIII, Sedbergh was refounded in 1551 under the grammar school legislation of Edward VI; from its early days the school has been closely connected with St John's College, Cambridge.

KINGSDALE

From Dent a narrow road between the hazel hedges and over-shadowed by immense sycamores runs along the western side of Deepdale. From the height the over-riding impression of the valley-bottom seen between the trees is the vivid intensity of its green. Beyond a waterfall that appears to tumble out of the trees by the wayside the gated road climbs White Shaw Moss on the flank of Whernside to the top of the pass into Kingsdale. From Kingsdale Head, at an altitude of 1,552 feet (472 metres), as the road descends the appearance of the landscape undergoes a striking change: the scars, the walls themselves in their shades of light grey, flecked with white, like lichen, proclaim that this is the Great Scar Limestone country, the terrain of the speleologists. The Yordas Cave, Jingle Pot and a number of potholes here give openings into that mysterious limestone underworld, a subterranean region of swift-flowing rivers, high waterfalls, lakes and pools, of narrow apertures leading to great cavernous chambers, of strange stalagmitic shapes—all formed by the erosive action of water on the limestone, where the acid-bearing waters have eaten their way through, until impervious strata have impeded their further passage. For some distance the Kingsdale Beck runs beside the road, its course as straight as if surveyed by a canal-builder, only to turn away before the hamlet of Thornton-in-Lonsdale, to plunge over Thornton Force and Pecca Falls in the verdant ravine that forms part of the wooded glens of Doe and Twiss at Ingleton. Ingleton with Settle is the popular headquarters for potholers, and these towns possess the advantages and the disadvantages that such popularity brings.

North-east of Ingleton, in the Ribble Head road, the White Scar Caverns, which are open to the public, illuminated and attended by guides, provide a comparatively painless way of seeing one of these underground river-systems. The brilliance of the light dry-stone walls of the limestone country in the bright sunshine and previous notions of crystalline formation of stalagmites and stalactites might lead one to expect these caves to reflect a similar lightness of tone and colour. But despite the electric lighting the rock through which one passes is of a sombre hue, glistening from moisture, dark, suggestive of nothing so much as the hide of a wet elephant. Any colour that there is appears to be a yellow-ochre, much like (to use another animal simile) the pelt of a waterlogged camel. If, then, the caves are a little disappointing aesthetically, they are nevertheless most impressive: everywhere one is in the presence of water, dripping, flowing, plunging silver over waterfalls and at every turn one is aware of the constant sound, from a just audible murmur to the swelling roar of the subterranean river. The White Scar Caverns and

Weathercote Cave are beneath the looming mass of Ingleborough. North of Ribble Head, where the road is met by that through Ribblesdale from Settle, are the Batty Moss viaduct and the Blea Moor tunnel, those considerable feats of engineering that cost so much in labour and in lives, in the construction of the Settle–Carlisle line in the 1870s. In the little church of Chapel-le-Dale a tablet was set up in 1876 by the Midland Railway Company and fellow workmen in memory of those men who lost their lives on this stretch of railway between Settle and Dent Head. It was within sight of Chapel-le-Dale that Robert Southey placed the farmstead of the Doe family in *The Doctor*, taking their name from the river which, joined by the Kingsdale Beck, becomes the River Greta—the second Dales' river to be so called.

The beauty of this limestone country in the aerial lightness of its predominant tone, with its bright green meadows partitioned by the pale greys, almost white, of the dry-stone walls, can be particularly well seen on the old road from Ingleton to Clapham. All the time among these rolling, grass-topped hills and frequent scars one is conscious, to the north, of the presence of Ingleborough. Away to the south, over the border in Lancashire, and seeming higher than it is from the level of the intervening countryside, rises the grey-blue contour of Pendle Hill (1,831 feet, 557 metres). George Fox climbed it in the summer of 1652 and here the Lord let him see 'atop of the hill in what places he had a great people' to save. A more perfect setting can hardly be imagined than that of the village of Clapham, the stone houses and cottages beside its beck and surrounded by the woods. Over the beck, that is crossed by ancient bridges, the nineteenth-century church of St James stands with its yews dark against the lighter background of trees, among them great towering beeches. Beyond the church, through the woods of Ingleborough Hall, following the beck past the still reflections of the lake, the 'nature trail' leads to the mouth of Ingleborough Cave between Clapdale and Thwaite Scars. Stone, water and the foliage of trees—this combination that the Dales offer so variously composed, is perfectly harmonised at Clapham. Still under the pervasive influence of Ingleborough, tucked away among the folds of the hills, are the unspoilt villages of Austwick and Wharfe, seemingly safe from the menace of the main A65 road, which runs through the Aire gap.

RIBBLESDALE

The northern edge of this natural pass through the Pennines is formed by the spectacular Giggleswick Scar, part of the North Craven fault, where the displacement of the earth's surface that has taken place is clearly visible in the wooded heights of the scar. Beneath it, a little way to the east of Giggleswick, is the strange phenomenon of the Ebbing and Flowing Well. Like Clapham and other Craven villages, much of the charm of Giggleswick (apart from its position by the stream in its hollow) comes from the quality of the building stone, which adds to the distinction of the seventeenth- and eighteenth-century architecture of its houses and cottages. The mainly fifteenth-century parish church of St Alkelda (a somewhat mysterious saint) contains a fine Jacobean pulpit and reading desk, once forming together a three-decker pulpit and its sounding board. On the pulpit the carved initials G.W. stand for George Winship, who was the vicar when it was erected in 1680; the panels contain the so-called badges of the twelve tribes of Israel. The reading desk is inscribed with the curious words: 'Hear is the Standardes of the Israelites when the Canan cam agenst the Cananites.' Much of the life of Giggleswick centres around the school, which was founded in 1553. High above the playing fields, which appear as an arena among the hills, is the school chapel, presented by the munificence of Walter Morrison in 1897.

Adjoining Giggleswick across the River Ribble is the market town of Settle. Old photographs show flocks of geese being offered for sale in the marketplace in front of the Shambles. This seventeenth-century building consisted originally of an open arcade of shops or booths on the ground floor, above which in Victorian times a first floor of living quarters was added. Pride of place among Settle's more interesting houses must go to the Folly in the High Street—which is perhaps not inaptly named, Pevsner finding the architectural style both 'capricious and wilful'. Its three-storeyed façade is remarkable for the lengths of mullioned windows and for its most curious doorway. In this the architect seems not to have made up his mind as to what style he should follow, the jambs being perhaps Italianate and surmounted by a lintel of what Pevsner could only describe as 'playfully arched Gothic forms'. A short way from the Folly is the little Museum of North Craven Life, that contains among its exhibits objects from the important prehistoric Victoria Cave, which is on the moors to the north-east of Settle, not far from the village of Lang-cliffe. Settle has its association with Sir Edward Elgar, who from 1882 frequently visited his friend Dr C. W. Buck there, the two men sharing a love of music and of walking over the moors. In 1885 Elgar dedicated his Gavotte for Violin to Buck and fifty years after his first visit he wrote, 'In this August weather I always live over again the holidays I had with you and the taste of *potted Ribble trout* comes with ineffaceable relish: nothing so good in eating or company has occurred to me since 1882.'

In the churchyard of St Mary the Virgin at Long Preston stands a Jacobean sundial dated 1667, and within the church a Saxon tomb in the chancel floor bears a cross and a pair of shears. The font too is of distinctive Saxon workmanship, although its date may be about that of the Norman Conquest. A ballad of a Long Preston milkmaid, Peggy Rathmell, tells of the equivocal relations of the inhabitants here at the time of the Jacobite troubles of 1745. Peggy, singing at her gate, seems to have given the glad eye to 'a noble Scottish lord'. When questioned by Lord Murray of Bonny Prince Charlie's suite, whether she was for him or not, and what was the name of the song she was singing, she replied:

> Arthur o'Bradley was the song that I sung,
> A song of two lovers who wedded when young,
> And it tells of old customs, which still do prevail,
> In Craven, in Yorkshire, and sweet Ribblesdale.

Her political allegiance seems to have been unresolved.

North of Settle the road up Ribblesdale passes through the village of Langcliffe, where the Jacobean Langcliffe Hall has a doorway that has been conjectured to be the work of the architect of the Folly in Settle. From the village a road runs to the Victoria Cave. This was discovered in 1838, the year after Queen Victoria's accession to the throne. The deposits in the cave have yielded the bones of animals of remote eras and warmer climes—the hippopotamus, woolly rhinoceros, elephant and hyena; also human artifacts from the time of the Old Stone Age to that of the beginning of our period, when the Romano-British sought a refuge here from the Anglo-Saxon invaders. A little to the north at Stainforth a road on the left, for Little Stainforth, leads down to a crossing over the Ribble at Stainforth Force. Here stands a perfect example of a seventeenth-century bridge, so steeply humped and narrow with its meticulous stonework; it is now under the care of the National Trust. In its upper waters the Ribble is not a beautiful river, but this reach of it, with its bridge and its cascades set against a magnificent backcloth of trees, rivals in beauty anything that is to be found in the Yorkshire Dales. From Stainforth a road runs over the moors below Pen-y-ghent to Halton Gill in Littondale; at Sannet Hall another road, branching right, leads to Malham Tarn and Malham Cove.

Horton-in-Ribblesdale is a centre for walkers and potholers, the latter having their choice between such descents as Alum, Churn, Hull and Gingle Pots and Long Churn and Gaping Gill Holes. For walkers it offers the gruelling test of the Three Peaks' Walk—the ascents, that is, of Ingleborough (2,372 feet, 722 metres), Pen-y-ghent (2,277 feet, 693 metres) and Whernside (2,415 feet, 735 metres), all to be tackled in the course of a single day. The parish church at Horton is dedicated to St Oswald, the King of Northumbria and friend of St Aidan, who was regarded as a martyr after his death in 642 fighting against King Penda of Mercia. The church has retained much of its Norman origins—the south doorway, the nave arcades and the font. The roofs of the two lych-gates and the paving of the pathway to the south porch have been made from huge flags of Helwith Bridge slate. There are notable remains of pre-Reformation glass in the west window depicting the Blessed Virgin Mary, the mitred head of St Thomas of Canterbury and part of the arms of Jervaulx Abbey, the Abbot of Jervaulx having contested the rights of Fountains Abbey to lands hereabouts in the thirteenth century. From Horton-in-Ribblesdale the road continues in a northerly direction to its junction with the Hawes–Ingleton road at Ribble Head.

MALHAMDALE

From the A65 Malhamdale is approached through a maze of small roads. Here, at Aire Head, between the villages of Kirkby Malham and Malham is the ambiguous source of the River Aire, whose upper reaches are typical of Dales' streams as it meanders through meadows in which cows graze lazily. It is only after Skipton that it loses its pristine freshness and suffers the industrial pollution that makes it a begrimed and turgid river, when it flows beneath the city bridges of Leeds. Airton, 'the hamlet on the Aire', has on its green a seventeenth-century squatter's cottage enclosed in its walled garden; and in the village is a Quaker meeting house of 1700 and its adjoining graveyard. Not far away at Calton the hall (now a farmhouse) was the birthplace of the Parliamentary leader, 'Honest' John Lambert. The extensive parish, which comprises the whole of Malhamdale and Malham Moor, is served by the fifteenth-century church of St Michael the Archangel at Kirkby Malham. High on the south-eastern buttress of the tower appears the coat of arms of Fountains Abbey: *azure*, three horseshoes *or*. Unusual are the niches in the nave piers, which in pre-Reformation times contained the sculptured figures of Christ, the Virgin Mary and saints. Of interest too are the Jacobean high family pews with balustraded tops above the patterned dado, one dated 1631. The panelling in the chancel was done in 1923 in memory of Walter Morrison of Malham Tarn House, the patron of the church, who is buried here. Higher up the dale the village of Malham is the centre for visits to the tourist attractions of Malham Cove, Gorsdale Scar, Malham Tarn and the limestone pavements of Malham Moor. This is splendid walking country; and up on the moors, far from the crowds, there is a freedom of spirit to be gained in the generous sweep of the landscape and in the constant movement of clouds in the embracing sky.

AIREDALE

From Settle the A65 runs through Gargrave to Skipton, the latter part being within sight of the Leeds–Liverpool Canal and the River Aire. Skipton, which lays claim to being the 'capital' of Craven and the 'gateway' to the Dales, is a busy market town, with its broad High Street leading at its northern end up to the impressive parish church of the Holy Trinity and next to it, set back on the right, the massive twin round towers of the gatehouse to Skipton Castle, the mediaeval stronghold of the Cliffords. Although Malhamdale and these western uplands were settled largely by Norse Vikings, the broader middle reaches of the Aire, the region of the gap, were earlier penetrated from the east by the Anglo-Saxons and it is they who are recalled in the name of Skipton, 'the sheep farm'. William Rufus granted the castellany here to the Norman Robert de Rumilly (the family name is spelt in various ways), after 1085 and it is to him or to his immediate successors that the foundation is owed of the church, castle and the mill on Eller Beck, immediately below the rocky eminence on which the castle rises. High Corn Mill is still in operation and it is fascinating to see its two great water-wheels turning under the impulsion of what seems so little weight of water from the beck, grinding the corn, as it has ground it for some eight centuries. On the disposal of the mill by the estate in 1950, it was bought by George Leatt, who opened it to the public as an Industrial and Folk Museum in 1970. But if these foundations and that of Bolton Priory were undertaken by the family of Rumilly, the history of Skipton is inseparably associated with another Norman family, the Cliffords, the barony being granted to Robert de Clifford by Edward II in 1309.

Holy Trinity is again a typical West Riding church with its great west tower, its low nave, aisles (battlemented) and chancel. Much of the fabric is of the fifteenth century and is therefore Perpendicular in style (Richard III on his accession in 1483 ordered a sum of money to be paid to Skipton church), but in the wall of the south aisle are a sedilia and piscina, which seem to pre-date 1350, and so are most likely to be from the earlier church. Beautiful features are the roof, which is of oak with richly carved bosses (those of the chancel picked out in colour) and the chancel screen. The latter was placed there in 1533, it is said (though this is disputed), as a gift of the monks of Bolton Priory, under whose spiritual direction the church then was. Little carved figures supported the rood-loft, which miraculously survived the iconoclasm of the Reformation, since apparently it was only removed in 1802. During the Civil War Holy Trinity suffered from the bombardments of the Parliamentary force besieging Skipton Castle, extensive repairs being carried out by Lady Anne Clifford, when she finally came into possession of her long-withheld patrimony in 1649. The church is the burial place of the Cliffords. To the north of the chancel in a great tomb of black marble with fine effigies in brass lie Henry Clifford first Earl of Cumberland and his wife Anne, daughter of Lord Dacre. The first Earl, the boyhood friend of King Henry VIII, died in 1542. Behind this monument is that of the second Earl, another Henry, who died in 1570. On the right of the sanctuary is the magnificent tomb erected by Lady Anne in 1654 to her father, the third Earl, George Clifford, the hero of the Invincible Armada and of many piratical exploits along the Spanish Main, the favourite of Queen Elizabeth I and her doughty champion. This monument exhibits all Lady Anne's pride in the ancestry of her family, the coats of arms displayed showing Cliffords quartered with many of the greatest families in the realm. And of her pride, it may be agreed with the words of the ubiquitous Garter: *Honi soit qui mal y pense*.

Little of the Norman work in Skipton Castle remains, the important exception being the gateway into Conduit Court; much of what we see is early fourteenth-century building from the time of Robert de Clifford's coming into the estate; the eastern wing, with its long gallery and octagon tower, was built in the reign of Henry VIII for the reception of Lady Eleanor Brandon on her marriage to Henry Clifford, the second Earl; the remainder is restoration and rebuilding, carried out by that indefatigable builder, Lady Anne, after the destruction caused by the three-year siege in the Civil War. In the gatehouse is a charming grotto decorated entirely in seashells, traditionally said to have been brought back from his voyages by the buccaneer third Earl but more likely to have been created in the eighteenth century. It is in the irregularly shaped Conduit Court, with its great yew tree, that Lady Anne's influence is most strongly felt, partly because of the Jacobean polygonal bay-windows. Off this court an outer staircase leads to the great hall in the north range of buildings. From windows high in this range the strength of the castle's position can be gauged, there being a sheer perpendicular drop on this side to the Eller Beck. Much of the history of the North could be written with reference to Skipton Castle, but even at the time of Lady Anne Clifford it was already history. This lends an irony to the motto she had worked into the balustrades of the gatehouse: *Desormais*—Henceforth.

From Skipton a road runs north through the hamlets of Rylstone and Cracoe to Linton, Threshfield and Grassington in Wharfedale. On the hill to the right of the road before Rylstone are the ruins of Norton's Tower, built as a summer pleasaunce by a member of that family who lived in perpetual feud with the Cliffords. East of Skipton it is but a short run to Bolton Bridge and nearby Bolton Priory, a place inextricably entwined with memories of both Cliffords and Nortons.

CHAPTER 14

The Northern Dales

TEESDALE

At Scotch Corner a main road (A66) branches left from the old Great North Road (A1) to run roughly westwards and cross the lonely stretches of what was once the Stainmore Forest, through Greta Bridge and Bowes, to Appleby, Penrith and ultimately Carlisle. Both modern roads follow the lines laid down by their original Roman builders. In the triangle formed by them and the River Tees to the north the foothills of the Dales disclose today so many relics of their former inhabitants as to constitute, incongruously in this rich, smiling landscape, a mausoleum of history. At Stanwick St John the vast grassed-over ramparts and ditches remain of the fortifications built by Venutius and his Brigantes, and it was here that they suffered their decisive defeat by the arms of the Ninth Legion from the camp at Roman York. Within sight of these earthworks is the rebuilt Norman church of St John the Baptist, which contains Anglo-Danish stonework, including the shaft of a cross with a hart and a hound preserved in its sculptured interlacing. At nearby Forcett the Normans built a church dedicated to St Cuthbert, using for their purpose fragments of tombstones from Anglo-Danish graves, which in their practical, unfeeling way they had probably taken from an earlier church on the spot and incorporated in the walls—stones carved with the figures of men and animals. South of the Stainmore road beyond Sedbury Park, formerly a home of the Darcys and not far from Aske Hall, the present seat of the Marquess of Zetland is the neat grey stone village of Gilling West. Once the centre of an important Saxon settlement, it was mentioned by the Venerable Bede as the scene of the treacherous murder of the saintly Oswin, the last King of Deira. Taking refuge at the house of a trusted earl, Oswin was betrayed by him to King Oswy of Bernicia and slain at Inget-lingum—Gilling. There, in the church of St Agatha—which is Norman in origin but was much altered when rebuilt in the last century—have been brought together both Anglo-Saxon and Anglo-Danish sculptural remains. These include a fragment, with what may be the features of two angels, and the interlaced head of a church-cross, whose fashioned shaft changes from roundness to a tapering rectangle. Professor Collingwood referred to the existence here of an Anglo-Danish fragment with the figure of a dragon in the Ringerike style.

A steep and narrow lane leads down to the southern bank of the Tees, where stands, among a small group of houses (all that remains of what was once the mediaeval village of Wycliffe), an ecclesiastical gem, the little church dedicated to St Mary the Virgin. As one approaches, the low thirteenth-century nave and chancel appear curiously roofless; within, one is struck by the beauty of the nave ceiling, tie-beams supporting a lozenge-shaped coffering in wood —the recent work (1963) of William Whitfield. The pews and communion rail are also modern, the carving by the 'Mouseman', Thompson of Kilburn. Despite nineteenth-century restoration of the east window the church interior reflects with a peculiarly intimate directness the faith and fervour of the Middle Ages. The remnant of a remarkable hogback tomb has been placed there: the animal with spiky scales and the head of a bear. Here too are fragments of two early ninth-century Anglo-Saxon crosses, one with a bird's head peering among the interlacing. In the Decorated south windows much mediaeval stained glass has survived: a Virgin with minstrel angels, the Trinity, Christ and two angels. A northern window glows with the rich mediaeval colours of armorial shields.

As the tombs and the register of parish priests show, this was the church of the Norman family of Wycliffe. In 1362 Robert de Wyclif was rector, to be followed the following year by William; in 1681 Ambrose Wycliffe held the cure. The greatest member of the family was, however, John Wycliffe (c. 1320–84), whom Protestants see as the morning star of the Reformation. An early authority, John Leland, states that the reformer was of the family of Wycliffe-on-Tees but that he was born at Hipswell just outside Richmond. Possibly through connections with the neighbouring Baliols of Barnard Castle, Wycliffe went up to Balliol College, Oxford, founded by that family. His reforming zeal won the support of John of Gaunt, who was pursuing for political ends an anti-papal policy. Wycliffe went farther on theological grounds in attacking the Church in some of its cherished dogmas concerning matters of grace, transubstantiation and the use of the vernacular. With the aid of his friends Nicholas Hereford and John Purvey he translated the Bible into English and his followers (subsequently known as Lollards), like the Wesleys and their disciples 400 years later, sought to bring religion closer to the people. If his ideas did not bear immediate fruit in his own country, they profoundly influenced John Huss and, through him, Martin Luther and the continental reformers. John Wycliffe must be regarded as among the greatest of Yorkshiremen. It is strange that another early translation of the Bible should also come from the hands of a native of Yorkshire, Miles Coverdale, from the dale of that name off Wensleydale.

The family house, Wycliffe Hall, which stands in higher ground to the south-east of the church, has an Early Georgian exterior forming a shell to the still earlier Elizabethan dwelling. The Wycliffes died out in the male line only in the last century, the last member of the family being buried not far away at Kirby Hill. The village of Kirby Hill retains to perfection the shape of an Anglo-Saxon nucleated grouping of houses and church around a green, in the corner of which an ancient tree now gives shelter to playing children. It lies to the south of the Stainmore road through the hamlet of Ravensworth, where the crumbling gatehouse and sections of remaining masonry indicate the former grandeur of the castle, once the stronghold of the baronial family of Fitz Hugh. From Ravensworth can be seen against the skyline the great Perpendicular west tower of the Norman church of St Peter and St Felix of Kirby Hill. Here, above the south porch sits the little sculptured figure of a man (some say that it represents King David), who is fiddling away, perhaps on a rebeck. In the chancel a memorial tablet to the last of the male Wycliffes was placed by his surviving sisters after his death in 1820. On the south wall of the nave is another memorial, that erected in 1558 to the rector of the parish, Dr John Dakyn.

It seems that Dakyn was the incumbent at Ravensworth in 1536 when he was caught up, perhaps unwillingly, by the insurgents in the Pilgrimage of Grace. At least after its failure he alleged in exculpation that he had been compelled by threat of force to join the rebels. A man of some means, he founded the grammar school which adjoins the church in 1556 and left on his death two years later funds to provide a trust to establish and maintain in perpetuity the almshouses of the Hospital of St John the Baptist. (The school, with its mullioned windows, is best seen from the churchyard; the almshouses are on the further side of the green.) Not only did Dakyn leave carefully written rules for the conduct of the boys at his school (it closed only in 1957), but also for the curious way in which trustees were chosen to manage the valuable Dakyn Trust, which is still in existence. This election is known, for some unexplained reason, as the Kirby Hill Races. Six possible candidates are selected for two positions from 'the gravest and honestest men of the said parish'. On election day the rector calls a meeting in the common hall and there in the presence of the villagers he writes the names of those pre-selected on a piece of white paper and folds them in a brown paper covering. Then the local cobbler encloses these packets in cobbler's wax, and they are placed together in an earthenware pot filled with water. From this the rector picks out two, 'as chance shall offer them'; and these are duly appointed. Afterwards the pot is securely locked away, since, should one trustee die during his term of office, another name is drawn from the pot.

Sitting in the gardens of the Morritt Arms at Greta Bridge, which is a quiet backwater now that the A66 has by-passed the narrow bridge over the River Greta, the visitor has time to reflect on the idyllic tranquillity of the spot. Behind him on rising ground is the site of the Roman camp, now a green meadow where the animals graze; to his right is the beautiful bridge designed (some say) by Sir Thomas Robinson of Rokeby Hall and built by J. A. Morritt in 1773; in front of him the gates (Doric in style, with a key-pattern frieze) to Rokeby Hall open on to the drive, through a park of splendid matured trees—magnificent limes, beech, sycamores and oaks. The estate was in the possession of a family who took from it the name of Rokeby, or Rokesby, from the time of the Conquest to that of the Civil War, when, espousing the cause of Charles I, they suffered heavily in fines and confiscations. From the Rokesbys it passed to the Robinsons, the last of whom, Sir Thomas, was a connoisseur in the eighteenth-century sense, a collector of fine art and a notable amateur architect. He was also a director of Ranelagh pleasure gardens and, it is said, a spendthrift who was ultimately obliged to sell Rokeby to J. A. Morritt, whose descendants still own the estate. Thus the property has been in the hands of only three families since the Conquest. It was Sir Thomas who designed and built Rokeby Hall with its strong suggestion of Palladian influence.

All this Romantic countryside forms the background to Scott's popular poem *Rokeby*: so popular was it that his friend, John Bacon Morritt, with whom he frequently stayed, had cause for mild complaint about the number of sightseers that the poem drew. In a note Scott described the 'romantic glen, or rather ravine' through which the Greta flows to join the Tees (the meeting of the waters painted by Turner) between Rokeby Hall and the mediaeval Mortham Tower:

> The river flows with great rapidity over a bed of solid rock, broken by many shelving descents, down which the stream dashes with great noise and impetuosity. . . . The banks partake of the same wild and romantic character, being chiefly lofty cliffs of limestone rock, whose grey colour contrasts admirably with the various trees and shrubs which find root among the crevices, as well as with the hue of the ivy, which clings around them in profusion, and hangs down from their projections in long sweeping tendrils.

Scott said that the whole spot so suggested ideas of superstition that it had acquired the name of Blockula, from its association with the Sabbath of Viking witches. The locals thought it haunted by a spectre known as the Dobie of Mortham. The aptness of these descriptions can best be seen from the single-span bridge over the Greta in the approach to Mortham Tower. This house, which so perfectly retains its Middle Ages' appearance, is centred on a peel tower, built in the fourteenth century as protection against Scottish raids. In its court, whose walls are trellised with roses and clematis, a weathered stone shield let into the wall shows the three heraldic rooks of the original Rokebys.

Upstream the Tees has cleft its way through a deep gorge, where the surface of the water and the banks are overshadowed by the greens of shrubs and trees in these beautifully wooded reaches of the river. Here, in an open space, rise the ruins of Eggleston Abbey, a spot today of great pastoral seclusion, where the white-robed Premonstratensian monks once worked and prayed. Nearby are two bridges, built at different times to serve different purposes: the old pack-horse bridge which crosses Thorsgill Beck and that which spans the Tees, the castellated Abbey Bridge, which was constructed in 1773. A mile to the west another bridge stands directly below the cliff, where 'the castelle of Barnard standeth stately upon Tees', as John Leland put it; the bridge of his time consisting of three arches, now diminished to two. William Rufus granted the place to Guy de Baliol in 1098 and it seems that the castle was begun by Guy's son, Bernard or Barnard, about 1112. John de Baliol, who founded Balliol College, Oxford, married into the Scottish royal family, whence his descendants claimed the throne of Scotland, only to lose it and with it Barnard Castle.

From Greta Bridge the Roman road runs with its characteristic directness due west to Bowes, then on over the moors, desolate enough in winter, with wide sweeping views to the south, the fells stretching away in seemingly endless succession to the skyline. If Bowes has its memories of Dickens and Dotheboys Hall and of the Normans whose massive keep stands by the church of St Giles, it is the Romans who chiefly come to mind on this, the legionaries' road across inhospitable Stainmore. In the church has been placed a dedicatory stone, found in the vicarage garden, with an inscription carved into the millstone grit. It was from the Roman camp of Lavatrae here.

To the Emperors and Caesars Lucius Septimus Severus Pius Pertinax, conqueror of Arabia and Adiabene, greatest conqueror of Parthia, and Marcus Aurelius Antoninus Pius, Augusti (and to Publius Septimus Geta, most noble Caesar), by order of Lucius Alfenius Senecio, imperial propraetorian Legate, by the first Equitate cohort of Thracians.

Its date would be c. AD 206.

There are the remains of two Roman signal stations between Lavatrae and their camp at Rey Cross; the first near Vale House and the other in the proximity of Bowes Moor Hotel, both stations situated a little to the north of the A66. During the Middle Ages a refuge was maintained about here for pilgrims and travellers, a house dependent on the Benedictine nuns of Marrick Priory in Swaledale. Its presence is recalled in the name Spital. The site of the Roman camp at Rey Cross is to the north of the road, that of the cross to the south. This very ancient cross once marked the border between England and Scotland. Holinshed in his *Chronicles* explains how peace was concluded between the English and Scottish kings, when it was agreed that:

> In the midst of Stainmore there shall be a crosse set up, with the Kinge of England's image on the one side, and the Kinge of Scotland on the other, to signifie that one is march to England, and the other to Scotland. The crosse was called the Roi-crosse, that is, the crosse of the Kinge.

It could, however, have had an earlier origin, as a boundary mark of the Norse Vikings.

The Tees above Barnard Castle flows through a countryside so 'picturesquely' described by Arthur Young in the eighteenth century, past the villages of Cotherstone, celebrated for its delicate cheese, and Romaldkirk. The latter is an attractive village, its houses and late twelfth-century church of St Romald grouped on or about the green, or rather greens—in fact, one is aware of the warmth of mellowed stonework and of the fine trees standing enveloped in their green lawns. Beyond Middleton-in-Teesdale the dale narrows and the geniality of its earlier character withdraws; the landscape takes on a grimmer aspect, a wildness that prepares the visitor for the basaltic uplands and the dramas of High Force and Caldron Snout. He is approaching, in the north-western corner of the Dales (not now properly the Yorkshire Dales, for he is in County Durham), a region of bleak moorlands, windswept fellsides, cascades and waterfalls, in winter unspeakably dreary and forlorn—the road between Middleton-in-Teesdale and Alston on the upper Tyne has been called the loneliest in all England. But in springtime this is a region that has much to delight the botanist, the habitat of flora left over from the Ice Ages, some not found elsewhere in England, rare species such as the little alpine gentian and others, like the common globe flower, the mountain pansy and masses of sweet blue violets.

SWALEDALE

Practically from its start, with its tributary becks rising on Birkdale Common and high Stonesdale Moors, the River Swale achieves a character that merits Swaledale's title as the grandest of the Yorkshire Dales. From its wild origins the Swale descends rapidly, fed by numerous becks, many with their waterfalls, so that when it has passed over Wain Wath Force and entered the narrow green valley below Keld and the rush of waters over Kisdon Force is joined by that of adjoining Catrake, it seems already to have triumphantly established its claim to grandeur. The movement of water of the two falls is enhanced by being seen through the foliage of the trees, the freshness of mountain ash, hornbeam and hazel. The walk by the rising riverside path to Muker, along the ravine between East Stonesdale and Kisdon, and descending to river-meadows, all encompassed by the high fells—first through the overhanging woods and then to follow the path over the fields, in spring carpeted with bluebells and with groups of primroses beneath the dry-stone walls —this walk confirms the judgement that few places in all the Dales can rival this in magnificence of natural scenery. As the place-names suggest—Keld, Angram, Thwaite, Muker—the upper dale was settled by Norse Vikings and they must have felt very much at home here, solitary in their mountain fastnesses. Later drovers and pedlars with their pack-trains passed through these remote uplands along the ancient Pennine Way.

Roads here, impassable at times in the long winter months, lead over the often desolate moors: up Birkdale to Kirkby Stephen; by way of West Stonesdale to Tan Hill and its lonely inn, reputedly the highest in England; over the Buttertubs Pass between Great Shunner Fell and Lovely Seat, with its splendid views of Swaledale and Wensleydale; and down the dale to Muker, Gunnerside, Reeth and Richmond, the 'capital' of Swaledale. Just off the road downdale, at the hamlet of Ivelet, is a curious, very beautiful high humpbacked bridge over the Swale, whose date is mysterious. Sir Nikolaus Pevsner said little beyond describing it as 'romantic'. It would seem that the present bridge was built in the last century but its design would surely suggest that it faithfully replaced a structure of the Middle Ages. From mediaeval times another rough track led down the dale to the parish church for the whole of the upper dale at Grinton; there were only chapels of ease at Keld and Muker. This was known as the Corpse Way from the custom of carrying the dead down the dale in wicker-made coffins on the backs of the dalesmen, to be buried in consecrated ground. Stones still exist by the wayside, where a halt was made for rest and on which the bier was placed, while the bearers took refreshment. A longer pause for the same purpose was had at Feetham at the Punch Bowl Inn, a very old hostelry, the present building dating from 1638. (The hamlet of Feetham has recently lost its name—which recalls the Norse presence here—by diktat of the Post Office, being absorbed in the ignominious nomenclature of neighbouring Low Row.) A road branches north-east from Feetham to Arkengarthdale, giving access to the ruins of the most famous of the worked-out lead-mines of Old Gang and Surrender. The entire district—Gunnerside, Whitaside, Harkerside, Arkengarthdale and Melbecks, Reeth, Hurst and Marrick Moors—is riddled with the disused shafts and levels of the former lead-miners. Reeth was once the animated centre of the upper dale. The population figures tell the tale of its decline: in 1821 it numbered, with its district, 7,433; by 1971 it had fallen to fewer than a quarter of this figure, a mere 1,639. At Grinton the parish church of St Andrew—a low-spreading Perpendicular building—was once served by the monks of Bridlington Priory. Next to it, on the site of the former monks' house, is Blackburn Hall, an attractive dwelling with hooded mullioned windows, built in 1635. Down the dale on either bank of the Swale are the remains of the two nunneries of Marrick and Ellerton Priories, the former being adapted for use as a farm as early as Elizabethan times. Marske, on the old Reeth to Richmond road north of the river, is a hamlet set in idyllic surroundings: a sunken water-garden, laid out by the former Hutton owners of Marske Hall, lies below the road; a fifteenth-century bridge crosses the beck, overshadowed by tall trees; and, on rising ground, the little church of St Edmund, essentially Norman, is half hidden among the yews. These reaches of the Swale, now become a lusty stream, glory in the luxuriance of the surrounding woods; in the spring by the roadside wild garlic shows white beneath great larches and in summer the road, lined with rosebay willow-herb, loses the glare of sunlight in tunnels of filtered green shade.

The newer Richmond road south of the river joins the old road from Richmond (passing through Downholme and Bellarby) to Leyburn. It was along this road that William and Dorothy Wordsworth walked in the winter of 1799, returning from a visit to the Hutchesons at Sockburn-on-Tees. Near Downholme they stopped and spoke to an old shepherd by a grassy mound and spring of water and learned the story of a famous chase of earlier times, which had ended here with the death of the stag. Cattle, they were told, still avoided the spot, refusing to drink from the spring.

'Something ails it now: the spot is curst.' Round this story

Wordsworth wrote the poem 'Hart-Leap Well'. Some little way further down the dale, the cliffs above the woods to the north of the Swale were the scene of another famous leap, that of a Richmond townsman named Willance, an event which took place in the first years of the seventeenth century. Robert Willance was returning from a hunt on a winter's evening when a mist suddenly came down. Missing his way and anxious to get home he spurred his horse over the cliff-edge, both horse and rider plunging 200 feet (60 metres) to the rock-strewn bottom. The horse was killed outright but Willance survived, although a leg had to be amputated. In memory of his escape he raised a monument at the foot of the cliff and presented to the Richmond town council, of which he was a member, a loving cup which is dated 1606. An ancient bridle path from Richmond leads past the spot, traversing Whitcliffe Woods, which have remained in a state of virgin forest, with age-old yews sombre among the dense thicket of trees and undergrowth. The walk is rewarding for the views over the wooded valley of the Swale and of Richmond itself, with its high Norman keep easily out-topping the houses and the Greyfriars' tower.

Not far beyond Downholme, between two sharp bends on the Leyburn road, stands a house of considerable historical and architectural interest, Walburn Hall, now a farmhouse. From the time of Henry IV this was a manor of the Scropes of Wensleydale, who possessed a fine deer-park here in Elizabeth's reign. Much of the present house, with its battlemented outer wall and pleasing oriel window, was built at that time. Parts of the buildings, however, may be earlier, dating from the fifteenth century; it is thought that the now ruined north-western range of buildings possibly contained a pre-Reformation chapel. The hall was long in Catholic hands and during the Civil War it was garrisoned on behalf of Charles I.

Richmond owes its very existence to its Norman castle, although as a military establishment it has never played a very stirring part in the town's history, save perhaps in serving as a refuge from Scottish raiders. The castle keep still dominates the town, particularly the large irregularly shaped marketplace. Here in an island of houses and shops stands John Leland's 'Chapel with straunge figures in the waulles of it', the Norman-founded church of the Holy Trinity, now the regimental museum of the Green Howards. The parish church of

St Mary is outside the old town walls. Its earliest fabric is of the twelfth century but the whole was much restored by Sir George Gilbert Scott in 1859. In the early sixteenth-century choir stalls, removed from Easby Abbey at the Dissolution, the seats have carved misericords, one depicting a pig bagpiper playing to two little dancing pigs. In the chancel high on the south wall is the monument to Sir Timothy Hutton of the Marske family, who died in 1629. The large effigies of Sir Timothy and his wife, Elizabeth Bowes, are kneeling and beneath them are the smaller figures of their children. From the coats of arms displayed it appears that one of the sons married a girl of the Yorke family.

The Yorkes had a mansion, now demolished, near the Green at the bottom of Bargate, close to the Swale. Part of their former estate still exists as a most beautiful enclosed park of 35 acres (14 hectares) almost in the centre of Richmond, the grounds today of Temple Lodge, whose entrance faces the western end of Newbiggin. Here rises the Culloden Tower, built by a Yorke in 1746 to commemorate the Jacobite defeat of that year, and a very remarkable edifice it is. Temple Lodge itself, which was erected by John Yorke in 1769, was described by Pevsner as a 'symmetrical essay in the Gothic', a castellated house with an arcaded front and ogee-headed windows. But it is the Culloden Tower that fills one with surprise. Little known architecturally, this is a delightful early example of the Gothick Revival, which antedates Horace Walpole's celebrated Strawberry Hill. The tower is high, built in good stone, in shape an octagon on a square base with pointed windows and a band of blind ogee arches between the upper storeys. The interior decoration is attractive: a room on the first floor has a very beautiful chimneypiece, Gothick with a suggestion of the influence of the Yorkshireman William Kent, and this decoration appears in the doorway and windows. The plaster ceiling shows Gothick ribbing. The floor above it has retained the earlier sober eighteenth-century classicism. Set in its park-like surroundings with a splendid view across the valley to Richmond town and castle, this building is quite unique in revealing the imaginative charm of eighteenth-century England.

Richmond holds much from this spacious period. The Georgian Theatre is not spacious; in fact it is tiny; but it is one of the oldest and best preserved of our Georgian theatres. It was built in 1788 when Richmond was a town favoured by the county gentry, with such amenities as assembly rooms (frequented by John Buncle) and a racecourse, a rival of nearby Catterick. (The course is something less than a mile on the high ground north of the town; the grandstand, built *c.*1775 by John Carr of York, and the starter's box have survived.) The theatre, where from their two tiers of boxes the audience applauded the performances of such leading actors of the day as Kemble, Kean and Macready, continued until the 1840s, after which it was used in various ignoble ways until it was restored with taste to its original condition in 1963 when Dames Sybil Thorndike and Edith Evans were present for its re-opening. Georgian echoes still linger in Richmond's many eighteenth-century houses and in one particularly on the heights to the north of Frenchgate, Hill House, the home at the close of the century of William I'Anson. The beauty of his daughter Fanny, who was born in Leyburn in Wensleydale, still remains in the well-known song:

> Whose charms all other maids surpass,
> A rose without a thorn,
>> This lass so neat,
>> With smile so sweet,
> Has won my right goodwill.
>> I'ld crowns resign
>> To call her mine.
> Sweet lass of Richmond Hill.

The writer of this lyric, Leonard MacNally, came rightly to call her his; at least, he married her. Another marriage of a young lady who inhabited Hill House was less romantic. At a somewhat later period Sir Noel Milbanke rented it as his Richmond town house. The Milbankes had possessed the estate of Barningham Park near Ravensworth since 1690; another beautiful house of theirs, Halnaby Hall on the Plain of Mowbray, was destroyed by fire this century. The Milbankes' claim on our memory perhaps rests on the ill-starred marriage of their daughter Annabella with that female-harassed, even henpecked, gentleman, Lord Byron.

A beautiful walk downstream from Richmond through woods and water-meadows leads to the ruins of the Premonstratensian Easby Abbey of St Agatha. Pevsner thought this 'one of the most pictures-que monastic ruins in the county richest in monastic ruins'. Near to the abbey gatehouse and within its walls stands the parish church, whose founding may have pre-dated that of the monastery. This is also dedicated to St Agatha, the serving priest, before the Dissolution, always being one of the abbey canons. Within the church is a replica of the Easby Cross (the original is in the Victoria and Albert Museum), the finest example of Anglo-Saxon sculpture (c. 800) in Yorkshire. The church also contains, among much of historical and aesthetic interest, wall-paintings from the mid-thirteenth century of Old and New Testament scenes. The connection of the Scrope family with the abbey is recalled by their sculptured arms on the porch of the church next to those of the families of Aske and Conyers. These links with the Roman religion are found again in neighbouring Brough Hall, formerly the seat of the Catholic Lawsons. The hall is at present being converted into modern flats but on rising ground before it stand the family chapel and adjoining presbytery in a state of seemingly sad neglect. It was not very far away, at Catterick, that St Paulinus once baptised converted dalesmen in the running waters of the River Swale.

WENSLEYDALE

The River Ure (anciently Yore) rises on Lunds Fell just south of Mallerstang and as it flows south and then in an easterly direction it is joined by numerous becks which have their sources on the broad expanse of Abbotside Common. It was up the Ure valley from Nappa Hall, near Askrigg, and over Cotterdale to Pendragon Castle in Mallerstang that Lady Anne Clifford led her bizarre household troop in the late months of 1663. The upper reaches of the river with its tributary becks are remarkable for their waterfalls: among them Cotter Foss, Hardrow Force (so accurately described by Wordsworth in a letter to Coleridge) and the majestic falls at Aysgarth. These last are seen at their best—and they have then in a high degree that awesome beauty required by the canons of the Picturesque —when the Ure is in spate, on a day of bright sunshine and preferably with a wind blowing. Then, from the bridge by the old mill (now a carriage museum) the upper force is seen, with no apparent source, against a high bank of trees: a tumbling mass of seething, foaming white waters, with touches of yellows and browns from the rock; its spray, caught up and billowing in the wind, momentarily reflecting the colours of a rainbow. Downstream the middle and lower forces are reached by a path beneath the low branches of a thick hazel copse: the roar of the waters reveals the presence of the middle falls in their narrow ravine before they are visible through the dense foliage.

At the lower falls the southern bank opens out and the stream, as if exultant in its release, surges and plunges in three symmetrical cascades over steps in the limestone rock. It is thenceforth a more leisurely Ure that flows serenely past Bolton Hall and below the beautiful bridge at Wensley. This seemingly Georgian bridge has, however, two pointed arches which may be as early as the fifteenth century.

Hawes, placed slightly to the east of the northern opening to Widdale, is a market town for upper Wensleydale, having taken over with Leyburn much of the importance held in the Middle Ages by the villages of Wensley and Askrigg. The history of this last has been faithfully and lovingly related by Marie Hartley and Joan Ingilby in their *A Yorkshire Village*. These two ladies have most generously presented their invaluable collection of objects relating to life in the Dales to the community. The Upper Dales Folk Museum is housed in Station Yard; not only are the objects of great interest in themselves but their presentation could not be bettered.

South of the Ure and feeding it by the little River Bain lies Semer Water, enfolded in the bosom of the fells. Something of the very early history of the peoples who once inhabited this enchanting spot is perhaps contained in the traditional story told of the deluge that overwhelmed the town which is said to have stood here, but now to rest below the placid waters of the lake. It was at the time of the midwinter solstice, so the story goes, that, when the druid priests were performing their rites within the town, an angel came, disguised as an old and penniless traveller, with news of the Christian tidings of charity and hope. But the priests and townsfolk rejected his message and hounded him out of the town. Passing on he came to a shepherd's hut, where the shepherd and his wife took pity on him and gave him food, warmth and shelter for the night. They accepted willingly the good news that he brought. Next morning standing on the fellside the traveller called down a retribution on the unbelieving and uncharitable inhabitants of the town, in words that all the children of the dale still recite:

> Simmer water rise, Simmer water sink:
> And swallow all the town, save this lil' house
> Where they gave me meat and drink.

On his words the heavens opened, the rain poured down and the offending town and its people were engulfed in its waters—all, save the shepherd couple and their cottage. On still evenings, it is said, people rowing on Semer Water have seen deep down beneath its surface the roofs and towers of the drowned town and heard the faint, far-off tolling of its bells. Such is the story.

Almost within the shadow of Brough Hill, on whose eminence the Romans built their fort, the houses of Bainbridge are grouped around the long beautifully kept village green. At nine o'clock in the evening from 27 September to Shrovetide benighted travellers have heard here since the Middle Ages the welcome sound of a horn directing them on their way—now to the warm fires of the Rose and Crown Inn, where the present horn is kept. This mediaeval sound has a particular appropriateness and continuity for the traveller down Wensleydale, as he proceeds from its wild beginnings, then is enclosed between its high fells—Abbotside and Askrigg Commons and East Bolton and Leyburn Moors to the north, and the heights of Wether Fell, flat-topped Addleborough and Penhill Beacon to the south; to emerge eventually in the very beautiful pastoral and wooded countryside of the middle and lower dale. For so much English history—from the Middle Ages, through the Tudor and Stuart periods into Hanoverian times—could be written with reference to the great monasteries and powerful families whose estates, with their abbeys, castles, mansions and manor houses parcelled out these rich and rewarding lands. Here is to be found persisting an epitome of the English nation.

To the north of Bainbridge over the Ure only the top storeys of Colby Hall can be seen above the bungalows built on the high ground in front of it—the planning people have slipped up here. Colby is a fine example of a Tudor manor house although it was built as late as 1633. Down the dale beyond Askrigg immediately below road level is the fortified house of the once influential Metcalfe family, still inhabited, although the great hall, which might have compared with the great chamber of contemporary Mortham Tower, is in a sorry state of disrepair. The original peel tower was probably erected by Thomas Metcalfe in c.1460. Tradition has it that Mary Queen of Scots was entertained here by a Metcalfe during her enforced stay at nearby Bolton Castle in 1568–9; and it was as guest of her Metcalfe relative that Lady Anne Clifford stayed in 1663.

Bolton Castle, which was begun in 1379 by Richard le Scrope, the first Baron Scrope of Bolton, represents the transition from the purely fortified castle to the more domestically conceived habitation, where considerations of comfort and even aesthetics influenced its design. Mary's sympathetic governor, Sir Francis Knollys, referred to it as a house rather than a castle, saying that it, 'appeareth to be very strong, very fair, and very stately after the old manner of building', and adding, 'It is the highest walled house that I have seen.' The Scrope stronghold to the north of the Ure had as its near neighbour to the south of the river the great castle of Middleham; of Norman origin it was a seat of the Neville family and 'the Court of the North' under Richard III. At Wensley the parish church dedicated to the Holy Trinity, which stands not far from the old bridge over the Ure and opposite the gateway to Bolton Hall, the present seat of Lord Bolton, contains memorials to the Scropes, in the late seventeenth-century family pew and in the beautiful rood-screen, which has been placed on the wall behind it. This is inscribed with the names of members of the family and came to the church after the Dissolution from Easby Abbey, of which the Scropes were lay patrons. This ancient family, which has remained Catholic, is today in possession of Danby Hall at nearby Thornton Steward, a much altered house, incorporating a peel tower of the fourteenth or fifteenth century. About half a mile from Thornton Steward, standing by itself among the woods and meadows, is the little Anglo-Saxon church of St Oswald, which the Normans repaired, retaining much of the previous stonework. Within is an earlier Anglo-Danish cross-head, with the Crucifixion on one face and a seated Christ on the reverse.

In the Middle Ages baronial power hereabouts was matched and perhaps at times softened by the influence of the monasteries—by the Cistercian house at Jervaulx and the Premonstratensian at Coverham. The Cover Beck, which disappears in places beneath the overhanging trees, runs through pleasant Coverdale and by its side rise what few ruins remain of Coverham Abbey. In the spring the dale is a delight with its wildflowers and it is likely that some of those found there—agrimony, hemlock, hellebore, mallow, cuckoo-pint, figwort and yarrow—derive from the herbal and flower gardens of the former monks. It seems appropriate that nurseries should have been established in the grounds of the house now standing on the site of the monastery and that these ancient plants are again being cultivated here. From the abbey the old road, running under the fells, leads past the fine mid-seventeenth-century Braithwaite Hall (now the property of the National Trust) to the charming village of East Witton, and thence to Jervaulx Abbey.

Today the ruins of Jervaulx, set in a beautiful wooded park—the church and chapter house, the dorters and fraters of the monks and *conversi*, their kitchens and offices lying, like the original cloisters, open to the sky—evoke a sense of calm and peace, of perfect tranquillity. By way of contrast the events that took place here at the time of the Dissolution come to mind—the brutal destruction of the monastic buildings and the treatment and fate of the last abbot, Adam Sedbergh. After carefully stripping the roofs of their valuable lead and despoiling the place of anything that would fetch a price, the Crown's agents finally employed gunpowder as the most expeditious way of demolishing the fabric. How beautiful the abbey furnishings were may be seen in Aysgarth parish church, where some of the exquisitely carved woodwork has been used to form a screen on the south side of the chancel and again in the vicar's chair, the latter with its rebus of Abbot William de Heslington—a 'W' and a hazel tree above a tun. The broad east window in St Gregory's church in Bedale is said also to have come from Jervaulx.

Abbot Sedbergh, imprisoned with leaders of the Pilgrimage of Grace, wrote from the Tower of London a graphic account of these final days in the life of the abbey:

It was on a Wednesday about Michaelmas Day then last past [29 September 1536] there came to the garth or court of the abbey of Jervaulx two or three hundred of the inhabitants of Richmondshire and Kirkbyshire, and among them the captains Middleton and Staveley. When [the abbot] heard that they were there, he conveyed himself by a back door to Witton Fell . . . bidding his other servants get every man to his house and save their goods and cattle. He remained upon this fell . . . for the space of four days, returning to the convent every night. During this time the commons wandered about the surrounding country and went to Coverham Abbey; then to Wensleydale, and thence to Richmond. At length, having heard that he, the abbot, had said that 'no servant of his should ever after do him service . . . that should go with them', they therefore turned back to Jervaulx, and enquired for him. They were answered that he was absent. . . . The brethren sent several ways to seek the abbot; and at last one William Nelson came to the place . . . and showed him that the commons would burn down the place unless he returned home. Through fear of this being done he went back. When he came to the outer gate, he was torn among the people and almost killed, they crying, 'Down with that traitor'. . . . When he arrived at the hall entry, Leonard Burgh, one of the ringleaders, drew his dagger, and would have killed him, but for them that stood by. Then he came further, where one William Asleby, chief captain of these parts, was, who said to him, 'Whoreson traitor where hast thou been?' and cried, 'Get a block to strike off his head upon'. There the abbot was commanded to take the oath, which he did; the said Burgh ministering it to him.

Poor Abbot Sedbergh was then to be caught between two fires and to perish at Tyburn. One of those who were appointed to administer affairs at Jervaulx on behalf of the insurgents was a 'Dr Dakyns' (*sic*), probably that other reluctant (but more fortunate) rebel, the rector of Ravensworth and Kirby Hill. In a cell in the Tower of London is inscribed on the wall the name of Adam Sedbar and the date 1537.

In 1329 the manor of Masham was bought by Sir Geoffrey le Scrope, passing on his death in 1340 to his son Henry, who became first Lord Scrope of Masham. It was the latter's son, Richard, who as Archbishop of York, sided with the Percies against King Henry IV and paid for it with his life—the 'good Archbishop Scrope'. A grandson of the first lord, another Henry, was blasted to obloquy by the rhetoric of Shakespeare's *Henry V* for his part in the South-ampton conspiracy:

> But, O,
> What shall I say to thee, Lord Scrope, thou cruel,
> Ingrateful, savage, and inhuman creature!

In the parish church of St Mary the Virgin at Masham, which is part Norman, are monuments to the Danbys, who succeeded the Scropes as lords of the manor; one is that in alabaster of Magdalen Danby and her husband Sir Marmaduke Wyvill, with their reclining figures attended by Father Time and a cherub who is blowing soap bubbles. The neighbouring Wyvills were the possessors of two interesting houses: the early (perhaps thirteenth-century in part) Low Burton Hall and Constable Burton Hall, a most beautiful example of the English Palladian style, built in 1762 by John Carr of York. Outside the entrance porch to St Mary's stands the substantial shaft of an early ninth-century Anglo-Saxon cross, decorated with figures in four tiers, animals, and scenes from some unidentifiable legend.

A high avenue of ancient limes leads to Snape Castle, once a stronghold of the Nevilles and long in the possession of a junior branch of the family with the title of Lords Latimer. Richard, the second Lord Latimer, led the troops from Mashamshire to victory at Flodden Field in 1513. His eldest son, John third Lord Latimer, was implicated in the Pilgrimage of Grace and was one of the four nobles who on the part of the rebels treated with King Henry VIII. He had married Catherine Parr and on his death in 1542 his widow married the king, whom she was fortunate enough to survive. Catherine subsequently married again (for the fourth time), her choice being a former lover, Sir Thomas Seymour. In 1577 Dorothy Neville, the heiress of the manor of Snape, married Thomas Cecil, son of William Cecil, Lord Burghley, the chief minister of Elizabeth I, and it is to Cecil that much of the present buildings, including the Perpendicular chapel, is owed. Later, towards the end of the eighteenth century the estates of Snape and nearby Well were bought by the Milbankes of Barningham, Halnaby and Thorpe Perrow.

The church of St Michael the Archangel at Well has been seen as a fitting memorial to the Nevilles, one of the greatest families of the North of England. Ralph Neville, who inherited the manors of Snape and Well from his grandmother, Mary of Middleham, together with Henry Lord Percy led the English forces at the battle of Neville's Cross in 1346, when the Scots were routed and King David II taken prisoner. It was Ralph who some time between 1320 and 1350 rebuilt the Norman church dedicated to St Michael. In the east window of the south chapel the victory over the Scots is recalled in the contemporary stained glass window: the arms of Neville, Percy and Ros appear above four knights, each bearing the Neville saltire —this lower part of the window has been most unfortunately restored. The font cover with its delicate tracery would appear to have been placed there by Ralph Neville, its date 1352 suggesting that it is among the earliest to survive in the country. Ralph also founded and endowed the adjoining Hospital of St Michael, a refuge for twelve poor men and twelve poor women, governed by a master and two priests who were lodged next door in Well House. The present most beautiful almshouses are said to have been erected in 1758 by the Cecils but seem from the architecture to be earlier. The tomb of Sir John Neville, the fourth and last Lord Latimer, who died in 1577, which is in the south chapel, has on it graffiti bearing the names of neighbouring gentry: among others, those as well known as Danby, Bowes, Lumley and Ireton. Of the existing memorials—many of the Nevilles not having survived the drastic restoration of the church in 1852—are those of the Milbanke family, and there is also one to Francis Burdett Money Coutts, in whom the barony of Latimer was revived in 1912, after being in abeyance for over 300 years. A section of floor mosaic from the nearby Roman villa was placed in the church after it had been recovered in the last century.

The village of West Tanfield stands on the northern bank of the Ure: right by the riverside rises the fifteenth- to sixteenth-century Marmion gateway, with its lovely oriel window, all that remains of the castle of the Marmions. Beside it is the parish church dedicated to St Nicholas, and within are Marmion family tombs of the thirteenth and fourteenth centuries. One (possibly of Sir John Marmion, who died in 1387, and his wife) in alabaster is of a type extremely rare, in that it is placed below an iron hearse, for holding dedicatory candles. Miraculously it escaped the iconoclasm of the reformers. In the church of St Mary the Virgin in neighbouring Wath the west window of the transept (the Norton Chapel) has a heraldic shield of fourteen quarterings, thought to be that of Sir Henry Fitz Hugh, of the Ravensworth family, lord of the manor of Wath, who died in 1472. This impales the arms of his wife, Alice Neville, sister of Richard Earl of Warwick, the 'Kingmaker'. In the chapel are the brass effigies of Richard Norton, who was chief justice in 1413, and his wife Katherine. The beautiful house of Norton Conyers in the parish of Wath was remodelled some time in the seventeenth century. This has incorporated the earlier house of the warlike Nortons, the inveterate enemies of the Cliffords and the Catholic upholders of the traditional feudalism of the North against the innovation of a centralised (southern) monarchy. From here Richard Norton rode off in November 1569 to join the earls in the Rising of the North, and with him went his six sons and his brother Thomas. The failure of the rebellion meant his attainder, the execution of two of the family and the forfeiture of their estates. In 1630 Norton Conyers was bought by Sir Richard Graham and his descendants still possess it.

It would be hard to imagine a more typically English landscape than these middle reaches of the Ure, as it flows past well-wooded hills and fertile water-meadows. These are a perfect foil to those upland regions of high moors, mountainous tracts and beautiful intervening valleys. Together they present to an uncommon degree that conjunction of great scenic beauty with deep historical interest which distinguishes the Dales of Yorkshire.

Select Bibliography

Amory, T., *Life and Opinion of J. Buncle, Esq.*, London, 1904

Aveling, H., *The Catholic Recusants of the West Riding of Yorkshire*, Leeds, 1964

—— *Northern Catholics*, London, 1966

Aveling, J. C. H., *The Handle and the Axe*, London, 1976

Ayling, S. E., *John Wesley*, London, 1979

Bede, *Ecclesiastical History of the English Nation*, London, 1870

Butler, R. M., (editor), *Soldier and Civilian in Roman Yorkshire*, London, 1971

Chitty, S., *The Beast and the Monk*, London, 1975

Collingwood, R. G., and Myers, J. N. L., *Roman Britain and the English Settlements*, Oxford, 1936

Cooper, E., *A History of Swaledale*, Clapham, 1973

Darby, H. C., and Maxwell, I. S., *The Domesday Geography for North of England*, Cambridge, 1962

Defoe, D., *A Tour through the Whole Island of Great Britain*, London, 1962 edition

Dewhurst, I., *Yorkshire through the Years*, London, 1975

Dickens, C., *Nicholas Nickleby*, London, 1839

Fieldhouse, R., and Jennings, B., *History of Richmond and Swaledale*, Chichester, 1978

Fiennes, C., *The Journeys of Celia Fiennes (1698)*, London, 1947

Fletcher, J. S., *Picturesque Yorkshire* (3 vols.), London, 1899–1901

Gillingham, J., *The Wars of the Roses*, London, 1981

Gilpin, W., *Observations Chiefly Relating to Picturesque Beauty*, 2 vols, London, 1786

Graham, R., *English Ecclesiastical Studies*, London, 1929

Gray, T., *Correspondence*, Oxford, 1933

Harland, O., *Yorkshire North Riding*, London, 1951

Hartley, M., and Ingilby, J., *The Yorkshire Dales*, London, 1956

—— *Life and Tradition in the Yorkshire Dales*, London, 1968

—— *A Dales Heritage*, London, 1982

Hindle, A., *Literary Visitors to Yorkshire*, Ormskirk, Lancs., 1981

Holmes, M., *Proud Northern Lady*, London and Chichester, 1975

Hussey, C., *The Picturesque*, London and New York, 1927

Kendal, P. F., and Wroot, H. E., *The Geology of Yorkshire*, Wakefield, 1972

Kendall, P. M., *Richard the Third*, London, 1955

Kingsley, C., *The Water Babies*, London, 1891

Knowles, D., *The Religious Orders in England*, Cambridge, 1962

—— *The Monastic Order in England*, Cambridge, 1966

Mainwaring, E. W., *Italian Landscape in 18th-Century England*, New York, 1925

Mancini, D., *The Usurpation of Richard III*, C. A. J. Armstrong (ed.), Oxford, 1936

Mee, A., *Yorkshire, West Riding*, London, 1969

—— *Yorkshire, North Riding*, London, 1970

Mitchell, W. R., *Wild Pennines*, London, 1976

Moorman, M., *Wm. Wordsworth: Early Years*, Oxford, 1957

—— *Wm. Wordsworth: Late Years*, Oxford, 1965

Morris, J., *The Age of Arthur*, London, 1973

Pocock, M., *A History of Yorkshire*, York, 1978

Raistrick, A., *The Romans in Yorkshire*, Clapham, 1972

—— *Vikings, Angles and Danes in Yorkshire*, Clapham, 1965

—— *West Riding of Yorkshire*, London, 1970

— and Jennings, B., *A History of Lead Mining in the Pennines*, London, 1965

Ruskin, J., *Proserpina*, London, 1879

Scott, H. J., *Yorkshire Heritage*, London, 1970

—— *Portrait of Yorkshire*, London, 1965

Sedgwick, A., *A Memorial of Cowgill Chapel*, London, 1868

Smith, A. H., *Place-Names of North Riding of Yorkshire*, Cambridge, 1928

Southey, R., *The Doctor*, London, 1898

Speight, H., *Romantic Richmondshire*, London, 1897

Stenton, F. M., *Anglo-Saxon England*, Oxford, 1943

Tacitus, P. C., *Annals*, London, 1907

—— *Agricola*, Furneaux, H. (ed.), Oxford, 1922

Taylor, E., *The Valiant Sixty*, London, 1951

Victoria County Histories: Yorkshire, North Riding, West Riding, London, 1907

Wainwright, F. T., *Scandinavian England*, Chichester, 1975

Wesley, J., *Journals*, London, 1938 edition

Wheeler, M., *The Stanwick Fortifications*, London, 1954

Whitaker, T. D., *History of Craven*, London, 1803

—— *History of Richmondshire*, London, 1823

Wildes, H. E., *Voice of the Lord*, Philadelphia, 1965

Williamson, G. C., *Lady Anne Clifford*, Kendal, 1922

Wood, G. B., *Yorkshire Villages*, London, 1971

Wordsworth, *Poetical Works*, London, 1930

Young, A., *A Tour through the North of England*, 2 vols, London, 1770

INDEX